An Ethiopian Reading of the Bible

An Ethiopian Reading of the Bible

Biblical Interpretation of the Ethiopian Orthodox Tewahido Church

Keon-Sang An

Foreword by William A. Dyrness
Preface by Joel B. Green

James Clarke & Co

To
Mi-Young, my wife and best friend
Isaac, Sol, and Eunbee, my beloved children

James Clarke & Co
P.O. Box 60
Cambridge
CB1 2NT
United Kingdom

www.jamesclarke.co
publishing@jamesclarke.co

ISBN: 978 0 227 17591 0

British Library Cataloguing in Publication Data
A record is available from the British Library

First published by James Clarke & Co, 2016

Published by arrangement
with Pickwick Publications

Contents

Tables

Foreword

THANKFULLY, MOST PEOPLE WORKING in Christian mission and in theological education today recognize the importance of the cultural context in which Scripture is read. This context, we have come to see, plays a role not only in how Scripture is read, but also in the theological reflection that follows such readings. The significance of this lies in the fact that Scripture is read in a wide (and increasing) variety of settings. Keon-Sang An's study of biblical interpretation of the Ethiopian Orthodox *Tewahido* Church (EOTC) explores one important—and mostly overlooked—cultural reading.

Keon-Sang An's book makes very clear that a contextual reading of Scripture does not mean anything goes—that any reading of Scripture is just as good as any other. Quite the contrary, he carefully describes the way contextual readings emerge out of clearly defined community configurations and express the traditions embodied in those communities. Such readings are thus constrained by their context, while at the same time they are also enabled by this. And in the case of EOTC, as in many other contextual readings, the end goal is that the Bible is truly "heard" in that place, that the power of Scripture is allowed freely to have its way.

Keon-Sang frames the conversation within the recent Evangelical reflection on Scripture and culture—which represents his own setting. Evangelicals have been known for their desire to let Scripture be the final authority in faith and practice. But in their attempt to find the one true reading of Scripture they have sometimes acted as if cultural influences were optional or even harmful. The aspiration for a true and undistorted biblical reading is certainly laudable, but it does not allow them, as they think, to escape from reading contextually—it rather expresses a particular hermeneutical tradition that derives from Evangelicalism's roots in the Reformation and subsequent revivals and renewal movements.

Important as this tradition may be, it is not privileged. And this study demonstrates how much Evangelicals have to learn from a tradition founded and developed in a completely different setting.

Keon-Sang An's important study of the hermeneutics of the Oriental Orthodox Church uncovers a centuries-long tradition of faith and practice that is carried by a living tradition of preaching. Moreover he shows how this pattern of interpretation is not simply an ecclesial tradition but also a cultural and political repository. Embedded within these practices are not only primal elements of Ethiopian indigenous religion, but also theological accents stemming from ancient Hebrew and Syriac sources. And in them he also discerns political impulses that have been formative in Ethiopian history.

Central to explication of the EOTC treatment of Scripture is an understanding of the carriers of that tradition (which might usefully stimulate Evangelicals to ask a parallel question: what are the primary carriers of their interpretation of Scripture?). In the case of EOTC, Keon-Sang introduces us to the *Andemta* Commentary which has brought together the combined voices of readers of Scripture over time (initially an oral tradition) that interlaces a striking diversity of strands, and that in turn allows preachers to discover richer meanings—a procedure resonating especially with the Syriac notions of symbolism, one figure with many senses. The written commentary then is the aggregation of many voices—much like the Jewish accumulation of Rabbinic sources—to clarify texts for subsequent believers.

But the commentary is not an end in itself; it serves the larger purpose of informing the ongoing practice of preaching, which for the EOTC becomes an oral transcription of God's truth for the sake of present-day application. As for Evangelicals, though with strikingly different patterns, preaching for the EOTC is central to the practice of worship. For the EOTC preaching is meant to open narrative windows, based on a rich variety of voices, to reach a spiritual goal: "to bear good fruit." Here too Evangelicals will find material for reflection. While they are proud to move from history to symbol, the EOTC moves in the opposite direction, from symbol to history. Both value the historical and the theological, though they arrive there by different paths. And both find their theological center in the person of Jesus Christ, though they represent Christological traditions developing in different landscapes and over terrain unrecognizable to the other.

Their different geographies have meant these traditions have long lived in isolation from one another. Keon-Sang An's important study gives evidence that, happily, this isolation is coming to an end. This fresh opening allows us to contemplate a collective future, of mutual learning, as we together grow up into Christ in all things.

William A. Dyrness
Dean Emeritus and Professor of Theology and Culture
Fuller Theological Seminary

Preface

"WITHOUT A CONTEXT, EVERY text is a pretext . . . " Biblical scholars today are fond of quoting this saying—a saying that has for many achieved almost proverbial status. In fact, however, stated in this way this saying is nonsensical. Every text is read against some sort of contextual backdrop. Interpreters can argue over whether this or that is the better context, but they can hardly claim that reading, any reading, takes place apart from any context at all.

That this emphasis on context has achieved popularity in modern times is undoubtedly due to the rise of the historical-critical method, which continues to enjoy near-hegemonic status as the heart and soul of critical biblical studies. This is because the historical method takes as axiomatic that a text's original context is determinative of its meaning. Accordingly, in New Testament studies, what matters is what John or Paul or James intended, originally, understood in their ancient setting. What matters is the point of a text's composition. For this reason, our interpretive energies should be marshaled in the service of determining what the author meant back then and there, at the point of origin. In the wake of the rise and flourishing of modern biblical studies, this way of thinking about "meaning" has achieved the status of a taken-for-granted point-of-departure. It is unassailable. It goes without saying.

People tend not to think much about the air they breathe or the water they drink, so accustomed to it they have become. It often takes an outsider, someone unschooled in "the way things simply are," to point out the sweetness of the water or the smelly air. This is precisely the role Keon-Sang An has assumed in this insightful monograph. Historical criticism was supposed to rescue Scripture from its captivity to modern interests by returning it and its significance to their pristine origins. This meant liberating the biblical materials from their service to modern contexts. Dr. An demonstrates, however, that this attempt to locate the meaning of, say, 1 Corinthians in relation to the city of Corinth in the mid-first century is itself a product of interpretive aims and commitments that have their home in the modern west. Stated simply, the historical-critical attempt to deny the modern context in its attempt to discover ancient meaning is itself an example of the contextual nature of all biblical interpretation. Approaches to reading Scripture that prioritize dispassionate, inductive, historically determined interpretation are not thereby critical or neutral approaches; rather they serve modern, western sensibilities. No one reads the Bible on its own terms, for the knower is forever involved in what is known, all readers are shaped and guided by their assumptions. This is true irrespective of how concealed those assumptions might be, even from readers themselves. No one reads inductively, though not everyone is aware that this is so.

Recognizing the persistently contextual nature of biblical interpretation does not provide one with a license to make Scripture say whatever one wants it to say. The Bible is not a wax nose to be twisted this way or that. Rather, this recognition allows us to admit that the biblical materials are capable of more than one sense, depending on the commitments and aims of the interpreter. And it is to allow that those different commitments and aims may find sometimes more and sometimes less coherence with the data with which the Bible presents us. Missional interpreters rightly imagine that God's mission animates the Scriptures, for example, leading to readings of scriptural texts shaped by a mission-minded God. Such readings could be falsified, however, if it could be demonstrated that, in fact, the Scriptures have no such missional interests.

What is fascinating about Dr. An's work is not simply his critical evaluation of the contextual nature of all biblical interpretation, but also the captivating exemplar he provides of this reality. I refer to his work with the time-honored, living, interpretive traditions of the Ethiopian Orthodox *Tewahido* Church, codified in the *andemta* commentary. Making the larger church aware of this tradition is already a significant contribution, but Dr. An goes further to show how the *andemta* commentary continues to influence the central, formative, ecclesial practice of preaching. He shows that preachers in the Ethiopian Orthodox *Tewahido* Church drink from their own wells—both in the sense that their homiletical concerns arise out of Ethiopian culture and address Ethiopian people and concerns, and in the sense that they draw on this hoary exegetical tradition.

For theological interpreters of Scripture, missional interpreters included, the point is clear. Here is a living example of an ecclesially located, tradition-minded engagement with Scripture; that is, here is a fascinating illustration of the axiom that all biblical interpretation is contextual. Historical interests imported from the west may come to influence this hermeneutical tradition. After all, it is a living tradition, not a frozen one, and Ethiopian institutions of theological training have already come under western influence. Whether that influence will be for good or ill will likely be determined by the degree to which voices like Dr. An's are heeded, voices that name all forms of biblical study as contextually shaped and guided and that recognize that western, historical approaches are not self-evidently correct, but reflect modern assumptions about the nature of biblical texts. Indeed, given the triumph of historical approaches in the west, we in the west may long for the influence of a theologically committed, ecclesially located interpretive tradition such as that reflected in the *andemta* commentary of our brothers and sisters of the Ethiopian Orthodox *Tewahido* Church.

Joel B. Green
Dean of the School of Theology
Professor of New Testament Interpretation
Fuller Theological Seminary

Acknowledgments

I GIVE ALL PRAISE, honor, and glory to God, my Father. He is the Alpha and the Omega, and all things are from him and through him and for him. He carried me all the way until I reached this place.

I wish to acknowledge my mentor, William A. Dyrness, and my committee members, Wilbert R. Shenk and Joel B. Green. Dr. Dyrness thoughtfully guided and directed me throughout this long project, and gave me valuable insights on contextual theology. Dr. Shenk set an example of noble scholarly character and considerately instructed me. Dr. Green demonstrated pastoral heart and offered me wholesome theological perspectives. I am blessed to have such excellent scholars as my teachers. I am also indebted to Dr. Elizabeth Glanville for her consistent concern and encouragement during my Fuller days. I also wish to thank Jennifer Shaw for her faithful and wonderful editorial work.

I wish to acknowledge my KHMTC students, who are dispersed and who strive for the advance of the gospel. We learned from each other in a container classroom. They taught me how to persevere by faith in suffering. "Oh, Lord, have mercy on them." I am also grateful to my ETC students for their interaction and practical help in my research. This dissertation blossomed out of our fellowship in Christ.

I wish to acknowledge my friends and supporters. My ecclesia friends are in my heart as coworkers for the kingdom of God. My Fuller prayer friends participated in my work by sharing and praying, which I greatly enjoyed. I also thank my SIM colleagues for their expectations and careful considerations. My supporters have prayerfully supported me throughout the years of my ministry and study. Their love and generosity assured me of God's presence with me and His purpose for my study. Without their help I could not have completed this monograph. "Oh, Lord, repay their love with abundant blessings."

Special gratitude is due my parents. This monograph is God's answer to their earnest wish and prayer. I extend my gratitude to my father and mother-in-law for their warmhearted care and prayer. I express my heart of appreciation to my sisters for their love, sacrifice, and prayer. In my absence they took care of my parents and shared an intimate family bond in the midst of challenges. This was a great consolation and encouragement to me.

My deepest gratitude and thanks go to my wife, Mi-Young. We walked together through this journey, talking, laughing, crying, and praying. In this journey, we were growing to fit God's purpose. Her gentle smile lit up my life. We have done it "together." I also hope and pray that this monograph will be a gift for my children, Isaac, Sol, and Eunbee. Their hugs and kisses always took away my fatigues and energized me to go forward. Whenever they mentioned "daddy" in their prayer, I became confident that God would answer.

Most of all, it was the amazing grace of God that made this monograph possible. It was a precious joy to be with God in the Prayer Garden. He listened and talked to me. He consoled, recovered, and strengthened me. I was a child playing around in my Father's garden before His tender eyes. This monograph includes the confession of faith in my life: "The Lord is my Shepherd! I shall not want." This is Yours as I am Yours. Amen!

Abbreviations

EOTC	Ethiopian Orthodox *Tewahido* Church
ETC	Evangelical Theological College
KHMTC	*Kale Hiwot* Ministry Training Center

Introduction

Recently, there has been growing recognition and acceptance of the contextual nature of biblical interpretation. As a result, various contextual readings of the Bible have been explored in different local contexts throughout the world. Although it is encouraging that the number of contextual studies of biblical interpretation is increasing, the study of contextual biblical interpretation has yet to be developed more extensively. In particular, more historical case studies are needed in order to expand our understanding of the nature of contextual biblical interpretation.

This monograph is an exploration of contextual biblical interpretation through the investigation of the biblical interpretation of the Ethiopian Orthodox *Tewahido* Church (EOTC). The EOTC has a long history with a unique ecclesiastical tradition. Particularly, the EOTC has its own approach to biblical interpretation, an approach that has been shaped and developed under the substantial influence of the EOTC's tradition in the historical and cultural context of Ethiopia. Consequently, it has interpretive characteristics that are distinctive from those of other Christian traditions. Thus, the biblical interpretation of the EOTC demonstrates the contextual nature of biblical interpretation.

The thesis of this monograph is that tradition and context significantly influence biblical interpretation and that the EOTC provides a compelling historical example of contextual reading of the Bible.

This introductory chapter provides the focus of this research. It begins with a presentation of the background of the research. This is followed by presentation of the purpose, goal, significance, central research issue, research questions, limitations and delimitations, definitions, and overview of the study.

BACKGROUND

In Ethiopia, a biannual council meeting of a certain mission agency was taking place. National church leaders and missionaries were seriously discussing the issue of interdependence. One church leader said, "Interdependence means those who have give things to those who do not have." His remark expresses a general perception of interdependence that is found especially in the relationship between national churches and foreign organizations. Even the discussion of accountability in mission tends to focus only on how to wisely and effectively give from one side to the other. This attitude leads to the permanent dependency of national churches on foreign churches and/or mission agencies. I believe that this is one of the most serious challenges yet to be overcome in the current missional context of the world.

This attitude of dependency is found in theological education in many parts of the world, as well. The basic attitude of the students is, "Teach us the truth. We will learn." The expatriate teachers respond, "I will teach you. Listen carefully." This gives rise to the theological dependency of many national churches, as well as the churches of emerging mission countries, on Western churches. This theological monopoly is prevalent in many different places in the world. It is my conviction that genuine interdependence is possible only when the entities in a relationship are independent. A healthy relationship is not one-sided—the "give" of one side and the "take" of the other side—but reciprocal—the "give and take" of both sides.

I experienced this unhealthy relationship of dependence in theological education through my past ministries in East Africa. Beginning in 1999, I served as a theology teacher first at *Kale Hiwot* Ministry Training Center in Asmara, Eritrea, and then at Evangelical Theological College in Addis Ababa, Ethiopia. A foreign mission agency started both schools. Even though the two schools were quite different in size, both had curriculums that were similar to those of Western theological schools.

When I began my teaching ministry, I simply assumed that my task was to teach my students the theology I had learned. I was under the significant influence of Western theology because of my own theological education. I graduated from a Presbyterian theological seminary in Korea. Theology students in major seminaries in Korea were exposed to and significantly influenced by Western theology, since many professors received their advanced theological training in schools in the West. Later,

I studied theology in England and the U.S., where I increasingly absorbed the theological viewpoints and methodologies of the West. Thus, an interesting cultural dynamic was taking place in my classroom: a Korean theology teacher was delivering Western theology to African students.

As time went by, I found an unfortunate phenomenon happening among my students. They were struggling with the gap between what they learned at school and what really happened in their local ministry contexts. They were becoming more isolated from the community of believers in their own contexts. It seemed that in this situation many of the students regarded their theological education simply as a means of promotion, in order to get a better job, for example. In their actual ministry, however, they continued to do what they were accustomed to doing, because they could not find relevant contact points between their theological education in school and their practical ministries in the local church.

Especially I observed the students struggling with Western modes of biblical interpretation. They were unable to come up with abstract and rationalistic hermeneutical concepts and methodologies. They simply made efforts to memorize them for exams. Western hermeneutics was not helpful to the exegetical practices of these students for the local churches they served. Furthermore, such sophisticated hermeneutical approaches led these students to ignore their own ways of reading the texts, which had been passed on and practiced in their historical and cultural contexts.

With this recognition, I encouraged my students to understand the importance of constructing their own theologies in their historical and cultural contexts, rather than simply and passively accepting foreign theologies. Particularly, I worked diligently with my students to discover culturally relevant ways of reading the Bible in the Ethiopian context. Fortunately, there was a time-honored church tradition in Ethiopia: the Ethiopian Orthodox *Tewahido* Church. It has developed and maintained its own ecclesiastic tradition in the Ethiopian context for almost as long as the history of the Christian church. Significantly, the EOTC has its own distinctive way of reading the Bible, which has been shaped and developed in the context of Ethiopia's long history.

At that time, I had opportunities for fellowship with the teachers of the Theological College of the Holy Trinity, an Orthodox seminary in Addis Ababa. I visited the school and spoke with theology teachers there. They were happy about my interest in the EOTC and the theology of the church. They were willing to help me in my research on the biblical interpretation of the church. This interaction enriched and transformed my theological perspective, especially in the area of biblical interpretation. I came to affirm the contextual nature of biblical interpretation and the significance of tradition and context in biblical interpretation. As a result, I was motivated and encouraged to pursue this monograph on the biblical interpretation of the EOTC as a historical example of contextual biblical interpretation.

PURPOSE

The purpose of this study is to explore the EOTC's reading of the Bible with a focus on the significance of tradition and context in biblical interpretation.

GOAL

The goal of this research is to demonstrate the contextual nature of biblical interpretation, and to present the EOTC's reading of the Bible as a historical example of contextual biblical interpretation.

SIGNIFICANCE

First, this research is significant for the EOTC's biblical interpretation, in particular. It is an attempt to present the biblical interpretation of the EOTC. Though the church has a distinctive interpretive tradition, which developed over its long history, it has not been recognized appreciatively by other church traditions. Even the EOTC has not clearly articulated its own hermeneutical tradition. There are relatively few scholarly studies on the EOTC's interpretation of the Bible, and most of these studies focus only on the *andemta* commentary.

Second, this research is significant for the discussion of contextual biblical interpretation, in general. As I propose, the appropriate approach in constructing contextual biblical interpretation is descriptive rather than normative. In other words, in order to construct contextual biblical interpretation, it is necessary to conduct various case studies on the reading of the Bible performed in particular contexts. This research into the biblical interpretation of the EOTC provides a compelling case of contextual biblical interpretation.

CENTRAL RESEARCH ISSUE

The central research issue is how the EOTC reads the Bible in the historical and cultural context of Ethiopia.

RESEARCH QUESTIONS

1. What is contextual theology? How can contextual theology be constructed?
2. How can the contextual nature of biblical interpretation be demonstrated?
3. What is the role of tradition and context in biblical interpretation?
4. What is the ecclesiastic tradition and context of the EOTC as a hermeneutical community?
5. What is the interpretive tradition of the EOTC found in the *andemta* commentary?
6. What are the characteristics of biblical interpretation revealed in the preaching of the EOTC?

LIMITATIONS AND DELIMITATIONS

This study limits the area of research into biblical interpretation to the *andemta* commentary and the preaching of the EOTC. The *andemta* commentary represents the tradition of EOTC's biblical interpretation and it still significantly influences the biblical interpretation of the church. In addition, the preaching of the EOTC most practically reveals the distinctive characteristics of the church's biblical interpretation. Thus, this study does not include other areas that might also disclose the biblical interpretation of the EOTC, such as other Ethiopian literature, liturgy, hymns and prayers, icons, etc.

This research is also delimited in terms of its regional scope. The sermons in this research were collected mostly in Addis Ababa, the capital city of Ethiopia, and its vicinity. There may be discrepancies in preaching between those who have official theological training and those who do not. This research does not consider the levels of theological education obtained by the preachers.

DEFINITIONS

In this monograph, I use certain important terms with the definitions given below. Other significant terms will be defined and treated in detail in subsequent sections.

Biblical Hermeneutics

"Biblical hermeneutics" is the study of the principles of interpretation of the Bible. Here it is used interchangeably with "biblical interpretation." The term "biblical exegesis" is also used as identical with these terms, even though it can be more narrowly defined.

Western Theology

It is difficult to clearly define the term "Western theology," even though it is frequently used in theological discussions without any specific definition. Geographically, "the West" designates Europe and North America (i.e., the North Atlantic). The term "Euro-American" refers to "persons of North Atlantic origins and cultures."[1] Though there are variations in the forms of culture in Euro-America, scholars assert that there are also underlying similarities and commonalities shared and exhibited by Euro-America as a cultural entity. In this regard, Louis J. Luzbetak notes that the term "culture" is used in an extended sense, referring to a number of closely related cultures.[2] By employing this perspective, we can speak of "Western culture" and "Western theology."

Accordingly, Western theology can be defined as theology that has been formed and developed by Euro-Americans in their historical and cultural context. Scott Foutz gives a relevant definition of Western theology: "that body of doctrine and tradition developed solely in terms of the temporal and cultural situations within the West."[3] This definition presupposes that "all doctrinal development takes place within a historical and ideological context which defines not only the issues raised but also the language and concepts used in attempting solutions."[4] In other words, theology is always context-laden, and this includes Western theology.

1. Patte, *Ethics of Biblical Interpretation*, 14.
2. Luzbetak, *Church and Culture*, 171.
3. Foutz, "Theology of Slavery."
4. Ibid.

The Non-Western World

"The non-Western world" is defined as that part of the world that does not include the countries of Western Europe and North America, such as those of Africa, Asia, the Middle East, Latin America, and Oceania.

OVERVIEW

Chapter 1, "Contextual Theology," explores contextual theology. First, I offer definitions for basic terms, such as culture, context, and contextualization, and then, based on these definitions, I demonstrate the contextual nature of theology. Second, I investigate the construction of contextual theology through a critical interaction with the Western mode of doing theology. Finally, I address the role of tradition in theology.

Chapter 2, "Contextual Reading of the Bible" is an investigation of contextual biblical interpretation. First, I demonstrate the contextual nature of biblical interpretation through a critical interaction with historical criticism. This analysis is particularly telling due to the so-called objective nature of historical criticism, and its claims to be context-neutral. Next, I address the aim and task of biblical interpretation from this perspective. Finally, I discuss the role of tradition in biblical interpretation in its theological and historical aspects.

Chapter 3, "The Ethiopian Orthodox *Tewahido* Church: Tradition and Contextualization," explores the tradition and context of the EOTC as a hermeneutical community. First, I briefly describe the history and position of the EOTC in Ethiopia. Next, I address the unique tradition of the EOTC, which is woven out of various strands of influences. Last, I discuss the characteristics of the contextualization of the EOTC, along with a consideration of the present context in which the church is situated.

Chapter 4, "The Interpretive Tradition of the EOTC: The *Andemta* Commentary Tradition," examines the *andemta* commentary tradition of the EOTC. First, I describe the general features and history of the *andemta* commentary. Next, I discuss various exegetical issues in order to clarify the interpretive character of the *andemta* commentary. Then, I investigate the internal and external sources of the *andemta* commentary. Finally, I address the ways in which different interpretive traditions have been integrated in the context of Ethiopia to produce the unique interpretive tradition of the *andemta* commentary.

Chapter 5, "Biblical Interpretation in the Preaching of the EOTC," analyzes the preaching of the EOTC in order to illuminate the characteristics of the EOTC's biblical interpretation. First, I analyze nine sermons given by EOTC preachers. Then, I discuss the characteristics of biblical interpretation exemplified in these sermons.

In the "Conclusion," I summarize the findings of this research, and discuss its implications and contributions. Then, I offer suggestions for further studies. I finish this monograph by presenting some concluding remarks.

1

Contextual Theology

In recent years, there has been a growing recognition of the critical place of contextuality in doing theology. Contextual theology takes into account the important place of a people's culture and location in doing theology. This chapter presents an exploration of contextual theology. In contrast to modern Western modes of doing theology, which demonstrate an abstractionist tendency with its assertions of universal and perennial values, contextual theology recognizes theology's contextual nature and the significance of tradition in doing theology. It also proactively applies this recognition to developing various contextual theologies.

I propose that all theology is contextual theology. In other words, theology is formed and developed by the people of a faith community in a given time and place. I also propose that there have been multiple traditions in Christianity throughout its history, and that each particular tradition of a people plays a critical role in their way of doing theology. In order to support these proposals, this chapter presents an exploration of contextual theology.

Given the overall proposal of this monograph that tradition and context significantly influence biblical interpretation, and that the Ethiopian Orthodox *Tewahido* Church (EOTC) provides a compelling historical example of contextual reading of the Bible, it will be helpful to investigate contextual theology in several different but interconnected ways. First, I will define and clarify basic terms and concepts, such as culture, context, and contextualization, used in this monograph for the development of the discussion. Second, I will lay a theological basis for contextual biblical interpretation, in general, and the biblical interpretation of the EOTC, in particular. This will include a critical interaction with Western modes of doing theology. Third, I will address the significant role of tradition in theology.

CULTURE, CONTEXT, AND CONTEXTUALIZATION

In the past decades of debate on contextual theology, no clear consensus has emerged as to the meaning of the term. I suggest that part of the reason for this is that the term and its associated words—culture, context, and contextualization—are used without first being clarified. This leads to confusion and misunderstanding. Therefore, a discussion of contextualization ought to begin by defining the key terms and concepts. These definitions are presented below in the expectation that this will elucidate many important aspects of contextual theology.

Culture

The term "culture" is not easily defined. Historically, it has undergone changes in its connotation and understanding. Currently, there are various definitions of culture. As Daniel Shaw aptly states, "Definitions of culture are almost as numerous as anthropologists."[1] In its broadest sense, culture is a people's way of life. I favor this definition for its basic emphasis on human corporate life. Specifically, this definition of culture reveals some important conceptual elements and implications.

First, culture is a common lifestyle shared by a group of people. This is the social dimension of culture. Culture is not private, but communal; it is a people's corporate way of life. Therefore, it is "the possession not of individuals but of people who have a sense of their (separate) identity and express this in patterned action."[2] Persons live their daily lives as a group according to the pattern of their culture. In this sense, culture may be called the corporate personality of a people. As Luzbetak defines it, culture is "a society's code for behavior" and "a social heredity."[3]

Second, culture is the sum-total of a people's life, inclusive of all areas of human life. M. P. Maggay and W. A. Dyrness define the four components of culture as "the public, observable patterns of behavior" (*conduct*), "the norms and rules for behavior" (*code*), "the belief systems,

1. Shaw, *Transculturation*, 24.
2. Maggay and Dyrness, "Culture and Society," 218.
3. Luzbetak, *Church and Culture*, 170–71.

worldviews and ways of explaining the meaning of things" (*creed*), and "the recurrent rituals, festivals and other enactments that provide rhythm and regularity to the life system of a people" (*cult*).[4] Here I would add the products of a people as a component of culture. A people's culture is expressed in what they make in their location. Thus, the concept of culture embraces all aspects of human life, including behaviors, practices, assumptions, and products.

Third, culture is not a mere aggregate, but an integrated system of all these elements. Culture is a whole; it is "a single, albeit very complex, unit" of a people's life.[5] According to Paul G. Hiebert, culture is "a patterned lifestyle" which a group of people share.[6] Similarly, Charles H. Kraft refers to culture as "a society's complex, integrated coping mechanism."[7] Culture is not simply the random activities and achievements of a people, but a framework in and with which a people live.

Culture as patterned human practices has theological meaning. According to Paul Tillich, "Religion as ultimate concern is the meaning-giving substance of culture, and culture is the totality of forms in which the basic concern of religion expresses itself. In abbreviation: religion is the substance of culture, culture is the form of religion."[8] Dyrness defines culture as "what we [humans] make of creation."[9] He states, "Our making is a response to—indeed it engages with—who God is and what God has done and continues to do in creation."[10] This is a theological understanding of human culture.

Fourth, culture is context-relative, meaning each and every culture has its own particularity. Dyrness states, "Culture itself is a metaphor that has come to stand for what humans have made of their particular corner of the earth."[11] Culture is always a particular culture of a particular people in a given time and place. Culture is always embodied. There is no universal culture that all peoples have shared at all times, and such an understanding of culture is nothing but an abstract concept that exists

4. Maggay and Dyrness, "Culture and Society," 222–23.
5. Tanner, *Theories of Culture*, 29.
6. Hiebert, *Anthropological Insights*, 30.
7. Kraft, *Anthropology*, 38.
8. Tillich, *Theology of Culture*, 42.
9. Dyrness, *Earth Is God's*, 58.
10. Ibid.
11. Ibid., 62.

only in theory. Rather, there are many different peculiar cultures in the world. As Clemens Sedmak properly notes, "culture is multifarious and varies with geographical, social, and historical context; the way cultures are shaped and come into existence is contingent."[12]

Fifth, culture is not static, but continually changes throughout time as a result of both internal and external influences. Traditional anthropology tended to focus on isolated people groups in its culture studies. However, this approach has limitations and weaknesses. As Sherry Ortner notes, it can "easily turn into stereotype (ethnic, racial, class), and sometimes in fact dangerous stereotype—groups can be labeled (even "profiled") as intrinsically culturally prone to this or that (good or bad, model minorities or terrorists) pattern of behavior."[13] This concept of culture fails to address dynamic cultural changes presently taking place in the world. Currently, peoples in different cultures experience mutual cultural influences among each other and cultural changes in various ways. Thus, recent studies have placed more emphasis on the dynamic aspect of culture.

These recent studies appreciate that the changing global situation has accelerated dynamic encounters and interactions among cultures. Media culture, in particular, plays a crucial role in shaping cultures across the globe. Even in remote areas in Africa, people are exposed to current technology—primarily television, DVD, radio, cinema, internet, and the press. These media have a significant impact on culture throughout the world, and function as the major conduit for spreading different types of cultures. In fact, media culture has transformed the concept of culture itself.

There is a growing recognition that a culture is mobile, not geographically limited to a certain people. According to Ortner, "culture has . . . become an at least partially mobile object. Not only does it move around (like media) across social, cultural, and political boundaries. It also, and perhaps because of that mobility, can be seen to be much more variably deployed or appropriated than had been assumed of culture in the classic sense."[14]

As a result, diverse hybrid cultures, derived from the active contacts and interactions of different cultures, have emerged. Therefore,

12. Sedmak, *Doing Local Theology*, 12.

13. Ortner, *Anthropology and Social Theory*, 12.

14. Ibid., 13.

recent culture studies pay close attention to "the porous boundaries between cultures" and "various forms of cultural hybridity."[15] Similarly, Tanner asserts, "Cultural identity becomes, instead, a hybrid, relational affair, something that lives between as much as within cultures. What is important for cultural identity is the novel way cultural elements from elsewhere are now put to work, by means of such complex and ad hoc relational processes as resistance, appropriation, subversion, and compromise."[16] Contemporary cultures across the globe are characterized by cultural hybridity.

Finally, cultural mobility and hybridity notwithstanding, traditional local culture remains highly significant, even as it is shaped by external influences. In many cases, global influences are integrated into the local culture, so as to produce a new shape of a peculiar culture in a local context. Typically, a people's consciousness of their culture remains significant, in the midst of its dynamic interaction with other cultures in the world. In addition, the people in a culture continue to have a sense of their distinct identity and express this in patterned action in relation to peoples in other cultures. This cultural distinctiveness significantly influences their corporate life in general and their religious beliefs and practices in particular, including doing theology.

Context

The term "context" is used in many different ways. Typically, its meaning is simply assumed in its usage without being clearly defined. Hence, there may be many different meanings in mind when persons use the word, which often causes misunderstanding or confusion in ministrial and academic discussions. This calls for some clarification of the term, which is a foundational concept in the discussion of contextualization.

Thomas Austin defines context as:

> (Con + text: with or next to text) comes from the Latin word texere, from which the word textile comes, meaning a woven fabric. This word may also mean the social and human environment (all that surrounds the human being) where the individual and their collective build a way to understand the world and to live in it. The context shows that those that share it notice likeness of cultural identity as well as similarities in geography,

15. Maggay and Dyrness, "Culture and Society," 218.

16. Tanner, *Theories of Culture*, 57–58.

> climate, history, and the productive processes. The context is the marker of nets of meanings and relationships in which human beings participate daily.[17]

This definition embraces both human and non-human forms of settings that surround people. Typically, the human factor of context is called culture, while the non-human factor including geographical location is called nature. However, it is difficult to make a clear demarcation between them, since they are interconnected with each other. Thus, a people's cultural context is inclusive of human and non-human factors.

In contemporary global society, a people do not exist in an isolated context. Due to the rapid development of technology, communication, and transportation, people in the world are exposed to many mutual influences. Thus, it is nearly impossible to imagine a purely independent context of a people. In discussion of local context, it is important to consider both internal and external elements. As Virginia Fabella states, the internal element of context has "historical, socioeconomic, political, cultural, ethnic, racial, and religious dimensions." The external element of context is the impact of outside forces, such as "the imposition of a global market and a homogenized culture."[18]

Thus, context is a complex concept that combines several realities: human and non-human factors, geographical features, history (including the past and present experience), and local and global elements. These realities are the dimensions of context. In sum, context is the total environment in which a people live and events happen.

This understanding of context can be applied to theology: context is a set of circumstances in which theology is done. For example, a local church is situated in the particular context in which it formulates and develops its particular theology and religious practices. Furthermore, it is important to recognize that the term 'context' itself is a theological notion, if it is understood in terms of creation. Therefore, a people's context has a critical influence on their way of doing theology. As Stephen B. Bevans correctly states, "rather than simply to speak of culture . . . I would prefer to speak of context . . . to use the shorthand expression, we should not speak of 'gospel and culture,' but 'gospel and context.'"[19] Thus, context must be considered in our discussion of doing theology.

17. Segura-Guzmán, "Practice of Theology," 127.

18. Fabella, "Contextualization," 58.

19. Bevans, *Models of Contextual Theology*, xvi–vii.

As demonstrated above, context has not only synchronic, but also diachronic, dimensions. The past of a people's life resides in and influences the present life of the people. This is the historical dimension of context. Tradition is a significant element in the history of a people and, therefore, strongly influences their present experience.

In light of biblical interpretation, Joel B. Green states that "context" could be used in terms of three different referents: (1) sociocultural setting: "sociohistorical setting, within which a text was generated, within which the events to which a text provides witness took place, or within which the traditions that came finally to expression in a text were shaped and handed down"; (2) cotext: "the portions of something written that precede and follow a word or passage in a text"; (3) readerly situation: "the situation of the reader, understood in sociohistorical as well as theological terms, which helps to shape how the reader accesses and construes the significance of a text."[20]

The term "context" in this research is mostly used in the sense of "readerly situation." More specifically, it means, first, the situation in which a specific interpretive approach has been originated and developed. It refers, then, to the present historical and cultural situation of a church as a hermeneutical community that influences the way of interpreting the text.

Contextualization

"Contextualization" is one of the most frequently used terms in academic and ministerial discussions. The term emerged and developed in theological discourse in the 1970s through a series of missiological conferences and consultations. It was first introduced in 1972 in a report of the Theological Education Fund entitled "Ministry in Context: The Third Mandate Programme of the Theological Education Fund," which was headed by Shoki Coe[21] and Sharon Sapseziah. The mandate states, "Contextualization has to do with how we assess the peculiarity of third world contexts. . . . [Contextualization] takes into account the process of secularity, technology, and the struggle for human justice, which characterize the historical moment of nations in the Third World."[22]

20. Green, "Context," 132–33.

21. Shoki Coe is the Japanese transliteration of C. H. Hwang. From the time he joined the TEF staff in 1964, he went by "Shoki Coe." Wilbert Shenk, e-mail message to author, January 1, 2014.

22. Theological Education Fund, *Ministry in Context*, 20.

Shoki Coe made a significant contribution by leading in the work to define "contextuality" and "contextualization" (1973). He recognized, through his personal experience as the principle of Tainan Theological College, the inappropriateness of the theological education offered in Third World theology schools for training ministers for their local congregations, because it simply repeated and imitated the Western pattern. In this view Western theology was assumed to be normative throughout the world. He states, "Ever since, there has been a growing uneasiness within me—an uncomfortable questioning as to whether in trying to improve the levels of our theological education we are in fact uncritically repeating and imitating the particular pattern which we happened to inherit."[23]

Thus, he underlines the importance of considering the context of local churches in theological education: "theological training for the ministry in the younger churches today can take place faithfully and creatively only in the existential encounter with the religious and cultural revivals in the nations in which they are called to serve."[24] He continues that theological training for ministry must "take place in the midst of the existential and exacting context," not "in an ivory tower."[25] This highlights the importance of recognizing context in the Third World, especially in theological education.

In 1974, two years after the publication of the report on "Ministry in Context," the Lausanne International Congress on World Evangelism was held with the theme, "The Gospel, Cultural Contextualization and Religious Syncretism." It focused on the evangelization of the world and especially emphasized cross-cultural evangelism. It has subsequently stimulated a number of consultations. In 1978, the Lausanne Committee's Theology and Education Group and Strategy Working Group organized a consultation on "Gospel and Culture" in Willowbank, Bermuda. This meeting produced the "Willowbank Report," which acknowledges "the central importance of culture for the effective communication of the Gospel."[26] This consultation encouraged evangelicals to accept "contextualization" as a replacement for the older "indigenization" theory.

23. Hwang, "Rethinking of Theological Training," 8.

24. Ibid., 30.

25. Ibid., 31.

26. Stott and Coote, *Gospel and Culture*, ix.

In sum, contextual theology takes into account the importance of a people's culture and their context in doing theology. Since the movements of the 1970s, the term contextualization has gained widespread acceptance in theological and ministerial discussions. Regarding this development of contextual theology, Wilbert Shenk notes:

> This acceptance was due to the fact that western theologians began to accept the fact that all theology must, by definition, be contextual. Thus, western theology was rooted in western culture. Conservative western scholars, especially evangelicals and fundamentalists, were the most reluctant to concede this point. But even they have been forced to recognize, to some extent, the truth of "contextualization theory."[27]

As a result, literature on the issue has dramatically increased over the past several decades. In particular, theologians have attempted to establish various categories in order to schematize contextualization and thereby, develop contextualization models, which continue to grow in number and diversity. However, many of the Western models of contextualization are abstract and theoretical, which means that they do not fit the real contexts of people in the world. This will be addressed in subsequent discussions.

Several significant factors ignited the growing interest in contextualization. These are noted by Robert J. Schreiter: "the coming to voice of so many Christian communities, the dissatisfaction with some inherited ways of doing theology, the need to find theological expressions more attuned to changing realities."[28] I would add one additional factor: the emerging recognition of different theological traditions that have a long and rich history, yet have not been recognized by people outside of their contexts.

Currently, there are quite distinctive approaches to contextualization, which bring different perceptions and intentions. For example, contextualization emerged with the concern for liberating persons from the distorted socio-political and economic realities in specific contexts. Liberation theology, Minjung theology, black theology, and feminist theology share this concern. Their critique of the traditional theological approach has stimulated discussions on contextualization.

27. Wilber Shenk, e-mail message to author, January 1, 2014.

28. Schreiter, "Foreword," ix.

Another approach to contextualization emerged with a concern for the contemporary missionary movement coupled with the development of anthropological and missiological insights. Some decades ago, Hiebert argued, "missions must be far more sensitive to people and their cultures," and noted, "there has been growing awareness . . . in anthropology, of the need to understand people in their cultural settings."[29] The main question of this approach is how to contextualize the gospel in specific cultural contexts. It has engaged in finding effective ways of communicating the gospel to the people in a particular context. In this approach, it is vital to understand the receivers' culture in order for the gospel to be comprehensible and relevant to the local people.

Yet another approach has come with a fresh understanding of the nature of theology proper. It emphasizes the contextual nature of theology along with the critical place of culture and context in doing theology. It asserts that all theology is contextual, including traditional theologies and contemporary Western theology. In this approach, people have endeavored to articulate a variety of contextual theologies, with different names, such as local theologies, vernacular theologies, theologies in the Third World, etc. For the purpose of this paper, I will use the term contextual theology. Contextual theology is the central concern of this chapter.

THEOLOGY IN CONTEXT

Constructing contextual theology must begin with an understanding of the nature of theology. Thus, this discussion will commence by defining theology. It will then address the important aspects of doing theology including culture, context, and form and content. Finally, it will present a critical assessment of Western theology in the light of theology's contextual nature.

Definition of Theology

Etymologically, theology is the "study of God." I define theology as reflection on and discourse of God and his truth. Theology in the West has typically been devoted to investigating the nature of God. This derives from the assumption that human beings come to know God by knowing the nature of God. However, I will argue that knowing God's nature does not give us proper knowledge of God. It is God's identity rather

29. Hiebert, *Anthropological Insights*, 9–10.

than God's nature by which we know and have relationship with God. As Charles M. Wood eloquently states, "We may come to know, not what God is, but who God is; not God's nature, but God's identity."[30] By this definition, theology engages in inquiry regarding God's identity in order to know him.

Identity is a relational term, and we come to know the identity of God in his relation to creation. This relationship is primarily revealed in the Bible, and therefore, doing theology is mainly mediated through the Bible. The Bible relates the story about God, his character and work in relation to creation, particularly his people. Thus, we seek to know God's identity by exploring the Bible. Therefore, the biblical texts are the lens through which we come to know God. Theology entails comprehending what the biblical texts say about God.

The Bible has been represented by the use of various specific expressions, words, or phrases. "The gospel" is one of the most frequently used terms to describe the Bible. However, this use is problematic. It tends to understand "the gospel" as certain summary statements of concepts or principles. This is a reductionistic understanding of the gospel, making it abstract and, consequently, isolating it from its biblical context.

Similarly, the phrase "the message of the Bible" is also intended to be representative of the Bible. This phrase indicates the work of drawing a message from the Bible, which is then understood as the core truth of Christianity. In this use, communicating the gospel becomes "a matter of decoding and encoding a message" from the Bible.[31] It also risks isolating the message from its biblical context. With an appreciation for cross-cultural communication, Dyrness argues, "it is Scripture, and not its 'message,' that is finally transcultural . . . what is transcultural is not some core truth, but Scripture—the full biblical context of Christ's work. It is this that must be allowed to strike its own spark in the light of the needs of particular cultures."[32]

It is important to note that a condensed or summarized form of the Bible, whether called "the gospel" or "the message," employs a theological approach that presupposes a particular way of understanding the gospel or the message. In other words, this process is a way of theologizing that reduces the bringing of the gospel to a matter of delivering a specific

30. Wood, *Foundation of Christian Understanding*, 38.

31. Dyrness, *Theology from the Third World*, 28.

32. Ibid.

theology. Harvie M. Conn notes this problem in "the equation of the gospel and theology, and the meaning of theology implied in this equation."[33] In this case, a particular theology, mostly Western theology, is asserted to be universal and perennial and, thus, applicable everywhere. It also isolates the message from the context.[34]

Theology must be distinguished from the Bible. The whole Bible, not its summary or its core message, is the gospel. I agree with John Stott: "The Bible does not just contain the gospel; it is the gospel. Through the Bible God himself is actually evangelizing, that is, communicating the good news to the world."[35] Christians must beware of communicating our theology as the gospel and, instead, must faithfully communicate the Bible, which is the gospel, to the world.

Finally, theology is not simply a theoretical exercise undertaken in order to satisfy intellectual curiosity. Rather, it is "faith seeking understanding" (to use Augustine's expression) accompanied by faithful action. Thus, in doing theology there is no separation between theoria and praxis. As Conn states:

> Theology is always theology-on-the-road. And, in this sense, it is not simply a question of relevance or of application. It is not a twofold question of, first, theological interpretation, and then, practical application. Interpretation and application are not two questions but one . . . to ask what Scripture says, or what it means, is always to ask a question about application.[36]

Theology always seeks the way of accomplishing our God-given task in the world by way of obedience to God. As Dyrness states, "Theology is always a question of, first, 'what does God want me to do?' and then 'how do I understand this?' Because Christian faith is like marriage, it cannot be understood in the abstract but only in the experience of it."[37] The Bible is a call to action, not an invitation to understanding only.

The Dynamic Interaction of Cultures in Doing Theology

Authentic theology is done by a people of a faith community in a particular cultural context. This statement expresses important aspects of doing

33. Conn, "Contextualization," 100.
34. Ibid.
35. Stott, "Bible in World Evangelism," A6.
36. Conn, "Contextual Theologies," 54.
37. William A. Dyrness, e-mail message to author, April 2, 2013.

theology. The agent of doing theology is a people of a faith community. The faith community is located within a particular cultural context. The culture of the people is a critical element that influences every aspect of theology, such as content, form, and communication. Many people have tried to write theology from other viewpoints and assumptions. This becomes problematic because they are not aware or explicit about the kind of theology they are writing. Theology is never done in a vacuum, but always embedded in a culture.

Stott's rhetorical question expresses the foundational place of culture in the cross-cultural communication of the gospel: "How can I, who was born and brought up in one culture, take truth out of the Bible which was addressed to people in a second culture, and communicate it to people who belong to a third culture, without either falsifying the message or rendering it unintelligible?"[38] As Stott articulates, the communication of the gospel takes place in the dynamic interaction of cultures, and three cultures, in particular, are engaged in this process: the culture(s) in the Bible, the culture of the communicator(s), and the culture of the receiver(s). Culture is the critical element in each stage of cross-cultural communication of the gospel.

The first critical culture in the communication of the gospel is the Bible itself. Culture has been viewed as just the wrapping that covers the content of the Bible. However, culture is not simply a husk for the gospel as the kernel. As Krikor Haleblian states, "To separate the content of the gospel from its cultural forms is similar to peeling an onion in order to find its core."[39] Culture is part of the gospel, as the whole Bible is composed of different cultural forms. We cannot discard culture from the Bible. In other words, as Martin Goldsmith notes, "The whole of the biblical revelation is acculturated."[40]

Specifically, the truth of the Bible comes to us in forms of culture that are predominantly Hebrew and Greco-Roman,[41] and partly Asian and African. Stott explains the cultural dimension of God's Word: "his Word has come to us in extremely particularized form. Whether spoken or written, it was addressed to particular people in particular cultures using the particular thought forms, syntax and vocabulary with which

38. Stott and Coote, *Gospel and Culture*, x.

39. Haleblian, "Problem of Contextualization," 102.

40. Goldsmith, "Contextualization of Theology," 19.

41. Maggay and Dyrness, "Culture and Society," 221.

they were familiar."[42] The Word of God, the Bible, was enculturated, as the Word of God, Jesus Christ, was incarnated. Cultural particularity is a very important characteristic of the Bible.

The next two cultural dimensions are found in the communication of the gospel, which is carried out in a dynamic interaction of the cultures of the communicator and the receiver. The communicator delivers the gospel according to his or her cultural understanding of it. Likewise, the receiver hears and interprets the gospel in his or her specific cultural context. In this dynamic interaction of cultures, unique local theology is formed. I believe this is the work of the Holy Spirit, who enables people to understand the gospel in a particular way in their particular context.

Niebuhr addresses these cultural interactions in *Christ and Culture*, and raises serious questions regarding the relationship between Christianity and culture. He asserts that the word "Christ" represents Christianity. He then comments on the relationship between Christianity and culture as follows: "It is not essentially the problem of Christianity and civilization; for Christianity, whether defined as church, creed, ethics, or movement of thought, itself moves between the poles of Christ and culture."[43] On this basis he establishes the now well-known framework: Christ against Culture, Christ of Culture, Christ above Culture, Christ and Culture in Paradox, and Christ the Transformer of Culture.

Dyrness articulates the philosophical background of this understanding of culture:

> We don't start with things, something called Christianity (or as Niebuhr put it even more narrowly, "Christ") and something called culture, which we then need to bring together. This way of putting things seems to assume that Christianity is something "pure" that either will become contaminated by culture or will enter it as a cleansing agent. The approach is simply a version of the purity that Descartes sought in his darkened room, when he sought to locate fundamental reality in certain indubitable ideas. Neither Christianity nor culture can be adequately approached in this way.[44]

The problem with Niebuhr's framework is the polarization of Christianity and culture. There is no such thing as "pure" Christianity that

42. Stott and Coote, *Gospel and Culture*, ix–x.

43. Niebuhr, *Christ and Culture*, 11.

44. Dyrness, *Earth Is God's*, 67–68.

exists apart from culture. In addition, culture is not an entity isolated from Christianity. Christianity is always embodied in culture and expressed in cultural form.

The Contextual Nature of Doing Theology

Theology is formulated and developed in an encounter of the Word of God and the world, in other words, the text and the context. According to Osías Segura-Guzmán, "The task of theologizing involves bringing the Context and the Text into dialogue. . . . It is the interaction of the Context with the Text and vice versa that create theology. This reflection on the Text and the Context is an ongoing task."[45]

As discussed above, context is the totality of human circumstances, that is, the total sum of situations that surrounds people, including geographical, historical, and cultural. Thus, doing theology is carried out by a people in their specific context for a given time and place. Sedmak articulately expresses the situatedness of theology: "Theology is done where people care about life. And theology is always done by people who are 'somewhere'—somewhere in a context, somewhere in a net of relationships, somewhere in their lives, somewhere in their intellectual and spiritual journeys."[46]

Goldsmith stresses the importance of context in understanding and practicing God's Word as he criticizes the demythologizing approach of Bultmann and others:

> Bultmannian approaches have tended to stress the need to strip the message of its cultural accretions, as if the kernel of the true message were hidden in an envelope of meaningless historical wrapping. But when we seek to remove this historical wrapping, we actually find there is nothing left. The whole message is interwoven within its context. We need therefore to understand the Word in its context and then interpret it and reapply it in our context today.[47]

Similarly, Schreiter points out the dangers in ignoring context in doing theology: "Without a sensitivity to the cultural context, a church and its theology either become a vehicle for outside domination or lapse

45. Segura-Guzmán, "Practice of Theology," 127–28.

46. Sedmak, *Doing Local Theology*, 16.

47. Goldsmith, "Contextualization of Theology," 20.

into docetism, as though its Lord never became flesh."[48] The early church rejected Docetism because it sought to preserve the Divine Christ by denying his incarnation in the material world. The dangers Schreiter mentions, theological domination and theological docetism, are especially evident in the contemporary history of theology. They remain serious challenges yet to be overcome in the contemporary understanding and practice of theology, especially in the context of cross-cultural ministries.

Thus, there is no such thing as universal theology, but theologies are as numerous as cultures. Schreiter states it well, "The theologies once thought to have a universal, and even enduring or perennial character . . . were but regional expressions of certain cultures."[49] Recently, there has been a growing recognition of local theologies in contrast to a concept of universal theology. Local theologies, with their particularities, contribute to enriching the knowledge of God. Bevans offers a compelling articulation of the contextual nature of theology and the theological mandate based on it:

> There is no such thing as "theology"; there is only contextual theology: feminist theology, black theology, liberation theology, Filipino theology, Asian-American theology, African theology, and so forth. Doing theology contextually is not an option, nor is it something that should only interest people from the Third World, missionaries who work there, or ethnic communities within dominant cultures. The contextualization of theology—the attempt to understand Christian faith in terms of a particular context—is really a theological imperative. As we have come to understand theology today, it is a process that is part of the very nature of theology itself.[50]

In conclusion, all theology is contextual by nature, and thus all theology is contextual theology. In doing theology, Christians must take context seriously. If we do not, our theology will be a purely theoretical exercise that does not speak to the people who live in a particular context.

Content and Form of Theology

Theology comes out of people's real-life situations, and, therefore, must be composed of local materials. Theology begins with the felt needs of a

48. Schreiter, *Constructing Local Theology*, 21.

49. Ibid., 3.

50. Bevans, *Models of Contextual Theology*, 3.

people in a particular place. People have questions that arise in their real-life situations and seek answers to these questions. In order to find these answers, the faith community reflects on the Bible. Those outside of the community do not grasp these questions in the same way as those inside the community. In addition, the questions are typically different from "those posed immediately by other Christian churches or those necessary for a systematic understanding of faith."[51]

Much too frequently, Christians assume people have questions that they never ask, and then attempt to answer those questions, especially in a cross-cultural context. Those questions and answers do not hold much meaning for the people, since they do not come from the people's real-life situation. For example, the nature of God is a key component of systematic theology. Two words, transcendence and imminence, are preeminent in explaining God's relationship with creation. However, this philosophical concept of God's nature has little to do with real-life situations, at least as these are experienced. As Dyrness argues, "While their cognitive weight is large, their affective and emotional impact is minimal. How has this happened? How can we speak of God's presence or distance without touching things closest to our hopes and fears as human beings? Scripture certainly does not do this (these words are nowhere to be found in the Bible)."[52]

Most of the peoples in Africa and Asia are not very interested in metaphysical and rational inquiries into God's nature. For them, there is no clear distinction between the God who is separated from creation and the God who is present in it. By and large, they assume God is always present in their life. Their question, rather, is how to build and maintain a right relationship with God so that they can be delivered from the present problems they face. For most people in the non-Western world relationality is more significant than rationality. Their understanding of the gospel is more relationally oriented than rationally oriented.[53] They believe that their suffering derives from their relational problem.

In most African countries, people are facing issues of life and death, such as poverty, famine, diseases, AIDS, corruption, violence, injustice, ethnic and religious conflict, war, reconciliation, building up a new nation, and so on. They are eager to obtain answers to the questions that

51. Schreiter, *Constructing Local Theology*, 16.

52. Dyrness, *Earth Is God's*, 29.

53. Siu, "Theologizing Locally," 148.

arise from these issues, and to find solutions in their relationship with God. Theology must address the questions that arise as a cry from the heart of people in these real-life situations.

Theology must also take local form in its articulation. There are diverse forms of theology done among cultures, such as stories, liturgy, arts, dramas, singing, dancing, poems, etc. These different cultural forms are very important vehicles for formulating and expressing theology. Only when culturally relevant forms are used in doing theology, will theology touch the heart of the people.

Perhaps the most prominent form of expressing theology is storytelling. C. S. Song regards story as the matrix of theology. He states:

> Theology and story are inseparable. Where there is story, there is theology. A story worthy of its name is a story that grips you in the depths of your heart and mind, forces you to look deeply into yourself and into human nature, and compels you to examine relations between you and other human beings, between human beings and the world, nature and creation, and relations between human beings and God. If this is what story does, it is already profoundly theological. It invites us to reflect on the roots of who we are and what we are, what the world around us is, and ultimately who and what God must be. Story is the matrix of theology.[54]

The Bible has a narrative nature, telling God's grand story with various stories of biblical figures and events. The biblical narratives are powerful in a culture where orality is the major form of daily communication. In my experience, people in Africa show great empathy with the stories of God's people in the Bible. They easily identify themselves and their life situations with the biblical figures. They find hope and consolation from the stories in the Bible. In this way, the biblical narratives have immediacy for their faith and life.

As in other cultures in Africa and Asia, the Ethiopian people love stories. They have numerous stories of historical figures and events. They like to share their stories in daily life. Stories are an important means of education. In this cultural context, storytelling is the primary form of doing theology. People express their experience with God, who God is and what God has done for them, through stories.

Another example is found in Syriac theology, which is known for using poems to express theology. These poetic expressions contain

54. Song, *In the Beginning*, 18.

profound theological thoughts and spirituality. For example, Ephrem the Syrian, "the most outspoken representative of Syriac Christianity,"[55] expresses highly symbolic theology by way of poems with rich symbols and images. His theology enriches contemporary theology and spiritual life. In Ethiopia, important thoughts and ideas in people's lives are expressed through composing and reciting poems. I observed people reciting their poems during important ceremonies on many occasions. This was a significant way of doing theology in the Ethiopian church tradition.

In addition, in the Ethiopian church, both Orthodox and Protestant, songs have a prominent position in liturgy and theology. Composing and singing songs was an essential curriculum of traditional Ethiopian theological education. Currently, Ethiopian church music delivers the truth of God and the reality of the world in a manner that is relevant to the Ethiopian culture. Theology is also beautifully expressed in visual art forms, especially in the Orthodox context.

In Ethiopia, I offered a course entitled "Paradigms of Mission." After studying biblical and historical mission paradigms, I gave the students a group assignment to do research on the mission paradigm of a church or an organization. Each group was required to have a presentation of their final report to the entire class. Notably, all of the groups presented their findings by using dramas. We had an enjoyable time together, sometimes laughing and clapping, and sometimes getting serious, especially in the scene in which an evangelist proclaimed the gospel against severe persecution. Even though these dramas were not logically organized, all of us understood what they were expressing. They were wonderful articulations and communications of theology in the cultural context.

Thus, diverse activities and artifacts of our daily life can be used as instruments in formulating and expressing theology. Unfortunately, however, they have long been overlooked in the modern Western mode of theology. As Dyrness notes, Western theology "has had to borrow language from science, philosophy, and even from economics to try to shape some recognizable image of God."[56] He continues with an affirmation of the aesthetic nature of theology. He understands aesthetics in a broad sense that "extends to all areas of our embodied and enculturated life together."[57] The poetics of our daily life is an important way of doing

55. Van Rompay, "Syriac Tradition," 622.

56. Dyrness, *Poetic Theology*, ix.

57. Ibid., 11.

theology. The forms I described above, such as story, drama, poetry, and icons, are aesthetic artifacts, and exemplify the diverse forms of doing theology. It is the task of Christians, therefore, to recognize and incorporate local materials in helping to construct local theologies. Only then will theology be authentic for the people who live in the particular context.

A CRITICAL ASSESSMENT OF WESTERN THEOLOGY

In light of the contextual nature of theology, serious problems are revealed in understandings and practices of Western theology. Western theology has dominated the theological world. It has been taught and preached all over the globe as if it is the universal theology, applicable to all times and all places. This derives from the dominant political and economic power that the Western countries have held for the past several centuries, along with the active engagement in cross-cultural mission of Western churches. Ironically, this phenomenon is currently fortified by many national church leaders and theology teachers of the non-Western world who undertook their theological education in Western countries.

Serious questions have been raised about the dominance of Western theology. The critique of Western theology is also currently expressed from within the West itself. The defective theological character of Western theology is noted in several important aspects. First, there is a general tendency for philosophical abstraction in Western theology. As the foundational theological method, it searches for essences, expresses them by using abstract concepts, and then attempts to build theological systems. Conn notes that in the Western theological agenda, "the Bible as norm" is confused with "theology as a neutral search for the rationality ideal," the "heavenly principles."[58] He continues: "true theology is seen as *sui generis*, the liberating search of the mind for essence, core, unhindered by any kind of historical, geographical, or social qualifier."[59] The rationalistic tendency of Western theology is a theological reductionism.

Problematically, theological abstractionism disregards the biblical contexts: the historical and cultural contexts, as well as the narrative contexts. The biblical texts were not written in a vacuum, but in particular historical and cultural contexts. In addition, each biblical text is located in its narrative context. Thus, each biblical text must be interpreted in its narrative context. Theological abstractionism destroys the biblical

58. Conn, "Contextual Theologies," 59.

59. Ibid.

narratives that are the basic structure of the Bible. To discard the various biblical contexts is to turn the Bible into a philosophical or theoretical system, which is isolated from the Bible itself.

In addition, abstract theology is isolated from the realities of the life of the people. Its claim of universal applicability notwithstanding, in actuality, the abstract philosophical and theological principles and statements of Western theology do not address the real issues of people's lives. Western theology risks being simply an intellectual exercise done by a limited number of scholars and, as such, it does not have any meaningful relevance to the daily life and faith of the vast majority of people. As Song argues, theology must deal with "the concrete issues that affect life in its totality and not just with abstract concepts that engage theoretical brains. . . . Theology has to wrestle with the earth, not with heaven."[60]

Similarly, Willie James Jennings notes the importance of "the deepest reality of the Christian social imagination" in doing theology.[61] He argues that the social imagination of today's theological academy is diseased, in that it does not reflect "the central trajectory of the incarnate life of the Son of God, who took on the life of the creature, a life of joining, belonging, connection, and intimacy."[62] He goes on to state that the proper posture in doing theology is to "present the likelihood of transformations not only of thinking but of ways of life that require the presence of the risks and vulnerabilities associated with being in the social, cultural, economic, and political position to be transformed."[63] These insights come from critical reflection on theological abstractionism in the West.

Another important criticism of Western theology is its arbitrary nature. It is assumed within Western theology that it is applicable in all times and all places. Western theology has enjoyed its sole position as the theology and, even today, it is taught as such throughout the world. Paul Siu asserts, "Western theologians have given the impression that they have a monopoly on God, the gospel, and the way of constructing theology."[64] Dyrness also draws attention to "the misconception that good theology has already been discovered and developed (usually in the

60. Song, *Tell Us Our Names*, 6–24.

61. Jennings, *Christian Imagination*, 6.

62. Ibid., 7.

63. Ibid.

64. Siu, "Theologizing Locally," 148.

context of Western Christianity), and it needs only to be exported and taught in Third World training schools."[65]

Such attitudes persist, even as discussions of contextualization continue. Steve Straus, who was a missionary in Ethiopia for many years, addresses the paternalistic attitude of the Western church:

> The importance of intercultural theologizing has generally been ignored by the Western church. Many in the Western church harbor a paternalistic attitude that their theology is "objective" and uninfluenced by Western culture. Consequently, they believe that non-Western theologians should simply accept theologies worked out in the West or that, at most, fresh non-Western theologies should be adaptations of the "objective" theology Westerners have already done.[66]

I suspect that this is not an official claim of many practitioners of Western theology. However, I have observed the arbitrary attitude of Western theology in schools I have visited in Asia and Africa. Despite a new realization of the importance of contextualization in theology, it is still not actualized in many places. As Coe notes, many theology schools in the world repeat and imitate the pattern of contemporary Western theological education that has been exported through the contemporary mission movement. Shenk argues that this "has proved to be a serious impediment to training church leaders in other cultures whose task was to develop contextually appropriate churches. Everything about this theological educational program was geared toward inculcating ideals and values."[67]

This reality has brought about problems in the theologizing of churches in the non-Western world. Most significantly, they fall captive to alien concepts, categories, and methodologies that are hard to understand for the ordinary people and, consequently, are not relevant to the real-life questions of the people. One example of this is Western theology's concern for demonstrating the existence of God. It is typically a first component in the prolegomena of Western systematic theology. Generally speaking, however, people in Asia and Africa have no problem with believing in the existence of God. For them it is not a matter of demonstration, but of reality. They simply know that God exists and they

65. Dyrness, *Cross-Cultural Theology*, 17.

66. Straus, "Role of Context," 120.

67. Shenk, "Theological Education," 221.

experience the presence of God in their daily life. Their questions relate to who God is and what God does in relation to their life.

Another example is Western theology's intense interest in the legitimacy of the Bible. For decades, Western theologians have engaged in debate over the legitimacy of the biblical texts. For many, the determining criterion has been scientific evidence. Liberal or progressive theologians insist that the Bible does not stand up to scientific scrutiny and, therefore, it is not authentic. Conservative or evangelical theologians have endeavored to demonstrate that the Bible is scientific and, therefore, it is authentic. The cause behind this heated debate is the belief that scientific evidence is the critical norm by which the legitimacy of the Bible is guaranteed. I join those who argue that both parties are obsessed by modern scientific rationality in which the norm of truth is believed to be scientific evidence. This is the philosophy of post-Enlightenment scientism in Western society.[68]

People in the non-Western world—along with, I believe, most believers in the West outside academic circles—do not have any serious problem with the statement that the Bible is the word of God. They do not need to testify to its authenticity with any observable scientific evidence. They believe that the Bible is the word of God, and the book of the Christian church. The important questions for them are how the Bible addresses their life situation and their response to what the Bible says.

Finally, it is important to recognize that Western theology itself is a contextual theology that has been formulated and developed in a specific historical and cultural context. Western theology has a long history in the Western church. Conn finds the root of Western theology in Greek philosophy. He maintains that the goal of Western theology was "a rational display of the Platonic ideal." He continues, "the Latin Fathers, with their legal training, reinforced this perception. The Cappadocian Fathers, Basil of Caesarea and the two Gregorys, in the second half of the fourth century, carry it on."[69]

This theological tendency intensified under the influence of scientism in the Post-Enlightenment era. For example, the theological reductionism of Western theology is a product of the individualistic rationalism of Western society under the influence of Enlightenment philosophy. As Schreiter indicates, "It was becoming increasingly evident

68. Peter Enns addresses the issue throughout his book, *Inspiration and Incarnation: Evangelicals and the Problem of the Old Testament* (2005).

69. Conn, "Contextual Theologies," 59.

that the theologies once thought to have a universal, and even enduring or perennial character (such as neo-scholastic Thomism in Catholicism or neo-orthodoxy in Protestantism) were but regional expressions of certain cultures."[70]

This recognition leads to the task of critically reflecting on previous ways of doing theology and ministry and then constructively seeking new ways of theological and ministerial engagement that are contextual. Justin Ukpong's statement nicely articulates this assertion:

> Naturally this awareness of the contextual particularity of Christian expression has led to a critique of the traditional missionary and theological methods which regarded the forms of Christian expression belonging to the cultural contexts of the evangelizers as perennial and universal to be adopted by the new cultures into which Christianity was introduced. It has also opened up new vistas of missionary and theological methodologies in our age. In particular this has meant the search for new forms of Christian expression that will take the new cultural contexts seriously and be relevant to them.[71]

The "contextual theology" movement, which started in 1972, has subverted the monolithic understanding of theology. The recognition of the contextual nature of all theology will accelerate the interest in contextual theology and help in the construction of diverse local theologies in particular contexts. It is encouraging that different perspectives on doing theology have emerged and have been freshly re-recognized in different parts of the world.

CONSTRUCTING CONTEXTUAL THEOLOGY

Over the past few decades, as interest in contextual theology has increased, different approaches to constructing contextual theology have been suggested. In this section, I will argue that the approach to constructing contextual theology must, above all, focus on what happens when a people hear or read the Bible in their particular context. In this light, some weaknesses in previous approaches to contextualization, especially using models of contextualization, are revealed.

One example of an earlier approach is Bevans' *Models of Contextual Theology*, which is widely used in the current discussion of contextual

70. Schreiter, *Constructing Local Theology*, 3.

71. Ukpong, "Contextualization," 168.

theology. In his book, Bevans recognizes the contextual nature of theology, and affirms that every theology is contextual. He appropriately argues, "The contextualization of theology—the attempt to understand Christian faith in terms of a particular context—is really a theological imperative. As we have come to understand theology today, it is a process that is part of the very nature of theology itself."[72]

He then proposes the use of models in order to present "a different way of theologizing that takes a particular context seriously." Each represents "a distinct theological starting point and distinct theological presuppositions." He explains, "The various models emerge out of the various ways that theologians combine the elements," that is, theological sources (scripture and tradition), and present human experience. Contextual theology emerges from the combination of these elements.[73]

Based on this understanding, he suggests six models of contextualization. The countercultural model "recognizes the importance of context, but radically distrusts its sanctity and revelational power." The translation model "while certainly taking account of experience, culture, social location, and social change, puts much more emphasis on fidelity to what it considers the essential content of scripture and tradition." The anthropological model "will emphasize cultural identity and its relevance for theology more than scripture or tradition." The praxis model "will zero in on the importance or need of social change as she or he articulates her or his faith." The synthetic model "will attempt the extremely difficult task of keeping all of the elements in perfect balance." The transcendental model "focuses not on a content to be articulated but on the subject who is articulating."[74]

As I studied these models, I reflected on my ministry contexts and tried to determine which model was appropriate to the situations in which I worked. Unfortunately, it was very difficult to find any specific model that fit the contexts I had experienced. For example, Eritrea had nine ethnic groups. Most of the people were religious: half of the population was Muslim, slightly less than half Orthodox Christians, about five percent Catholic, and a small percentage Protestant. Within the Christian population, different church traditions had existed with their own unique theologies. It seems to me that all of them were contextual theologies that

72. Bevans, *Models of Contextual Theology*, 3.

73. Ibid.

74. Ibid., 31–32.

originated and were formed in the dynamic interaction of ecclesiastic traditions in the particular context.

Given my experience, a series of significant questions arose regarding Bevans' approach to constructing contextual theology. Most significantly, his intention was not clear to me. Does he attempt to describe theologies that have already been constructed in a context? Or does he suggest ways of constructing theology in a context? In other words, does he describe the types of contextualization that have taken place? Or does he prescribe what should be done in a specific context by choosing the model that seems appropriate to the context? In short, is his method descriptive or normative?

According to his explanation, it appears that the latter is the case: "we will be speaking about models of operation, models of theological method. Each model, therefore, presents a different way of theologizing that takes a particular context seriously, and so each represents a distinct theological starting point and distinct theological presuppositions."[75] From this statement, other questions follow. Who is the author constructing theology in this context? How is it possible to contextualize theology? What does Bevans actually mean by theologizing contextually?

There are some dangers in Bevans' approach to constructing contextual theology. First, if the models are ways of theologizing, Bevans' approach in practice will become a matter of delivering a specific theology from one culture to another. The theology of the predominant political, economic, and religious power holders will dictate the contextualization of the gospel according to their understanding of the particular context of the people. As a result, the agents of contextualization are outsiders, especially theologians,[76] who suggest or impose their understanding of contextualized theology on the people living in the context. This is not contextual theology but foreign theology that claims to be contextual. As Rob Haskell states, "The basis for contextualization ought to be the biblical text as it is read in a particular culture, not a prepackaged theological system."[77]

Second, these models of contextual theology do not inclusively represent the peculiarities of all contextual theologies. Theology is done by

75. Ibid., 31.

76. According to Bevans, theologians are the ones who construct contextual theology by combining the elements of Scripture and tradition on the one hand, and present human experience on the other (*Models of Contextual Theology*, 31).

77. Haskell, "Introduction," x.

the people of a faith community who live in and with a particular culture in a specific context. Theology is embedded in culture and context-laden. Therefore, theology is constructed differently from context to context. Stating that theology is contextual implies that each and every theology is unique, because each and every human context is unique in various ways.

Third, Mika Vähäkangas criticizes Bevans for making a categorical mistake in his models of contextual theology. He argues that "some are theological methods, while others general attitudes towards cultures, etc."[78] For Vähäkangas, transcendental and praxis models are "theological methods," and anthropological and synthetic models are "a general attitude towards cultures and religion." The translation model deals with "the general question of how to contextualize."[79] I believe this resulted from a theoretical approach to theologizing that does not pay appropriate attention to the real-life situation of persons in particular cultural contexts. The underlying problem of the "model" approach is that the approach itself is very much the product of modern rational thought. Imposing an abstract model is by definition "non-contextual."

Reflecting on previous approaches leads to the conclusion that contextual theology must be descriptive rather than normative. By this, I mean that the proper way of constructing contextual theology is to observe and describe what happens in a specific context when people in that context hear or read the Bible. My contention is that constructing contextual theology is not about applying certain models to particular contexts, but about observing and describing how people construct theology in their context. Thus, the task of contextual theology is descriptive rather than prescriptive.

This understanding of contextual theology is found in the belief in the contextualizing power of the gospel of Jesus Christ. Shenk offers valuable insight on the power of the gospel:

> I am convinced that no "outsider" can ever fully contextualize the gospel. In fact, I reject this way of speaking. We never "contextualize the gospel." The gospel, as God's good news, is always contextually appropriate. . . . The Christian faith was divinely designed to be completely contextually relevant in [a particular] culture. Indeed, there is no culture in which the gospel is not completely relevant. Note that this does not mean the host culture will gladly accept the fullness of the gospel, but it is fully

78. Vähäkangas, "Modeling Contextualization," 279.

79. Ibid., 287.

> available. But it does mean that for the gospel to become fully present "human" foreignness as a distraction or hindrance must be overcome.[80]

This does not exclude "outsiders" in the process of formulating contextual theology. As Shenk states, "the outsider—regardless of qualifications or title—should always come as a servant sharing whatever gifts the Master Servant had entrusted to the outsider on behalf of the world."[81] The task of outsiders is not to create their theology in other people's contexts, nor to propagate their understanding of contextual theology to the people. Rather, they play a role as dialogue partners and motivators, encouraging the people to construct and articulate their theology in their particular context.

As a corollary, constructing contextual theology takes an inductive approach in doing theology. Typically, Western theology has employed the deductive approach. Western theologians have attempted to articulate universal principles or proposition by using abstract concepts and ideas in constructing theology. It is assumed that those principles or propositions can be universally applied to all human contexts. Thus, the task of constructing local theology becomes faithful and effective communication of the universal theology to the people in local contexts.

On the contrary, the starting point of contextual theology must be the local context with the questions of the people "genuinely posed by the local circumstances."[82] Diverse contextual theologies, formed and developed in particular cultural contexts, will contribute to enrich a more holistic understanding of God's truth. In this sense, genuine contextual theology is theology from below, while Western theology is typically theology from above.[83]

In conclusion, the point of departure in doing theology must be the questions and priorities of the people who live their life in a particular context. With those questions and priorities, the people explore the Bible in order to find the answers to their questions, and apply them to their life situation. Therefore, the situation, in which people read the Bible, seeking answers, is already a theological situation. In other words, God is there and they are encountering him. Theology must be articulated with

80. Wilbert Shenk, e-mail message to author, June 18, 2013.

81. Shenk, "Theological Education," 240.

82. Schreiter, *Constructing Local Theology*, 14.

83. Vähäkangas, *Modeling Contextualization*, 281–82.

local materials, that is, a people's particular cultural content and forms. In this way, theology will be authentic theology emerging from reflective interaction of people in their local context and the biblical text.

TRADITION AND THEOLOGY

In this section, I address the significant place of tradition in doing theology, which has long been overlooked in the discussion of religious studies in general, and contextual theology in particular. I will argue that theologians must acknowledge the role of tradition in doing theology. This section will begin with a definition of Christian tradition. This will be followed by a discussion of the role of tradition in theology. This section will conclude with an exploration of various Christian traditions.

Definition of Tradition

Christian tradition has been defined as "the handing down of the Christian faith from generation to generation," it is "the sum total of the Christian heritage passed down from previous ages."[84] This is an inclusive definition. According to Stephen R. Holmes, the content of tradition is "all I have received and am still receiving from the various people who have inducted me into the Christian faith and who continue to lead and teach me."[85]

Specifically, Holmes includes as the content of tradition, "texts, embodying beliefs, concepts and ideas . . . language, behaviors, ethical intuitions, rites and ceremonies . . . ," as well as, "hymn books; ecclesial practices; doctrines; forms of language and movement used in prayer, social and ethical attitudes; ways of relating to various people—and whatever else can be thought of."[86]

The Orthodox Church finds profound meaning in tradition. Orthodox theologians define tradition not only as an artifact of the past, but "in terms of the future to be anticipated and prepared."[87] Tradition is not static but "the life of the Holy Spirit within the Church"[88] The Orthodox definition of tradition emphasizes the living tradition working within the church that has a critical impact on the present and the future.

84. Lane, "Tradition," 809.

85. Homes, *Listening to the Past*, 5–6.

86. Ibid.

87. Meyendorff, *Catholicity and the Church*, 84.

88. Breck, *Scripture in Tradition*, 4.

Thus, tradition is not traditionalism. As Jaroslav Pelikan states, "Tradition is the living faith of the dead; traditionalism is the dead faith of the living."[89] Traditionalism is an attitude that rejects any new influences. A living tradition, on the other hand, is produced through an ongoing process of negotiation in which useful and valid new ideas and practices are accepted and those judged invalid or threatening are rejected.

The Role of Tradition in Theology

Doing theology is practically guided, perhaps even determined, by a particular tradition or traditions. Tradition itself is an important element in comprising our context. All humans are embedded in tradition and, therefore, cannot escape its influence. Tradition mediates our faith. Holmes views tradition as part of our "historical locatedness." He argues, "To attempt to do theology without noticing the tradition, then, is to deny, or at least to attempt to escape from, our historical locatedness. It is worth stressing initially that this locatedness is unavoidable: it cannot be escaped from."[90]

Thus, various Christian church traditions must be taken into consideration in the discussion of contextual theology. Unfortunately, however, the role of tradition has been overlooked in the study of religion, especially regarding contextualization. For example, Clifford Geertz views religion as "a system of symbols."[91] This view of religion is abstract. Its attempt at analyzing religion is somewhat artificial, in that it employs Western categories of human faculty. I argue, on the contrary, that religion is not limited to people's minds, but resides in people's lives and is concretely demonstrated in their practices. Outside of academic circles, most people are not conscious of their theological belief system, but rather organically engage in the practices of their religious life.

It is important to note that religious practices are prescribed and regulated by tradition. Tradition enables people to live out their corporate religious life and express their religious identity. Accordingly, the nature of religion is most clearly expressed in religious tradition. Tradition is established through the process of contextualization in particular cultures and historical contexts.

89. Pelikan, *Vindication of Tradition*, 65.

90. Holmes, *Listening to the Past*, 6.

91. Geertz, *Interpretation of Cultures*, 90.

Multiple Traditions and Multiple Contextual Theologies

My goal in what follows is to critique and correct the monolithic understanding of theological tradition. Behind even diverse designations, such as gospel tradition, theological tradition, or simply tradition, there is typically the assumption of only one such tradition. This assumption is found in many discussions of contextual theology, as well. Such a monolithic understanding of tradition arises from ignorance and/or disrespect of other traditions, and results in exclusive and arbitrary attitudes in doing theology.

In reality, there are many different church traditions and many different theological traditions. Thus, instead of using the singular "tradition," it is more appropriate to use "traditions" or "theological traditions." Christian traditions share commonalities, yet they are also distinct in their religious practices and theologies. It is my contention that all Christian traditions are contextual, and it is important to consider the theology of each tradition in constructing contextual theology. Thus, in the following discussion, I will explore different traditions in the history of the Christian church.

Different Traditions during the Early Church Period

Theological diversity and unity existed from the early church period. Although various traditions all claimed to be in line with the apostolic tradition, they exhibited significant differences in their religious practices and theologies. J. A. Douglas argues for the existence of different traditions in the early days of the church. He asserts that the divisions derived from the clash of nationalities and religiosities of different peoples. According to Douglas, there were two different Christendoms under the Roman Empire. The one was a Greco-Latin Christendom, which consisted of the Greeks and Latins, and accepted Greco-Latin "supra-nationality." The other was a non-Greco-Latin Christendom. It was comprised of the Egyptians, the Syrians, and the Armenians and the peoples who accepted their "religio-nationalities."[92]

Thus, Douglas notes four distinct types of Christianity in the Roman Empire: the Greek, the Latin, the Egyptian, and the Syrian. Each had distinctive characteristics in theology, liturgy, versions of the Bible, hagiology, canonical system and polity, church customs, and so on.[93] Al-

92. Douglas, "Introduction," xi–xii.

93. Ibid.

though they were conscious of catholic unity as the Christian church, they demonstrated diversity in their faith, lifestyles, and religious practices, which were "national in expression."[94] This diversity in unity resulted in the development of different ecclesiastic traditions in subsequent history.

Each of these four church traditions evolved a distinctive theology. Douglas describes the distinctive characteristics of Greek and Latin theology as follows:

> The interest of Greek theologians was cosmological. Applying philosophical methods to Revelation, Greek theological thought began with the Being of the Godhead itself and worked out a metaphysical cosmology in the heavens which stretched down to include the earth, and systematized and interpreted all things mundane. . . . In contrast, the first interest of the Latin theologian was in this world. He coordinated the facts within his observation, including those of Revelation itself into a logical system which, beginning in earth, rose stage upon stage until its massive structure filled Heaven and included the Godhead itself.[95]

Egyptian and Syrian Christianity in the early days of the church formulated and developed quite different theologies from those of Greek and Latin theologians:

> Their minds continued to move in the simplest, uncoordinated theological categories. The concepts of the Latin and Greek theologies belonged to a plane which was incomprehensible to them. Their languages had no idiom to express the processes of Latin and Greek theological thought, and possessed no real equivalents, e.g., for such terms as being, substance, person and nature. . . . In brief, the Coptic and the Syrian Christianities have remained as static as anything in earth can remain static, and appear to consist today, as they consisted in the first centuries, of what to use a current term may be described as Ur-Christianity. That is to say, they conform in everything to the common Catholicity of the primitive Church, but possess theologies which only state the facts of Revelations as recorded in the Scriptures and in Tradition, and neither coordinated nor interpret them as a system.[96]

94. Ibid.
95. Ibid., xxiv.
96. Ibid., xxvi–xxvii.

These theological variations indicate that different theological traditions have existed from the time of the early church. Significantly, these various theologies arose from geographical, religious, and national differences. However, "not all traditions were considered equal, just like theology, some were felt to be orthodox, others not. Some were actually suppressed by violence."[97] Therefore, it is an important task in constructing contextual theology to overcome such skewed notions of theological traditions.

Great Schisms and Different Church Traditions

These Four distinct types of Christianity developed in different ways and shaped the major Christian traditions in subsequent church history. The differences among these early church traditions were evidently concretized through several large schisms. These schisms also resulted in subdivided traditions within the church.

The Council of Chalcedon (451) solidified the split over Christology, especially regarding the nature of Christ, in Christendom under the Roman Empire. The Council adopted *dyophysitism*, which maintains that Jesus Christ had two natures, one divine and one human, in one person. Egyptian and Syrian Christianity rejected Chalcedon, taking the *miaphysite*[98] *position, which holds that divinity and humanity are united in one nature in the one person of* Jesus Christ. Eventually, they broke off from Latin and Greek Christianity. The controversy, along with other sociopolitical and national factors, gave rise to a lasting schism between the Oriental Orthodox churches, on the one hand, and the Western and the Eastern Orthodox churches on the other.

This is the origin of the current Oriental Orthodox churches. Today, the Oriental Orthodox communion comprises six churches: Coptic Orthodox, Ethiopian Orthodox, Eritrean Orthodox, Syriac Orthodox, Malankara Orthodox Syrian Church (Indian Orthodox Church), and Armenian Apostolic churches. Whereas the Church of the East and the Church of the West were categorized as members of the official church under the Roman Empire, the Oriental Orthodox churches were more vernacular. They used vernacular languages in liturgy and theology that

97. William A. Dyrness, e-mail message to author, December 7, 2013.

98. The Oriental Orthodox Churches prefer this designation to *monophysite*, which they themselves reject.

spoke to the people in their cultural context. Because of this, they were separated from fellowship with the larger Christian church.

Though the Oriental Orthodox churches were isolated from one another for various reasons, they have held their common identity throughout history. These churches came under severe persecution by the Roman Empire and the Persian Empire, local political powers, and Muslims. Nonetheless, they maintained the traits of the early church as depicted in the Bible. They lived a communal life of unity under persecution and had significant influences among peoples in their societies. They also had a strong missionary passion and endeavored to preach the gospel among Muslims, going as far as India and China.

The Oriental Orthodox churches share commonalities with the Eastern Orthodox Church, but are also unique in many ways. The differences derived primarily from the cultural and historical contexts of the churches, and gave them distinctive ecclesiastic identities. While the Eastern Orthodox Church was formed and developed under the influence of the Roman Empire, and has remained one of the major church traditions, the Oriental Orthodox churches have maintained strong local traits in their particular contexts. Today, the existence of the Oriental Orthodox churches is becoming more recognized throughout the world, as some of the churches are experiencing revival and renewal. They continue to participate in dialogue with other churches in the world. In this way, the traditions of the Oriental Orthodox churches contribute to the global church.

Another Great Schism in Roman Christendom took place in 1054 between the Eastern church, on the one hand, and the Western Latin church, on the other. Later, during the Reformation that began in the sixteenth century, Protestant churches separated from the Roman Catholic Church. In subsequent history, the Protestant churches have further divided into many different denominations throughout the world. Both the Roman Catholic and Protestant churches have developed different ecclesiastic and theological traditions over their history.

Although the three large Christian church bodies—Eastern Orthodox, Roman Catholic, and Protestant—are typically recognized throughout the world, many people are ignorant of the existence of the Oriental Orthodox churches. As noted above, the Oriental Orthodox churches are beginning to receive more recognition. Given the history of the church discussed above, it is more accurate to state that there are four, rather than three, major traditions in church history.

Emerging Churches in the World

Another important factor in the appreciation of the diversity of Christian theology is the new shape and fresh recognition of World Christianity. Philip Jenkins notes, "We are currently living through one of the transforming moments in the history of religion worldwide. . .The center of gravity of the Christian world has shifted inexorably southward, to Africa, Asia, and Latin America."[99] This statement expresses the new geographical contour of today's Christianity. In the past, Christianity was regarded as the Western religion (which derived mostly from the ignorance of other church traditions). For the past several decades, however, the number of Christian churches has rapidly increased in Africa, Asia, South America, and the South Pacific Islands.

The churches in these locations have formulated and developed their own ecclesiastic and theological traditions. Thus, the local churches in these areas have unique expressions of Christianity—in faith, lifestyle, church order, ritual, theology, etc. These local church traditions provide new perspectives on doing church and doing theology. Andrew Walls discusses African churches, in particular, and asserts that they have composed new Christian traditions that are distinctive from Orthodox, Catholic, and Protestant churches.[100]

Walls asserts that these traditions are "the standard Christianity of the present age, a demonstration model of its character."[101] Today, in terms of number, Africa has a significant ratio of the world's Christians. In addition, the African churches present new ways of Christian thoughts and practices to global Christianity.[102] Further, in my experience in Africa, African churches are deeply rooted in their cultures and meet the life exigencies of people.

Another important factor is that the current missional context has changed significantly. Today's Christian mission is not a one-way movement from Christian countries to non-Christian countries, or from West to East, or from the global North to the global South. Rather, it is a multi-lane movement from everywhere to everywhere. The Lausanne Covenant proposes, "Missionaries should flow ever more freely from and to all six continents in a spirit of humble service" (par. 9), and this has turned into

99. Jenkins, *Next Christendom*, 1–2.

100. Fyfe and Walls, *Christianity in Africa*, 3; Jenkins, *Next Christendom*, 148.

101. Fyfe and Walls, *Christianity in Africa*, 3

102. Ibid.

reality. As Mark A. Noll states, "Obviously, once-fixed notions of 'sending country' and 'receiving country' have been tossed into the air."[103] Today, the statement that Western countries are mission fields is not unfamiliar. The churches in Africa, Asia, and South America send missionaries to many different places around the globe, including Western countries.

In addition, immigrant churches play a significant role in Western countries. Previously, the question was how to preach the gospel to immigrants who have come from non-Western countries to Western countries. Today, however, a significant mission movement is carried out by immigrant churches in Western countries. Along with the churches in the non-Western world, immigrant churches in the West provide new energy and dynamics to existing churches in Western countries. They are more community oriented, sharing and serving each other. They also have more passion for preaching the gospel to the people in their societies. Soong-Chan Rah, a Korean immigrant pastor asserts that immigrant churches shape the characteristics of New Evangelicalism in the context of the United States:

> The real emerging church is the church in Africa, Asia and Latin America that continues to grow by leaps and bounds. I believe that the real emerging church is the hip-hop church, the English-speaking Latino congregation, the second-generation Asian American church, the Haitian immigrant church, the Spanish-speaking store-front churches and so forth.[104]

Immigrant churches in Western countries shape the churches in those countries with different theology and spirituality. They are emerging churches in a real sense. Significantly, they have developed their own theologies in their particular historical and cultural contexts.

Thus far, I have come at a singular argument from different perspectives, that is, there have been multiple traditions in Christianity throughout its history. Therefore, the monolithic understanding of Christian tradition cannot stand. Each tradition has formulated and developed its theology in a particular historical and cultural context. Thus, each tradition is the result of contextual theology. Each tradition plays a critical role in the people's way of doing theology, as it serves to guide and sometimes regulate norms and principles in each particular context.

103. Noll, *New Shape of World Christianity*, 10.

104. Rah, *Next Evangelicalism*, 124.

In the discussion of contextual theology, therefore, it is vital to explore the theology of each tradition. Constructing contextual theology is not a matter of creating a new theology, but of understanding and describing the existing theologies already contextualized in particular contexts. Tradition plays a significant role in these theologies.

SUMMARY

In this chapter, I have proposed that all theology is contextual theology. I have also proposed that there have been multiple traditions in Christianity throughout its history, and that each particular tradition of a people plays a critical role in their way of doing theology. I have explored contextual theology in order to support these proposals.

Theology is done by the people of a faith community in a given time and place. Theology is embedded in culture and, therefore, context-laden. A universal theology, which can be applied to any context, does not exist. Each and every theology is formulated and developed in a particular culture. Thus, all theology is contextual theology.

There are dangers in approaching contextual theology by using models of contextualization. Frequently, such approaches do not fit a people's real-life situation. Using models of contextualization also risks imposing outsiders' theology with foreign theological categories and concepts on the cultural insiders. It prevents them from being the agents of doing theology. Thus, the discussion of contextual theology must be descriptive rather than normative. In other words, contextual theology seeks to discover what happens when a people encounter the gospel in their context.

Tradition, which functions as a guiding and regulating principle, plays a critical role in doing theology. There are many different church traditions and many different theological traditions. Each tradition has formulated and developed its theology in a particular historical and cultural context. Thus, in the discussion of contextual theology, it is vital to explore the theology of each particular tradition. Constructing contextual theology is not necessarily a matter of creating a new theology. Rather, it is primarily a matter of understanding and describing the existing theologies already contextualized in particular contexts.

In this chapter, I have demonstrated the contextual nature of doing theology. In particular, I have demonstrated the significance of tradition and context, which provide a theological basis for contextual biblical interpretation. Thus, I have established the theological basis for placing this investigation of the EOTC's biblical interpretation in a broader discussion of contextual theology. In other words, the biblical interpretation of the EOTC can be properly discussed in terms of contextual theology.

The contextual nature of doing theology is concretely exhibited in biblical interpretation. The tradition and context of a faith community significantly influence their way of reading the biblical texts. Therefore, in the next chapter, I will discuss contextual reading of the Bible with a focus on the contextual nature of biblical interpretation.

2

Contextual Reading of the Bible

IN THE PREVIOUS CHAPTER, I demonstrated that all theology is contextual theology and that tradition and context have a significant influence in doing theology. This recognition leads to a discussion of contextual reading of the Bible, which is the main area of interest in this monograph. This chapter explores contextual biblical interpretation.

I propose that biblical interpretation is inherently contextual. In other words, people in a particular context have a specific way of reading (or hearing) and understanding biblical texts. The social location of a people, their particular culture and tradition, significantly influences their way of reading the biblical texts. Thus, all biblical interpretation is informed by context. Accordingly, historical criticism, which has dominated theology in general and biblical interpretation in particular for over two centuries, is also contextual. It has been formed and developed in a particular philosophical and theological milieu. In other words, there are different ways of reading the Bible found in faith communities throughout the world. The particular biblical interpretations of peoples in the world can contribute to an enriched understanding of the Bible for the global church.

Therefore, investigating the contextual nature of biblical interpretation will contribute to the overall thesis of this monograph that tradition and context significantly influence biblical interpretation, and that the Ethiopian Orthodox *Tewahido* Church provides a compelling example of contextual reading of the Bible. Through this investigation, I will elucidate the contextual nature of biblical interpretation. By so doing, I will provide a rationale for overcoming the dominant Western mode of biblical interpretation, which still has a significant influence throughout the world. In addition, I will offer a perspective from which to investigate the biblical interpretation of the EOTC, which is an illuminating example of contextual reading of the Bible.

In order to achieve these goals, I will address four significant and related aspects of contextual biblical interpretation in this chapter. I will begin with a description of the character of historical criticism. This will be followed by an investigation of the contextual nature of biblical interpretation through a critical interaction with historical criticism. Next, the aim and task of biblical interpretation will be addressed from this perspective. Finally, the role of tradition in biblical interpretation will be discussed in its theological and historical aspects.

THE CHARACTER OF HISTORICAL CRITICISM

This discussion of contextual biblical interpretation will begin with a description of historical criticism. I believe this is a significant task, given historical criticism's position and influence in theology. The development of historical criticism since 1800 has played an influential role in theological studies. Particularly, it has been the dominant mode of biblical interpretation in the West for the past two hundred years. I will argue that the dominance of this form of criticism has kept students from appreciating alternative forms of interpretation and their significance for other settings, like the EOTC.

Definition of Historical Criticism

Historical criticism is not easily defined. It is not a monolithic entity subject to precise definition. Its history includes different philosophical bases, and it has cultivated a constellation of related methods. Thus, there are diverse views and perspectives on historical criticism. Complicating a definition of historical criticism is that it has recently taken on different shapes as it has been challenged by modern and postmodern responses to it.

Nonetheless, the term "historical criticism" itself offers substantial clues for how best to understand its character. Whether it is described as a method or an approach, it can be defined as both "historical" and "critical." It is historical in its intended goals, and it is critical in its adopted methods to achieve these goals. This provides the beginning of a working definition of historical criticism.

Definitions provided by major historical critics are helpful here. In his classic book, *The Historical-Critical Method*, Edgar Krentz defines the historical-critical method as "a disciplined interrogation of their [modern biblical scholars'] sources to secure a maximal amount of verified information."[1] According to John J. Collins, a more recent historical critic, historical criticism refers to "any method or approach that attempts to interpret the biblical text first of all in its historical context, in light of the literary and cultural conventions of its time."[2]

Two major orientations for this approach are found in these terms: "historical" and "critical." First, historical critics are concerned with exploring history. Thus, the Bible is used as a source for the pursuit of history. "Historical criticism seeks to answer a basic question: to what historical circumstances does this text refer, and out of what historical circumstances did it emerge?"[3]

Second, their concern for historicity prompts historical critics to adopt the critical methods of modern science. As sources, the biblical texts are treated in the same manner as other literature. As John R. Donahue states, when joined with "historical," "Criticism . . . simply designates the application to biblical texts of the same methods of investigation and the same norms for truth that are used with other documents from a past and different culture."[4]

Sense of History

Historical critics conceive of their role as historians rather than as theologians. It is necessary, therefore, to grasp the sense of history basic to this interpretive paradigm. Typically, historical critics have assumed the modern scientific understanding of history. History, in this model, is perceived as being comprised of objective or empirical facts, that is, "what really happened." History has as its object human activities in a specific context, such as time, space, and society. It does not deal with abstract concepts or ideas, but with "real" events and "real" persons, and the causes and effects of their activities.[5]

1. Krentz, *Historical-Critical Method*, 6.
2. Collins, *Encounters with Biblical Theology*, 2.
3. Burnett, "Historical Criticism," 290.
4. Donahue, "Modern and Postmodern Critical Methods," 147.
5. Krentz, *Historical-Critical Method*, 34.

These historical facts should and can be verified scientifically. In this regard, the historian's task is analogous to that of the natural scientist. As a scientist, the historian seeks to gain a systematic knowledge of the past by adopting the scientific method of rational analysis. Events and human activities are frequently expressed in written documents, which are used as sources. Therefore, the historian begins by attempting to recover from the sources the facts as they "really happened." Van A. Harvey describes "this drive to recover 'the facts as they really happened'" as a "Promethean will-to-truth."[6]

The historian then attempts to determine the connectedness of these facts, and subsequently reconstruct them in a chronological order. Facts are arranged or ordered chronologically in order to indicate the relation of causation (cause and effect) among them. Through this process, history is "produced" and functions as "canonical rules against which to measure particular stories about the past and to pronounce them uncertain or false."[7] On this basis, the historian might attempt to discover the general rules of humanity and, eventually, to predict the future. This could "function as a guide for the reshaping of human life."[8]

Principles of Historical Criticism

There is general scholarly consensus that the principles of modern historical criticism were first formulated by Troeltsch in his essay, "On Historical and Dogmatic Method in Theology" (1898). He struggled with "the degree to which the presuppositions of the historian determine the conclusion,"[9] and suggested some interrelated principles on which critical historical inquiry might depend in order to obtain a "purely objective causal explanation" of history in historical inquiry.[10] He set up three principles of critical historiography on which historical critics have generally relied in their work: criticism, analogy, and correlation.

First, according to the principle of criticism, any judgment about the past in historical inquiry is subject to criticism. No conclusion can claim to attain absolute certainty, but gain only a relative degree of probability. Conclusions cannot "be classified as true or false but must be seen

6. Harvey, *Historian & the Believer*, 4.

7. Provan, "Knowing and Believing," 229.

8. Ibid., 235.

9. Harvey, *Historian & the Believer*, 14.

10. Troeltsch, "Historiography," 720.

as claiming only a greater or lesser degree of probability."[11] This principle is the basis of methodological doubt in historical criticism. All historical narratives, including the biblical texts, must be treated with suspicion with regard to their authenticity and be subjected to revision. All historical narratives in the Bible should be verified through critical inquiry of their historicity.

Second, the principle of analogy is the basis for the first principle of criticism. It assumes that all events are similar in principle. If this assumption stands, then it can be argued that "our own present experience is not radically dissimilar to the experience of the past persons."[12] Therefore, present events and experiences can become the criteria of probability in the past. As a natural corollary, historical critics are able to make judgments of probability on the experiences and occurrences in the past. Troeltsch refers to this as "the almighty power of analogy."[13]

Hence, methodologically, critics must be suspicious of anything in the texts that is not encountered in their ordinary lives. Accordingly, for example, miracles in the Bible should be rejected as unhistorical, because historical critics believe these phenomena do not take place in their present experiences.

Third, the principle of correlation means that all historical phenomena are interrelated and interdependent. No historical phenomenon can be isolated from the sequence of cause and effect. A change in one historical event brings about a change in the causes that have led to it and in the effects it has. Historical explanation rests on this chain of cause and effect. A historical event must be understood and explained in terms of its antecedents and consequences. All historical events are conditioned in their time and space.

This principle also has significant methodological implications for historical criticism. In order to verify the historicity of narratives in the Bible, critics must go back to their supposed origins, since they were the outcomes (effects) of the previous events or sources according to the chain of cause and effect in the principle of correlation. Further, the meaning of a historical narrative must be understood in its original context, since the narratives are conditioned in their times and spaces. According to historical critics, there exists no time or place where supernatural things

11. Harvey, *Historian & the Believer*, 14.

12. Ibid., 14–15.

13. Collins, *Encounters with Biblical Theology*, 12.

can occur, thus, they are rejected by the principle of correlation. This principle rules out supernatural phenomena, such as miracles, found in the narratives of the Bible.

There are, however, significant questions regarding the three principles of critical historiography. First, who is the subject performing a historical inquiry, applying all of these principles? Second, how is it possible for the subject to avoid fallacies in practicing these principles? Addressing these questions, John J. Collins adds a fourth principle in more recent discussion on the method of historical criticism: "To these should be added the principle of autonomy, which is indispensable for any critical study. Neither church nor state can prescribe for the scholar which conclusions should be reached."[14]

This implies that the only possible subjects for this approach are scholars who adopt the historical-critical method, and who are free from any prescriptions imposed by outside powers in their critical study of the biblical texts. Critics must exclude any type of prescription from tradition or church, or specific types of theology in historical inquiry, since these would constitute alien impositions on the historical process and would inevitably contaminate pure scientific historical inquiry.

These four basic principles work together as underlying methodological presuppositions in historical criticism.

Task and Goal of Historical Criticism

The major task of historical criticism is comprised of two features. The first is validating the authenticity of the biblical text ("when it is judged to represent historical events with accuracy"), and the second is the reconstruction of history ("when it is not").[15] According to John Barton, this task can be divided into three areas.

First, historical critics are to reconstruct the historical events and experiences underlying the biblical text. The reconstruction of historical events is the most distinctive task in historical criticism. Out of this concern, historical critics have worked on a history of Israel, the historical Jesus, and a history of the church in the New Testament period.[16]

14. Ibid.

15. Green, *Seized by Truth*, 16.

16. Barton, *Nature of Biblical Criticism*, 33.

Second, historical critics are to seek the "historical development of the biblical text, itself, in its underlying strata and sources."[17] Historical critics focus on the earlier stages of the biblical text rather than the final form of the Bible. They attempt to get "behind" the biblical text to the earlier texts from which it is assumed to be composed. Then, they investigate the origins, transmission, and development of the text.[18] They explore "why an idea borrowed from some earlier source becomes significant at a particular time and place in history, no sooner and no later."[19] The biblical texts function as a window to earlier sources and, in some cases, to past events themselves.

Third, historical critics are to find out "the 'historical meaning' of the texts, that is the meaning that texts had in their original context."[20] The basic assumption of historical criticism is that the meaning of the biblical text resides in its original context. Therefore, "texts should be interpreted in their original historical context, in light of the literary and cultural conventions of their time."[21]

In addition to this type of diachronic inquiry, historical critics are engaged in synchronic inquiry in order to establish and compare, say, the narratives of the Hebrew Bible with other contemporary Near Eastern sources and thereby gain their verification. For example, according to Krentz, "Extra-biblical literature is the basis of chronology, archaeology illuminates the daily life and cultic fixtures of ancient Israel, and inscriptions and Near Eastern annals give the course of world history in which Israelite history must be fitted."[22]

Finally, historical critics attempt to re-narrate the historical events underlying biblical narratives. They assert that this re-narration of the historical events is the real history, "what really happened." Therefore, historical critics engage in the reconstruction of history. This may be said to be the goal of historical criticism.

17. Ibid.

18. Burnett, "Historical Criticism," 290.

19. Krentz, *Historical-Critical Method*, 36.

20. Barton, *Nature of Biblical Criticism*, 33.

21. Collins, *Bible after Babel*, 4.

22. Krentz, *Historical-Critical Method*, 48.

The Position and Influence of Historical Criticism

Historical criticism has strongly influenced theology in general, and biblical interpretation in particular, for over two centuries. It has, however, generated serious theological and practical difficulties during its dominance. Thus, significant questions have been raised regarding the effects of historical criticism. New paradigms have been introduced, challenging the hegemony of historical criticism in theological and biblical studies. Moreover, questions regarding the validity of historical criticism for theological studies and biblical interpretation have been raised. Historical criticism has become a target of critical assessment and, as a result, has been losing its prominence.

Nevertheless, historical criticism still maintains power, not least in theological education. There are several reasons for this phenomenon. First, historical criticism originated in the West, but it has not been limited to the Western countries. Even when historical criticism has come under scrutiny in the West, it has continued to exercise dominance outside of the West. This is because the theological educators were trained by earlier generations of Western scholars.

Among the many critiques that might be directed against historical criticism, the most significant is the ideological orientation of its practitioners. By this, I refer to the way in which practitioners of historical criticism impose this theory and practice as though it alone possesses validity. One might argue that historical criticism, by its very nature, disregards other approaches. Therefore, one means of overcoming the difficulties of historical criticism is to demonstrate its inherently contextual nature. In the process of the critical assessment of historical criticism, the contextual nature of biblical interpretation will be made clear.

THE CONTEXTUAL NATURE OF BIBLICAL INTERPRETATION

All biblical interpretation is contextual by nature. Walter Dietrich and Ulrich Luz note the problem of Western biblical interpretation in general: it has been abstractly carried out "without context." It has produced, as a consequence, abstract truths that do not relate to any context. More specifically, it is "unattached to the life and reading of 'ordinary' people, far away from their questions . . . detached from the present and from its problems . . . disconnected from the real concerns of present-day readers."[23] While their conclusion regarding the consequences of Western biblical interpretation is valid, their argument is naïve and self-deceiving, since there can be no such thing as "context-less" interpretation. It is important to note that Western biblical interpretation itself is contextual, having originated and developed in a particular historical and cultural context.

In what follows, I will investigate the rationales for the contextual nature of biblical interpretation based on two important philosophical and theological grounds: social location and narrativity. Together, they help demonstrate the contextual nature of biblical interpretation from two different, but closely connected perspectives.

Social Location

The first philosophical and theological ground of contextual biblical interpretation is social location. I will develop the discussion of social location through an exploration of two related areas. First, I will critically assess historical criticism's posture of positivistic objectivity. Second, I will discuss interpretive developments based on the recognition of social location.

The Myth of Positivistic Objectivity

Objectivity is the philosophical and methodological foundation of historical criticism. It is not difficult to find the assumption of the researcher's objectivity in the writings of historical critics. For example, Troeltsch argues that the critical assessments of traditional Christian dogmas are to be done with an "apparent objectivity," having recourse to "the purely factual claim of Christianity."[24] From this perspective, objectivity is essential to grasping reality. In order to be objective, the researcher needs to be separated from reality. Critics must be located outside of the object of their inquiry, so that they can attempt their inquiry completely independent from it. In historical inquiry practitioners of historical criticism adopt a posture of detachment from the object of their research.

This commitment to objectivity derives from scientific positivism, which claims that authentic knowledge can be gained only on the basis of the actual sense of experience. In this understanding, scientists should be

23. Dietrich and Luz, *Bible in a World Context*, ix–x.

24. Troeltsch, *Religion in History*, 30.

as value-free as possible. This natural scientific method has been adopted by critical historians as the foundation of historical inquiry. Elizabeth A. Clark observes that "many historians, past and present, deemed the quest for objectivity fundamental to their recognition as professionals."[25]

Peter Novick quotes Richard Bernstein as saying, "At the heart of the objectivist's vision . . . is the belief that there are or must be some fixed, permanent constraints to which we can appeal and which are secure and stable."[26] The ideal of objectivity is a "noble dream" to pursue "an Archimedean point upon which knowledge could be grounded."[27] In this way, modern scientific historians have found the ground of knowledge in the objectivity of the researcher.

Thomas L. Haskell brings important nuance to this discussion by arguing that objectivity is not neutrality. He asserts that objectivity is "compatible with strong political commitment. It pays no premium for standing in the middle of the road, and it recognizes that scholars are as passionate and as likely to be driven by interest as those they write about. It does not value even detachment as an end itself, but only as an indispensable prelude or preparation for the achievement of higher levels of understanding."[28] If his definition is accepted as appropriate, the critical historians' ideal of objectivity is actually closer to neutrality, since their assumption of objectivity has been "grounded in early modern notions of scientific objectivity."[29] Historical critics' claim of objectivity can, therefore, be more appropriately rendered as neutral-objectivity.

The assumption of objectivity has not only been nuanced, but has come under serious challenges on philosophical and practical grounds. In response, some historical critics have taken a more defensive attitude. Krentz suggests that his own understanding of objectivity "does not demand neutrality or freedom from presuppositions."[30] Collins admits the inevitability of presuppositions, but insists that "some presuppositions are better or more adequate than others. One criterion for the adequacy of presuppositions is the degree to which they allow dialogue between

25. Clark, *History, Theory, Text*, 15.

26. Novick, *Noble Dream*, 538.

27. Ibid.

28. Haskell, *Objectivity Is Not Neutrality*, 150.

29. Clark, *History, Theory, Text*, 16.

30. Krentz, *Historical-Critical Method*, 70.

differing viewpoints and accommodate new insights."[31] In this assertion, he seems to accord privilege to the nature of contemporary academic inquiry over a more traditional historicism.

Barton denies the sort of objectivity that others have criticized as "a straw man."[32] However, he still argues for the possibility of reasonable objectivity. He describes reasonable objectivity as "a refusal simply to read one's own ideas into the text or to have no sense of detachment from it even for the purposes of study."[33]

Historical critics have tried to respond to the serious challenges of more recent study. However, they still hold to the basic assumption of objectivity in their historical and biblical inquiries. This is because objectivity remains the philosophical and methodological foundation on which historical criticism stands or falls.

Notably, natural science, which provided the philosophical and methodological foundation for historical criticism, has undergone revolutionary changes in its philosophies and practices. The ideal of objectivity has been recognized as a naïve expectation of discovering reality "just as it is." Scientists have come to acknowledge the inevitability of the observer's involvement in the act of observing the natural world. The presuppositions of the observer unavoidably shape their perception of the world. Human beings always approach an object with our knowledge, prejudices, and values.[34]

Historical criticism started with the desire to stand as a scientific discipline by adopting scientific presuppositions and methodology. However, the practitioners of historical criticism have not acknowledged and accepted the paradigm shift in the philosophy of science.[35] They still attempt to maintain positivistic objectivity in their historical and biblical inquiry.

Another important motivation for practitioners of historical criticism has been freedom from traditional and dogmatic presuppositions that might, in their view, damage their objective historical research. For this reason, any factors beyond Troeltsch's principles of criticism are excluded from the historical reconstruction of reality. These include

31. Collins, *Encounters with Biblical Theology*, 16.

32. Barton, *Nature of Biblical Criticism*, 49.

33. Ibid.

34. Provan et al., *Biblical History of Israel*, 38.

35. In his influential book, *The Structure of Scientific Revolution*, Thomas Kuhn explains scientific change in light of paradigm shift.

supernatural revelation or the influence of other authorities, such as ideologies, dogmas, and church traditions.

Regarding this basic motivation, Elisabeth Schüssler Fiorenza argues that "the positivistic value-neutral stance of historical critical studies was shaped by the struggle of biblical scholarship to free itself from dogmatic authority and ecclesiastical controls."[36] She relates this attitude to "the professionalization of academic life and the rise of the university."[37] In order for biblical studies to take a firm place as an objective science in academia, "freedom of ideology and dogmatic imposition" was considered to be a necessary precondition.[38] Paradoxically, this reveals to us the political and ideological nature of historical criticism. The practitioners of historical criticism have not been freed from their own interests.

It is important to note that historical criticism is also a tradition. Craig Bartholomew observes that historical criticism "is itself traditioned and has its own 'prejudices.'" He continues, "Those prejudices are not neutral but specially oriented against the Bible as scripture."[39] One of the philosophical and methodological foundations of historical criticism is "the belief that the authors of the texts would have been unavoidably marked by the historical epoch in which they were embedded."[40] Historical critics, however, have not applied this recognition to their own historical inquiry. They themselves are also historically restricted to their epochs. F. W. Dobbs-Allsopp argues, "Like the texts they study, critics are hopelessly embedded in their own cultures with all of that culture's attendant prejudices and biases."[41] Historical critics' understandings of the biblical texts are also unavoidably influenced by the values and presuppositions, individual and corporate, of their time.

Therefore, historical criticism is also a form of contextual interpretation. It came out of a specific historical and cultural context in human history. It originated and has developed in specific philosophical milieus in which biblical interpretation is embedded. Collins acknowledges that historical criticism "too is a tradition, with its own values and presuppositions, derived in large part from the Enlightenment and Western

36. Fiorenza, "Biblical Interpretation and Critical Commitment," 6.

37. Ibid.

38. Ibid.

39. Bartholomew, "Uncharted Waters," 25.

40. Dobbs-Allsopp, "Rethinking Historical Criticism," 244.

41. Ibid., 242.

humanism."[42] Likewise, in his introduction to the historical critical method, Krentz names historical criticism as "the child of the Enlightenment."[43] The emergence of historical criticism has been closely connected to Western modernity, especially the modern intellectual revolution.

Specifically, historical criticism was formulated under the significant influence of several phenomena in the Enlightenment and post-Enlightenment era of the West. First, eighteenth-century deductive and critical rationalism was a seminal factor for historical criticism. Second, scientism also had a strong impact in determining the character of historical criticism. Finally, nineteenth-century historicism influenced the present shape of historical criticism. These examples demonstrate that historical criticism is a contextual interpretation, formed and developed in a specific historical context.

Although historical criticism remains highly influential, it has lost its privileged position. The limits and difficulties of the presumption of objectivity have been recognized and articulated. There is a fresh understanding that all biblical interpretation, including historical criticism, is contextual; it is influenced by the perspectives of people in a particular context. There is no such thing as value-free and disinterested reading of the Bible, because all readings are situated and interested. This leads to an important philosophical ground for the contextual reading of the Bible: the social location of all interpreters.

Social Location

Two decades ago, Fernando F. Segovia noted two important and closely related developments in biblical criticism at the end of the twentieth century. The first is the emerging recognition of the critical place of standpoint or perspective in biblical interpretation. The second is the increasing diversity of biblical interpretation that has derived from new perspectives and standpoints around the globe.[44] I would argue that these interpretive developments are primarily concerned with the contextual nature of biblical interpretation.

The situatedness of biblical interpretation has been adopted by modern and postmodern critical and two-thirds world hermeneutics. With regard to situatedness, Hans-Georg Gadamer attempts to uncover the

42. Collins, *Encounters with Biblical Theology*, 16.

43. Krentz, *Historical-Critical Method*, 55.

44. Segovia, "Culture Studies and Contemporary Biblical Criticism," ix.

nature of human understanding. He argues that humans are embedded in the particular history and culture that shaped them. Thus, they have a "historically effected consciousness," which "is itself situated in the web of historical effects."[45] He continues, "Historically effected consciousness . . . is an element in the act of understanding itself."[46] Therefore, Gadamer claims, "All self-knowledge arises from what is historically pregiven."[47] He describes situation as representing "a standpoint that limits the possibility of vision."[48] In other words, humans see and understand the world from a particular standpoint.

Historically effected consciousness is the primary consciousness of the hermeneutical situation. Following the work of Gadamer, Green notes that biblical interpretation has paid close attention to the fact that "we bring with us always and everywhere ourselves—our presuppositions and histories, our stories."[49] More specifically, Green emphasizes the importance of "conceptual schemes," which are the "imaginative structures by which we make sense of the world around us, which we share with others, and which find expression in our actions."[50] Just as humans cannot "jump out of our skins," we cannot avoid conceptual schemes because they are the basis on which we have a sense of identity and carry out our practices.[51]

Similarly, Graham Ward argues that interpreters engage hermeneutics from a situated standpoint. He describes "a standpoint" as "a shared knowledge; an understanding of the world that, in being articulated, is recognized and held to be a better account of the world than others available."[52] According to Ward, standpoints come from different sources: identifications made in social construction of situated knowledge; wider cultural traditions, horizons, and practices; and various communities.[53] These recognitions have significant interpretive implications.

In recent years, there has been a growing recognition of the social location of the reader, and its impact on the reading of texts. Consequently,

45. Gardamer, *Truth and Method*, 300.

46. Ibid.

47. Ibid., 301.

48. Ibid.

49. Green, *Seized by Truth*, 24.

50. Green, *Practicing Theological Interpretation*, 40.

51. Green, *Seized by Truth*, 24.

52. Ward, *Cultural Transformation and Religious Practice*, 76.

53. Ibid., 79–80.

social location has been privileged as a primary factor that determines people's understanding of the biblical texts. As C. René Padilla asserts, "For each of us, the process of arriving at the meaning of Scripture is not only highly shaped by who we are as individuals but also by various social forces, patterns and ideals of our particular culture and our particular historical situation."[54] People's social location provides the perspective from and in which they see and understand the biblical texts.

In this discussion, I am referring to social location inclusively, incorporating both the location of a society and an individual's position in the society. Corporately, social location includes the overall sociocultural and historical context of a society. Individually, social location may include "personal history, gender, ethnicity, race, nationality, place of residence, education, occupation, political perspective, economic status, religious views or commitments, and so forth."[55] All of these factors shape communal and individual human identities, and influence our interpretive practices.

Social location is important because it recognizes communal and individual dimensions as significant factors. As Michael Barram asserts, "Every interpretation comes from a 'place' to the extent that no interpreter can fully avoid the influence of [his or her social location] . . . As we read the biblical text, therefore, what we see, hear, and value is inevitably colored by our own situations, experiences, characteristics, and presuppositions."[56]

Segovia also emphasizes the role of flesh-and-blood readers and their social location in the reading and interpretation of the Bible. He argues, "all such readers are themselves regarded as variously positioned and engaged in their own respective social locations. Thus, different real readers use different strategies and models in different ways, at different times, and with different results (different readings and interpretations) in the light of their different and highly complex social locations."[57] In actuality, there is a multitude of voices reading and interpreting the Bible from different parts of the world.

For flesh-and-blood readers in the West, who live in a world shaped by the Enlightenment, historical criticism emanating from the

54. Padilla, "Interpreted Word," 18.

55. Barram, "Bible, Mission, and Social Location," 44.

56. Ibid.

57. Segovia, "Culture Studies and Contemporary Biblical Criticism," 7.

Enlightenment carries a certain weight. But readers in Africa, and specifically in Ethiopia, have no experience or understanding of the events and outcomes of the Enlightenment. Therefore, the use of historical criticism has little meaning for them.

Narrativity

The next important philosophical and theological ground of contextual biblical interpretation is narrativity. This important foundation is revealed in two different aspects: human narrativity and the narrative nature of the Bible. Both are significant points in understanding the contextual nature of biblical interpretation.

Human Narrativity

Narrativity deals primarily with the nature of humanity and human life. W. R. Fisher proposes a master metaphor, "*homo narrans*," to represent the essential nature of human beings.[58] Green points out recent developments in natural science in its understanding of humanity. In natural science, the centrality of narrativity to human existence has been brought into relief. Green states, "science itself has come full circle now to underscore the storied quality of distinctively human existence."[59] Human beings are story-tellers, and stories represent human beings.

Human life is characterized by narrative in various respects. First, our personal and communal life is composed of narrative. Life itself is understood in light of the structure and meaning of narratives. As Alasdair MacIntyre appropriately asserts, "We all live out narratives in our lives" and "we understand our own lives in terms of narratives."[60] In other words, our self-understanding is narratively determined. Our identity is narratively shaped. We also understand others in terms of narrative, and build relationships based on narrative. We make and tell stories in relationship with others in a specific context. Thus, narrative is the basis of human relationship, particularly communal life.

Second, humans perceive and interpret reality by way of narrative. According to Green, our conceptual schemes, mentioned above, are formulated in terms of narrative. They are embodied in the stories of our life by which we understand the world around us and take particular actions.

58. Fisher, "Narrative as a Human Communication Paradigm," 6.

59. Green, "(Re-)Turn to Narrative," 15.

60. MacIntyre, *After Virtue*, 212.

Green states, "Narrative is so crucial to the formation of one's identity and beliefs that humans will actually fabricate stories in order to give meaning to their present situations."[61]

Third, human actions are basically characterized by narrative. We make decisions and take action within the framework of narrative. As the essential mode of human representation of reality, narrative is the most common form of communication. All forms of human communication have narratives in some way. Accordingly, as Fisher states, "there is no genre, including technical communication, that is not an episode in the story of life (a part of the 'conversation')."[62] In these ways, narrativity is the essential mode of human existence.

Narrative Representation of History

The narrative perspective of human life enables us to address the relation of history and narrative, which is a significant issue in contemporary biblical interpretation. Recently, attention has been given to narrative representation among historians and philosophers. Some of them view it negatively. Historical critics have claimed that "narratives involve art, not science; are thus by nature interpretive; and are therefore insufficiently objective."[63] For historical critics, narrative is not history, but fiction, which has been invented. And invented stories cannot truthfully represent real life.

This negative view of narratives can be refuted on several solid bases. First, the term "fiction" has two different meanings. On the one hand, fiction is an invented story, which implies that it does not represent real life. This is the historical critics' understanding of fiction. On the other hand, fiction is a literary style, which is a way of delivering reality. Fiction, in this sense, does not necessarily mean falsity. It is rather to be understood as a strategy or skill employed to represent reality.

Accordingly, Meir Sternberg questions the truth claims of critical historians, and affirms the validity of fiction-writing for truth value. He argues that "history-writing is not a record of fact—of what 'really happened'—but a discourse that claims to be a record of fact. Nor is fiction-writing a tissue of free inventions but a discourse that claims freedom of invention. The antithesis lies not in the presence or absence of truth value

61. Green, *Practicing Theological Interpretation*, 27.

62. Fisher, "Narrative Paradigm," 347.

63. Provan et al., *Biblical History of Israel*, 75.

but of the commitment to truth value."[64] Thus, the narrative form of discourse does not exclude the historicity of the stories, but is an artistic way of writing history.

Similarly, Hayden White distinguishes between "historical" and "fictional" stories. He argues that it is not the form of the stories but their content that distinguishes them. The content of historical stories is not invented events but the events that happened. The narrative as a form of discourse does not change the content it represents. Rather, it aims at representing the events that really happened without adding anything to the content. As far as this representation resembles reality, "it must be taken as a true account."[65]

This assertion is supported by the narrative nature of human beings and human life. In order to share our personal histories, we construct and tell our stories to others. We also understand the actions of others in the way of narrative. As MacIntyre states, "In successfully identifying and understanding what someone else is doing we always move towards placing a particular episode in the context of a set of narrative histories, histories both of the individuals concerned and of the settings in which they act and suffer."[66] In this way, narrativity permeates everyday human life and every human relationship.

In addition, narratives themselves take part in the determination of the meaning of reality. Hans Frei points out that "meaning and narrative shape bear significantly on each other."[67] In order to represent reality, the form of narrative is decided in advance. Then, the reality is organized according to the narrative structure. In this process, the narrator's interpretation of the reality is involved. Accordingly, narrative is a representation of the interpreted reality. It reveals the writer's understanding of the meaning of the reality. Readers gain their own understanding of the meaning of the reality through the narratives of the text.

Thus, narrative can be rightly affirmed as a mode of historical representation. It is, in other words, "a legitimate mode of historical reportage."[68] Therefore, we can state with White, "Where there is no narrative . . . there

64. Sternberg, *Poetics of Biblical Narrative*, 25.

65. White, *Content of the Form*, 27.

66. MacIntyre, *After Virtue*, 211.

67. Frei, *Eclipse of Biblical Narrative*, 11.

68. Provan et al., *Biblical History of Israel*, 76.

is no history."[69] Historical critics' pejorative use of the term "narrative" in historical representation cannot be justified. Reality is represented in narrative, and it is in narrative that the writing of history is carried out. In addition, peoples' corporate lives are carried in narratives. For example, the narrative of the EOTC represents the history and culture of the church. It reveals the tradition of the church and life situation of the Ethiopian people, particularly believers of the EOTC.

The Narrative Nature of the Bible

The preceding discussion leads to the second important point regarding narrativity in biblical interpretation: the narrative nature of the Bible. The narrative nature of the biblical canon has been emphasized among various scholars. While the Bible includes different literary genres, significant parts of the Bible are narratives. In addition, significantly, the Bible as a whole has a narrative structure. Not just narratives *per se*, but also other forms of the biblical texts, are placed in the narrative structure, as parts of the overarching narrative of the Bible. This narrative structure of the Bible as a way of historical representation is a hermeneutical key to understanding the biblical texts.

Frei discusses the narrative that connects the biblical stories together in a unified whole: "If the real historical world described by the several biblical stories is a single world of one temporal sequence, there must in principle be one cumulative story to depict it. Consequently, the several biblical stories narrating sequential segments in time must fit together into one narrative."[70] Robert W. Jenson asserts that the canon of the biblical texts was construed by this narrative unity. Therefore, the biblical texts are to be read as "a single plotted succession of events, stretching from creation to consummation, plotted around exodus and resurrection."[71]

Green puts it more concretely: "as a whole, the Bible narrates the work of God: from Genesis to Revelation, from creation to new creation, with God's mighty acts of redemption, in the exodus from Egypt to the promised land and the new exodus of Jesus' life, death, and resurrection, the center points in God's grand story." He continues, "It is in this sense

69. White, *Content of the Form*, 5.

70. Frei, *Eclipse of Biblical Narrative*, 2.

71. Jenson, "Scripture's Authority," 29.

that Scripture itself promotes a narrative structure by which to comprehend the world."[72]

The Bible is the story of God with many stories in it, and many terms have been used to describe it: the grand narrative, the gospel, salvation history, divine economy, and theodrama. Regardless of the term used, the recognition that the Bible is the story of God provides a very important hermeneutical insight in biblical interpretation. The parts of the Bible compose the grand narrative of the Bible, which is, however, more than just an accumulation of the parts. Thus, each part of the Bible should be interpreted in light of the cumulative narrative. The grand narrative functions as a hermeneutical key to interpreting each and every biblical text. Therefore, all biblical texts must be interpreted in light of the unifying narrative of the Bible.

The narrative nature of the Bible leads to two significant understandings of the Bible. First, the Bible is a historical narrative. Second, the Bible is a theological narrative.

The Bible as Historical Narrative.

As discussed above, historical critics define history as "what really happened." They hold that the Bible is not real history, but merely contains sources for the reconstruction of real history. The Bible is one of many sources to be used for their historical inquiry. The biblical texts must, therefore, be treated like other sources. Krentz states that historical critics refuse "to take all documents at face value."[73] He asserts that sources are not themselves history and do not give immediate access to history.[74]

The view of history maintained by historical critics can be refuted on very significant grounds. History is not "what really happened" in the past, and the historian's task is not a chronological reconstruction of past events. Rather, history is an active engagement of the historian with the past. It includes the historian's selection and connection of events. In one sense, there are countless historical "facts" out in the world to be admitted. It is neither possible nor desirable to record all of these facts in the writing of history. The historian must select some evidence for historical inquiry. Certain evidence is selected as significant, while other

72. Green, *Practicing Theological Interpretation*, 29.

73. Krentz, *Historical-Critical Method*, 41.

74. Ibid., 42.

evidence is dismissed. As Albert Cook states, "All writing of history is synecdochic."[75] All historians assert that the selected evidence, and its presentation within a certain framework, is history.

In the process of selection, the historian has already made judgments regarding individual events. The selected facts themselves do not mean anything. As Haskell notes, facts do not speak for themselves.[76] Cook asserts, "What counts as an event is in itself initially unstable and cannot be fully stabilized."[77] Facts must be validated and verified as to their significance with reference to one another.

This necessarily invites the historian's further interpretation of the historical referents. The historian interprets the historical events within certain frameworks and criteria. Therefore, history is not just what really happened, but rather an interpretation of the historical events. The writing of history presupposes the historian's prior understanding of the meaning and relation of individual events. From certain perspectives and for certain purposes, the interpreted evidence is organized and presented as history. Individual events themselves are not yet history, as they wait for interpretation. In other words, no history can be written without interpretation. Therefore, all historiography is interpretive.

In this sense, the Bible is a historical narrative. The narrative representation of history does not negate the historicity of the Bible. The biblical narratives must be understood as both art and history, "not in terms of some fifty-fifty, fiction-fact mixture but in terms of true history artfully presented."[78] The Bible is historical narrative; it represents history in narrative form. Historical critics err in thinking of the biblical material only or primarily as sources, rather than as attempts to narrate a people's history.

The Bible as Theological Narrative.

The Bible is a theological, as well as a historical, narrative. The biblical narratives are not merely an artistic representation of history, but also theologically interpreted history. They relate how biblical authors comprehended historical events, and reveal the significance of the events as

75. Cook, *History Writing*, 137.

76. Haskell, *Objectivity Is Not Neutrality*, 146.

77. Cook, *History Writing*, 4.

78. Provan et al., *Biblical History of Israel*, 88.

the authors understood them theologically. Yet, the theological interpretation of the events does not obviate history. All history is interpreted history. It is interpreted by the historical inquirer, who works with certain presuppositions and purposes. It is such interpretation that makes sense of the historical occurrences and renders those events as history.

The Bible is the story of God and, therefore, it is a theological narrative. The biblical narratives talk about God's identity, character, and work. The Bible is the special revelation of God's involvement in history. Thus, history is "set within the context of God's purpose for all nations," and the biblical authors held "the conviction that a true account of history will relate the involvement of God in the successive unfolding of events."[79]

The core of the problem with historical criticism is its presupposition that "history cannot be the medium of divine self-disclosure."[80] This presupposition has led historical critics, as Krentz acknowledges, to exclude "God as a causative factor" and to deny the possibility of miracles.[81] Collins also admits "a clash between two conflicting moralities, one of which celebrated faith and belief as virtues and regarded doubt as sin, whereas the other celebrated methodological skepticism and was distrustful of prior commitments."[82] These assertions expose the secular nature of historical criticism. They also reveal the inescapably contextual nature of historical criticism.

The secular approach to history does not necessarily guarantee a higher possibility of discovering historical reality. In fact, historical criticism has ruled out the most important aspect of the Bible. As Murray Rae articulates:

> The Bible is a theological account of history. It is an account that is shaped by the conviction that all that takes place does so within the context of God's providential care for the created order . . . the writing of history is an undertaking that seeks and offers an explanation for the unfolding of events. . . . There is no good reason to suppose that a purely secular account of history, in which divine action is dispensed with as an explanatory category, brings the historian closer to the truth. . . . In quest of a status and supposed legitimacy comparable to that of the

79. Rae, "Creation and Promise," 283.

80. Ibid., 282.

81. Krentz, *Historical-Critical Method*, 58.

82. Collins, *Encounters with Biblical Theology*, 13.

> natural sciences, historical inquiry in the modern era has been undertaken . . . without recourse to the "God hypothesis."[83]

In sum, the Bible is a historical and theological narrative. It has a narrative structure, and is historically grounded and theologically interpreted. The stories in the Bible narrate historical events with theological assumptions and interpretations. As Green properly argues, the Bible has "the inherently theological nature of the narrative representation of historical events."[84]

Human narrativity and the narrative nature of the Bible are two important bases for the contextual nature of biblical interpretation. A people hear and read the narratives of the Bible in their narrative context. Western readers read in the light of their (Western) history, and African readers read in the light of the stories and myths that shape their understanding of the world. This generates particular understandings of the biblical texts and leads to particular practices in a people's life and faith situation. I will develop this in the following discussion.

TASK AND AIM OF INTERPRETATION

The contextual nature of biblical interpretation clarifies the two primary concerns in interpreting the Bible: task and aim. The discussion that follows will address these concerns by beginning with an exploration of the church as the interpretive community. This will be followed by a discussion of the task, and then the aim, of biblical interpretation.

Church as the Interpretive Community

Hearing and reading the Bible is an inherently communal event. As Ukpong states, "The readings are mediated through a particular *conceptual frame of reference* derived from the worldview and the sociocultural context of a particular cultural community. This differs from community to community. It informs and shapes the exegetical methodology and the reading practice and acts as a grid for making meaning of the text."[85] Each and every culture has its own way of hearing or reading, and understanding a text. Practically, in many cultures, reading or hearing the biblical texts is performed in the context of community.

83. Rae, "Creation and Promise," 283.

84. Green, *Practicing Theological Interpretation*, 52.

85. Ukpong, "Contextualization," 27.

The faith community, in particular, fulfills the role of the hermeneutical community in the process of interpreting biblical texts. As Scott Swain appropriately notes, "reading is a communal enterprise for the same reasons that Christianity is a communal enterprise."[86] God has charged the church to "obediently guard, discern, proclaim and interpret the word of God."[87] As God's people, the church is the intended addressee of the Bible. First, the biblical texts were written and read in the context of the community of God's people. As Green notes, "The biblical materials have their genesis and formation within the community of God's people. They speak most clearly and effectively from within and to communities of believers."[88]

In addition, the Bible addresses the contemporary church. God speaks to the church through the biblical texts; the immediacy of the Bible is experienced by the community of faith. Therefore, interpretation of the Bible is, primarily, the task of the church. Green asserts, "The best interpreters are those actively engaged in communities of biblical interpretation. . . . No interpretive tool, no advanced training, can substitute for active participation in a community concerned with the reading and performance of Scripture."[89]

Thus, the church is the primary context for biblical interpretation. Importantly, the local churches over the globe are the hermeneutical community, as these reflect ethnic and long term theological traditions. They are located in particular historical and cultural contexts. Each faith community reads or hears and understands the biblical texts, and generates practices in their particular contexts.

Task of Interpretation

It is generally held that the task of interpretation is to find the meaning of the texts. However, in practice, the attempt to seek the meaning of a text encounters difficulties. First, there are various definitions of "meaning" among interpreters. According to Jorge J. E. Gracia, the term "meaning" has many different senses: meaning as significance, meaning as reference, meaning as intention, meaning as ideas, meaning as use.[90] Therefore, if

86. Swain, "Ruled Reading Reformed," 180.

87. Ibid., 182.

88. Green, *Seized by Truth*, 66.

89. Ibid., 66–7.

90. Gracia, "Meaning," 492–93.

there is no consensus on the sense of the meaning, it is very difficult to develop a discussion of the meaning of the text. Thus, it is essential to define "meaning" in order to develop the discussion of establishing the meaning of the text as the interpretive task.

In this regard, E. D. Hirsch, Jr. distinguishes between two aspects of textual interpretation: meaning and significance. He states, "Meaning is that which is represented by a text; it is what the author meant by his use of a particular sign sequence; it is what the signs represent. Significance, on the other hand, names a relationship between that meaning and a person, or a conception, or situation, or indeed anything imaginable."[91] In this view, "meaning" is "fixed and immutable," but "significance" is open to change. Significance "typically embraces the present use of texts, and present use *is* present value."[92]

According to Hirsch, "A text means what its author meant,"[93] and the author's meaning is the only normative concept that can be universally accepted.[94] He clarifies his assertion as follows: "The significance and use of a text ought to be rooted in its fixed meaning."[95] Accordingly, in order to understand the texts, it is mandatory to know the meaning the authors originally intended in their writing. Many interpretive approaches are based on this understanding. Many scholars maintain that the author's intention establishes the meaning of a text and, therefore, they attempt to determine authorial intent.

Hirsch's distinction between meaning and significance is highly problematic, and has been criticized. Hirsch himself notes certain criticisms of his distinction: the distinction between authorial meaning and significance is artificial;[96] interpretive practice, the reconstruction of authorial meaning is impossible.[97] Later, Hirsch adjusted his distinction of the two terms. He states, "Meaning is the determinate representation of a text for an interpreter. An interpreted text is always taken to represent something, but that something can always be related to something else.

91. Hirsch, *Aims of Interpretation*, 8.

92. Hirsch, "Meaning and Significance Reinterpreted," 202.

93. Hirsch, *Validity in Interpretation*, 1.

94. Ibid., 25.

95. Hirsch, "Meaning and Significance Reinterpreted," 203.

96. Hirsch, *Aims of Interpretation*, 3.

97. Ibid., 81.

Significance is meaning-as-related-to-something-else."[98] Here, the sense of "meaning" is more nuanced.

However, despite these changes, Hirsch argues that his essential view remains the same. He continues to defend "the stable determinacy of meaning."[99] He argues, "Without the stable determinacy of meaning there can be no knowledge in interpretation, nor any knowledge in the many humanistic disciplines based upon textual interpretation."[100] Therefore, the primary task of biblical interpretation remains the same: to find the fixed meaning of a text.

Historical criticism also attempts to find the fixed meaning of the text, particularly in its original context. In this approach, the meaning of a text is identified by the past historical events of its original context. This identification leads historical critics to pursue the origin of the biblical text and its original historical situation. This has motivated historical critics to engage in an "endless regress toward the referent" in the past.[101]

There are several significant problems with this approach. First, it is questionable whether a sacred text belongs to its point of origin. In addition, as noted above, it is impossible to reconstruct the "real" history of the text's original context. Therefore, many of the suggested views on the original meaning of the text are based on mere hypotheses. They also frequently contradict one another. The attempt to find fixed meanings of the biblical texts results in a lack of consensus even among historical critics. It produces ever-growing complexity and conflicts regarding the supposed fixed meaning of the text.

I oppose the notion that there is only one fixed meaning of a text, which exists somewhere in author, text, or original context. Attempts to find the fixed meaning of a text presuppose that meaning is out there somewhere, waiting to be grasped by the interpreter. I suspect that this comes from the presupposition, conscious or unconscious, that if scholars grasp the meaning of the texts, then we can control them, rather than being controlled by them. In this paradigm, the ultimate goal of interpretation becomes establishing the fixed meaning of the text.

My argument is that the interpretive task in biblical interpretation is to understand the text, not to seek the fixed meaning of the text. Luke

98. Hirsch, *Aims of Interpretation*, 79–80.

99. Ibid., 1.

100. Ibid.

101. Cook, *History Writing*, 4.

Timothy Johnson asserts this in these terms: "Scripture itself imagines a world. By imagining a world, Scripture brings it into being."[102] He continues, "By imagining the world as always and essentially related to God, Scripture reveals the world and at the same time reveals God."[103] In this perspective, interpreting biblical texts must be focused on grasping the world the Bible imagines.

As Angus Paddison notes, the interpretive task concerns "what the text is talking about and pointing towards."[104] In this approach, to understand "the substance of what the text is ultimately trying to communicate" is the task of interpretation.[105] In other words, understanding the subject matter of the Bible is the task of biblical interpretation.

Significantly, the reader always understands biblical texts in his or her social location and with particular interests. In other words, understanding of the texts takes place in the encounter between the text and the reader, as Gadamer and Riceour assert. The text has its own textual interest, and the reader has his or her own interest. When the reader encounters the biblical text, he or she gains a certain understanding of the text. Therefore, understanding of the text is made possible where the textual interest and the reader's interest encounter each other.

In sum, the task of biblical interpretation is not seeking meaning with the assumption that meaning exists somewhere in author, text, or reader, but understanding the subject matter—what the text talks about and points toward. David C. Steinmetz states, "Those possible meanings are not dragged by the hair, willy-nilly, into the text, but belong to the life of the Bible in the encounter between author and reader as they belong to the life of any act of the human imagination."[106] Such an encounter always happens in a particular context. Therefore, the task of biblical interpretation is to seek an understanding of the text that arises from an encounter with the text in the interpreter's particular context—specifically, in the concrete narrative context of the interpreter.

102. Johnson, "Imagining the World Scripture Imagines," 165.

103. Ibid.

104. Paddison, *Theological Interpretation and 1 Thessalonians*, xi.

105. Ibid., 1.

106. Steinmetz, "Superiority of Pre-Critical Exegesis," 37.

Aim of Interpretation

The aim of biblical interpretation is to hear and respond to biblical texts faithfully so that we can come to know God and grow into the likeness of Christ. The Bible primarily talks about God. The biblical texts reveal who God is. In other words, God is the main character in the narrative of the Bible. Through attentive reading of the biblical texts, therefore, readers will come to know God. According to Green, biblical interpretation is concerned with "encountering the God who stands behind and is mediated in Scripture."[107] Biblical interpretation seeks to know God from the intrinsic testimony of the Bible, not to obtain abstract concepts of God imposed from extrinsic conceptual frameworks.

Human beings' knowledge of God is closely connected to our self-knowledge. We know ourselves genuinely only through our knowledge of God. This knowledge also enables us to know the world God made. Therefore, knowledge of God is the prerequisite for authentic knowledge of the self and the world. Through reading the Bible, we come to know and commit ourselves to the purpose of God for ourselves and the world. This knowledge of God and the formation of our lives into the purpose of God is the goal of biblical interpretation.

Here, the importance of biblical narrative comes into relief. As discussed previously, the Bible is the story of God. Thus, we know God through reading the narrative of God in the Bible. In other words, our knowledge of God is obtained in the context of the biblical narrative.

It is also important to note that knowledge of God is always relational. Knowledge of God gained in reading the Bible enables human beings to have the right relationship with God. Concurrently, our relationship with God leads us to a deeper knowledge of God in our understanding of the biblical texts. In other words, there is a hermeneutical spiral of knowledge of and relationship with God.

Knowing God is not just cognitive information about God. The biblical concept of genuine knowledge is always expressed by practice. *Theoria* and *praxis* are always, consistently joined. This is the transformational dimension of knowledge of God. As Kevin J. Vanhoozer appropriately asserts, "all textual understanding is a theological matter—an encounter with something that transcends us and has the capacity to transform us, provided that we approach it in the right spirit."[108]

107. Green, *Practicing Theological Interpretation*, 5.

108. Vanhoozer, *Is There a Meaning in This Text?*, 381.

Generally speaking, readers of the Bible tend to be concerned primarily with how we interpret the biblical texts for our use, but we do not often consider what God does through the texts. In our interpretative work, we must focus our attention on the purpose of God revealed in the Bible. God aims at the transformation of his people, and the global proclamation of the gospel, through which God eventually achieves his purpose. Therefore, we must attune ourselves to the purpose of God as the goal of our biblical interpretation. Faithful reading of the Bible forms and transforms us, and leads us to proclaim the gospel throughout the world.

Thus, biblical interpretation is to be directed to the change of life. Readers of the Bible must read biblical texts with this purpose in mind. Green describes the appropriate attitude of readers of the biblical text as follows:

> We remain open to God's challenge of developing those habits of life that make us receptive to God's vision, God's character, and God's project, animating these texts as Scripture and, then, textualized in and emanating from these pages. We come to Scripture with dispositions of risky openness to a reordering of the world, repentance for attitudes of defiance of the grace of God's self-revelation, hospitable to a conversion of our own imagination. . . . We would take on the persona of their addressees, allowing the terms of these texts to address us: to critique, to encourage, to motivate, to instruct, to redirect—that is, to shape us.[109]

Such an attitude will transform our life according to the will of God. This is the life that embodies the Bible. Speaking of transformative biblical knowledge in terms of narrativity, the Bible invites us into its narrative world. As Green asserts, "The biblical narrative is present as an alternative framework within which to construe our lives, and so challenges those who would be Christian by calling for a creative transformation of the stories by which we make sense of our lives and of the world."[110]

Such transformations always take place in narrative contexts. Human beings read and hear the biblical narratives in their narrative context. Consequently, the encounter of the biblical narratives and our narratives generates understanding of the text and brings about action. Eventually, it creates new narratives of formation and transformation in

109. Green, *Practicing Theological Interpretation*, 20.

110. Green, "(Re-)Turn to Narrative," 17.

our life situation. Our way of understanding biblical texts is significantly influenced by our particular narratives in our historical and cultural location. Thus, genuine biblical interpretation is always contextual.

ROLE OF TRADITION IN BIBLICAL INTERPRETATION

No human reads or hears the biblical texts in a historical or cultural vacuum. Tradition, in particular, plays a substantial role in biblical interpretation. Consciously or not, we read the Bible under the influence of tradition that has been formed and passed on in particular historical and cultural contexts. Gadamer emphasizes the importance of tradition in interpretation, "Understanding is to be thought of less as a subjective act than as participating in an event of tradition, a process of transmission in which past and present are constantly mediated."[111] Humans approach the biblical texts with certain pre-understandings that we have received from tradition. These pre-understandings have a critical effect on our reading of the biblical texts. They are not barriers to understanding; they actually enable it.

Tradition is the ground on which any interpretation of the text is made possible. Therefore, it is important to recognize the influence of tradition in our reading of the Bible. Specifically, it is an essential task to understand the tradition of any hermeneutical community in order to understand their characteristic interpretation of the Bible. In what follows, therefore, I will discuss the significant role of tradition in biblical interpretation, especially in regard to two prominent traditional areas: theological tradition in general and the Rule of Faith in particular.

Theological Traditions as the Guiding Interpretive Principle

The term "tradition" refers to "streams of influence": cultural, ecclesial, theological, and exegetical. While all of these influence readings of the Bible, I will focus mainly on theological tradition. Theological tradition functions as the guiding principle in biblical interpretation. As Rae asserts, we read the Bible from the theological context.[112] The theological traditions of the theological context may include religious practices (liturgy, Eucharist, baptism, and festivals), confessions (creeds, dogmas, and

111. Gardamer, *Truth and Method*, 291.

112. Rae, "Texts in Context," 41.

doctrines), art and music, and the experiences of the faith community in particular historical and cultural contexts.

As indicated above, along with theological traditions, we appropriate the biblical texts with our personal knowledge and experiences, as well. Robert W. Wall properly notes that the interpreter's personal experience influences the interpretation of the biblical texts.[113] I will refer to this aspect of interpretation as personal pilgrimage. Dyrness asserts that the interaction of tradition and personal experience may be understood as "the traditional formation" and "the individual appropriation" of tradition.[114] Even in this interaction, tradition stands out as "the primary interpreter of Scripture."[115] Readings of the biblical texts are typically done in line with particular theological traditions. Biblical interpretation is carried out within such a theological context.

More specifically, the influence of theological tradition permeates our interpretive task at critical points. First, human beings read the Bible with theological assumptions about the author, text, and audience that are given by tradition. These assumptions determine our basic attitudes toward the biblical texts in our interpretive task. As noted previously, our presuppositions and attitudes make a substantial difference in our interpretation of the texts.

Secondly, we prioritize theological concerns when we read the biblical texts. Green defines theological concerns as "the role of Scripture in the faith and formation of persons and ecclesial communities."[116] These theological concerns guide interpretation of the biblical texts. In this way, theological tradition sets the goal of our interpretation. In other words, our exegetical task becomes a way of achieving the goal set by our theological tradition. While the credibility of this kind of approach may be questioned, theological tradition is a reality in which people frequently engage in the interpretative task.

Third, interpretation of the biblical texts is practically guided by theology. Gracia argues that theology is necessary for the interpretation of biblical texts: "Theology governs . . . the interpretation of revealed texts."[117] He asserts, "Theology is not only a hermeneutical tool for inter-

113. Wall, "Reading the Bible from within Our Tradition," 94.

114. Dyrness, *Senses of Devotion*, 5.

115. Williams, *Evangelicals and Tradition*, 93.

116. Green, "What Is Theological Interpretation?"

117. Gracia, *How Can We Know What God Means?*, 144.

pretation, but more importantly, it is the ultimate determining factor of scriptural meaning."[118] In many cases, various biblical texts have already been theologically interpreted and taught in line with tradition. In some church traditions, interpretive novelty is not welcomed.

Further, as Rowan A. Greer assets, "the role of theology is not only decisive in shaping exegetical results, it is of great importance in the formation of exegetical methods."[119] In the actual process of interpretation, we adopt our interpretive methods in order to achieve our intended theological goals. The most significant factor in this type of exegesis is the theological tradition that drives the interpretation, which includes the selection of exegetical methods.

Finally, theological tradition sets boundaries and parameters in interpreting the biblical texts. It prohibits arbitrary readings of the text that do not cohere with the tradition, while encouraging readings of the biblical texts in line with tradition. As D. H. Williams points out, the church tradition functions as "the chief hermeneutic for discerning the difference between true and false doctrine," even though it "emerges from definite times and spaces."[120]

For example, the significant role of theological tradition is apparent in the patristic interpretation of the biblical texts. Recent patristic scholarship recognizes the critical role of theological tradition in biblical interpretation. Theology is considered to be one of the most prominent factors conditioning the exegetical differences in the patristic interpretive traditions. Donald Fairbairn argues that, in patristic biblical interpretation, "theology was the horse and exegesis the cart," not the other way around. He continues, "patristic exegesis . . . was a task of reading all of Scripture in light of a controlling theological idea."[121]

Fairbairn's claim depends heavily on Rowan A. Greer's book, *The Captain of Our Salvation* (1973). In his study of the patristic exegesis of Hebrews, Greer explores the role of theology in patristic exegesis. He contends that "theology . . . shapes exegesis in the sense that it determines the questions asked of the text." He continues, "The correlation between theology and exegesis is to be defined as that between the question

118. Gracia, "Meaning," 499.

119. Greer, *Captain of Our Salvation*, 5.

120. Williams, *Evangelicals and Tradition*, 23.

121. Fairbairn, "Patristic Exegesis and Theology," 10.

posed and the answer obtained from the text."[122] Particularly, "when the questions arise from theological controversy, the exegetical answers are theologically determined."[123] In this way, theology provides "a framework for interpretation."[124]

Patristic interpretation of biblical texts is a significant historical example that demonstrates the critical role of theological tradition in biblical interpretation. This is an important perspective in understanding the characteristics of patristic exegesis, and biblical interpretation in general. This patristic tradition is significant in this study, because it has heavily influenced the EOTC, including the biblical interpretation of the church.

Rule of Faith

The significant role of theological tradition is clearly demonstrated in the Rule of Faith for early Christians. The Rule of Faith is "a settled body of doctrine"[125] believed to be the tradition of apostolic teaching. The apostles had received it from Christ and had passed it on to the church. The church preserved it as the apostolic tradition. Therefore, the Rule of Faith refers to "the sum content of apostolic teaching."[126] Even before the formation of the biblical canon, the Rule of Faith existed as the tradition of apostolic teaching, both written and oral, in the early church.

The content of the Rule of Faith is not easy to confirm, since it is "a fluid array of doctrine."[127] Yet, according to Pelikan, the Rule of Faith had two consistent elements: first, "the triune name of 'Father, Son, and the Holy Spirit'"; and second, "the life, death, and resurrection of Jesus Christ."[128] The Rule of Faith, with these elements at the center, was expressed in the form of narrative. For Irenaeus, the Rule of Faith is "a synopsis of the basic plot of the biblical narrative from Genesis to Revelation."[129]

Frances Young associates the Rule of Faith with baptismal formulas. When a convert was baptized, the Rule of Faith was given as "a summary

122. Greer, *Captain of Our Salvation*, 5.

123. Ibid., 357.

124. Ibid.

125. O'Keefe and Reno, *Sanctified Vision*, 125.

126. Greene-McCreight, "Rule of Faith," 703.

127. O'Keefe and Reno, *Sanctified Vision*, 120.

128. Pelikan, *Christian Tradition*, 117.

129. O'Keefe and Reno, *Sanctified Vision*, 119.

of the overarching Christian story contained in scripture."[130] Later, more broadly, it was articulated in catechetical summaries, or later councilor creeds.[131] In this regard, the Rule of Faith may refer to "the codification of early Christian teaching that is claimed as a witness to the apostolic beliefs of the Church."[132]

The Rule of Faith can be properly understood in its relationship with the canon of Scripture. Green explains this relationship as "mutual influence."[133] On the one hand, the Rule of Faith functioned as the criteria in the determination of the biblical canon. John Breck states, "The canon of Scripture was born and shaped within a community of faith. . . . The Scripture . . . took shape within the matrix of ancient Church Tradition."[134]

On the other hand, after its completion, the canon of the Bible is the primary source in which the Rule of Faith is seen. Accordingly, the Bible is the primary source for identifying the Rule of Faith. With Irenaeus, Stephen E. Fowl argues that the Rule of Faith derives from Scripture.[135] Greer claims, "Scripture itself . . . supplies the categories in which the principle is expressed."[136] However, it is important to note that the Rule of Faith is not simply a summary of the Bible. Rather, it "is the principle or logic of scripture itself," "articulates the divine order within scripture," and "describes that actual architecture of the Bible."[137]

Ecumenical councils also played their parts in the Rule of Faith. The ecumenical creeds were produced by the early church faced with serious theological challenges in its contexts. The creeds are, therefore, also contextually dependent. In addition, they do not include exhaustively the content of the Rule of Faith, but articulate some of the essential issues in the specific contexts. Thus, the ecumenical creeds of the early church can be described as a codification of the Rule of Faith, and an articulation of the biblical principles on the core issues of Christianity. They function as a reference to the biblical Rule of Faith in its narrative structure.

130. Young, *Art of Performance*, 49.

131. Williams, *Evangelicals and Tradition*, 94.

132. Holmes, *Listening to the Past*, 2.

133. Green, *Practicing Theological Interpretation*, 95.

134. Breck, *Scripture in Tradition*, 3.

135. Fowl, *Theological Interpretation*, 30.

136. Greer, *Christian Bible and Its Interpretation*, 157.

137. O'Keefe and Reno, *Sanctified Vision*, 120.

The Rule of Faith took a central place in the beliefs and practices of the early church. With regard to the function of the Rule of Faith in early Christianity, Williams notes that it "led them through the steps of conversion, shepherded believers into the life of God—by the Father, through the Son, and in the Spirit—as realized within the church, helped them interpret the meaning of Scripture, and, when needed, supplied them with the word of hope in their suffering for Christ. The tradition was about salvation and how that salvation was nurtured once begun."[138]

The Rule of Faith also played a critical role in functioning as the interpretive key and guiding principle in interpreting the biblical texts. According to Wall, "The Rule of Faith is the grammar of theological agreement which Christians confess to be true and by which all of Scripture is rendered in forming a truly Christian faith and life."[139] The Rule of Faith serves as a norm that regulates the interpretation of the biblical texts. It circumscribes possible Christian interpretations of the Bible and thereby rules out other interpretations. If an interpretation collides with or destroys the narrative of the canon of the Bible, it is ruled out as not Christian. In this way, the Rule of Faith functions as a "rule" for reading Scripture.[140]

Historically, the Rule of Faith played a critical role in the early church's fight against heresies. It was used to defend the authentic teaching of the apostolic tradition in the vehement fight against false teachings. The interpretation of biblical texts was carried out in order to defend and advocate for the Rule of Faith. Thus, the Rule of Faith was the guiding interpretive principle in the interpretation of each biblical text. It determined interpretive goals and methods, and set the boundaries of faithful interpretation.

In addition, particular denominational distinctiveness concerning the Rule of Faith must be considered. As Wall states, "The Rule exists as various 'rules' of faith that bear a striking family resemblance to each other. Each rule conforms, more or less, to the core beliefs and deeper logic of the catholic Rule of Faith."[141] Denominational doctrines have been formed in specific historical and theological contexts. They address certain issues and concerns, and attempt to give answers. They articu-

138. Williams, *Evangelicals and Tradition*, 32.

139. Wall, "Reading the Bible from within Our Tradition," 88.

140. Green, *Practicing Theological Interpretation*, 96.

141. Wall, "Reading the Bible from within Our Tradition," 102.

late different aspects of the Rule of Faith along with basic commonalities of the Christian tradition, which are significant especially to those who belong to the denominations. These denominational doctrines function as rules of faith under the umbrella of the Rule of Faith in the catholic Christian church. Notably, the Rule of Faith in each tradition has a critical influence on the interpretive work of that tradition.

The Rule of Faith is an important historical and theological example that demonstrates the critical role of tradition in biblical interpretation. Its significance might raise this question: "Is the Rule of Faith not a barrier to contextual interpretation?" Two answers can be given in response. First, contextual biblical interpretation is different from subjective relativism, which denies any type of absolute truth claim. There is a nonnegotiable core of Christianity that the Bible reveals and church traditions interpret and teach. This provides the criteria for authentic Christianity. In other words, the Rule of Faith, as the tradition of the Christian church, provides boundaries for authentic Christian readings of the Bible. Second, the Rule of Faith functions as the guiding principle in biblical interpretation, but it does not urge any specific way of interpreting the Bible. Therefore, within the boundary of the Rule of Faith, different readings of biblical texts in local contexts are possible.

In sum, theological tradition is formed and developed in a faith community in a particular historical and cultural context. Particular theological traditions play a critical role in the biblical interpretation of a faith community. As Green states, "We live out our lives or engage in biblical interpretation not as 'generic Christians' but as followers of Christ embedded in particular faith communities and theological traditions."[142]

LOCAL INTERPRETATIONS FOR THE GLOBAL CHURCH

Thus far, I have come from different perspectives at a singular argument that every interpretation of the Bible is contextual. All biblical interpretation is carried out by faith communities located in particular contexts. We interpret the biblical texts from our particular locations.

Accordingly, there are many different readings of the biblical texts among peoples in the world. As Dyrness notes, "Just as history has been replaced by histories, theology now has been replaced by theologies. Each group, from its own perspective, is reading the biblical text and finding its

142. Green, *Practicing Theological Interpretation*, 10.

own place in the story of scripture."[143] Thus, the task of contextual biblical interpretation is exploring and describing different ways of a people's reading biblical texts in their particular historical and cultural contexts.

It is important to recognize that the contextual nature of biblical interpretation is not an obstacle. Rather, it is a valuable asset for the biblical interpretation of the Christian church. As Ukpong rightly points out, any given reading appropriates only "a certain aspect or certain aspects of a text."[144] No one way of reading the Bible can claim to appropriate the totality of understanding the biblical texts. A text has multiple aspects, dimensions, and perspectives, which no single reading can totally grasp. Therefore, "the more perspectival readings of a text we are aware of, the more dimensions of the text are disclosed to us, and the better we can appreciate it."[145]

In this respect, each local interpretation of the Bible in its historical and cultural context can make a unique contribution to a more holistic understanding of the Bible for the church of God. Christians can learn from each other's interpretation of God's word. We are being transformed by the word of God, and proclaim the word of God to the world. In this way, we build up the body of Christ for the glory of God. I would argue that this is the way that the church hears or reads, understands, and practices the Bible. As Green asserts, if "the church is one, holy, apostolic, and catholic," as in the traditional confession of the church, "there is only one church, global and historical"[146] with the local churches as its contextual manifestations. This ecclesial unity validates local interpretations for the global church.

SUMMARY

In this chapter, I have discussed contextual readings of the Bible. I have argued that biblical interpretation is contextual by nature. It is performed in particular historical and socio-cultural contexts.

I have demonstrated various philosophical and theological grounds for contextual biblical interpretation. The philosophical ground for the contextual nature of biblical interpretation is the situatedness of human

143. Dyrness, *Earth Is God's*, 8–9.

144. Ukpong, "Inculturation Hemeneutics," 26.

145. Ibid.

146. Green, *Practicing Theological Interpretation*, 16.

understanding. The social location of the reader critically influences his or her interpretation of the biblical texts.

The theological ground for the contextual reading of the Bible is narrativity, both human narrativity and the narrative nature of the Bible. I have argued that the interpreter's encounter with the biblical narratives in the context of his or her narrative of life makes possible particular understandings and brings about new narratives of formation and transformation. This is the aim of biblical interpretation. The task of biblical interpretation is to understand the texts, rather than to endlessly seek the text's meaning. Biblical interpretation seeks to understand what the text itself talks about and points toward.

Finally, I have also shown that tradition functions as the primary interpretive principle for the interpretation of the Bible. Tradition engages every stage of interpretive work. Therefore, it is appropriate to state that we read the Bible with tradition. Theological tradition, particularly the Rule of Faith, is regarded not as an obstacle to understanding the biblical texts, but as the basis on which the texts can be explored. All biblical interpretation practiced by local churches in their particular locations contributes to a more wholesome understanding of the Bible for the entire Christian church.

In sum, I have demonstrated the contextual nature of biblical interpretation. In particular, the significance of tradition and context in biblical interpretation has been demonstrated. Therefore, this chapter has established grounds for the investigation of the EOTC's biblical interpretation. The biblical interpretation of the EOTC is a contextual biblical interpretation that exemplifies the nature of biblical interpretation in general. Therefore, the biblical interpretation of the EOTC must be investigated in terms of contextual biblical interpretation. This chapter has provided the primary focus in the investigation of the EOTC's biblical interpretation: the tradition and context of the EOTC.

Thus, in the following chapter, I will discuss the particular ecclesiastic tradition and contextualization of the EOTC, which have a significant impact on the biblical interpretation of the church.

3

The Ethiopian Orthodox *Tewahido* Church

Tradition and Contextualization

In the previous chapter, I demonstrated that biblical interpretation is contextual. In particular, the tradition and context of a church have a significant influence in the biblical interpretation of the church. Thus, it is necessary to explore the tradition and context of the Ethiopian Orthodox *Tewahido* Church in order to find the characteristics of the EOTC's biblical interpretation. The EOTC has a long history and notably distinctive characteristics in relation to other Christian churches. It has developed its own unique ecclesiastical tradition in the context of Ethiopia. This tradition is a foundational element that significantly influences the biblical interpretation within the EOTC. I propose that the EOTC has developed a living tradition during its survival over nearly two millennia. This has been made possible because of its ability to continually negotiate its way forward by accepting and rejecting internal and external influences in its context.

Given my proposal that the biblical interpretation of the EOTC has been shaped and developed under the substantial influence of the EOTC's tradition in the historical and cultural context of Ethiopia, and that the biblical interpretation of the EOTC is a compelling example of contextual reading of the Bible, it is essential to understand the tradition and context of the EOTC for an investigation of its biblical interpretation.

Therefore, in this chapter, I will discuss the tradition and context of the EOTC. I will also discuss the contextualization of the church's tradition in the historical and cultural context of Ethiopia.

In order to do so, I will begin with a brief exploration of the history and position of the EOTC in Ethiopia. Next, I will discuss the unique tradition of the EOTC, which is woven out of various strands of influences. Last, I will discuss the characteristics of the contextualization of the EOTC, along with a consideration of the present context in which the church is situated.

The discussion in this chapter will illuminate the context and tradition that shape the biblical interpretation of the EOTC. This will establish grounds for the following explorations of the EOTC's biblical interpretation. Therefore, I will not address biblical interpretation in this chapter, but will do so in chapter four and chapter five.

A BRIEF HISTORY AND POSITION OF THE EOTC

Barbara Ann Smith notes that there have been several discrepancies between views of Western researches and those of Ethiopians on the origin of Christianity in Ethiopia.[1] Archaeological research confirms that Christianity became the official religion of Ethiopia in the fourth century AD. However, Ethiopians commonly believe that Christianity was introduced into Ethiopia long before this date. In this paper, I affirm that Christianity was first introduced into Ethiopia through various routes in the middle of the first century.

In his *Homily on Pentecost*, St. John Chrysostom stated that Ethiopians were present in Jerusalem on the day of Pentecost.[2] Rufinus, a fourth-century church historian, stated that, when the apostles divided the world by lot for the preaching of the gospel to fulfill the commission of Jesus Christ, the province of Ethiopia fell to Matthew.[3] Accordingly, Matthew went to Ethiopia to preach the good news, and eventually suffered martyrdom.[4]

Ethiopians believe that the Ethiopian eunuch introduced Christianity to Ethiopia (as narrated in Acts 8:26–39), and Eusebius and Irenaeus acknowledged the historical veracity of this. The treasurer of Queen Candace of Ethiopia went to Jerusalem to worship the God of Israel. On his return he met Philip the Deacon,[5] received Jesus Christ as his Savior,

1. Smith, "Role of the Ethiopian Orthodox Church," 169.
2. The Ethiopian Orthodox Church, *Church of Ethiopia*, 3.
3. Rufinus, *Church History*, 18.
4. The Ethiopian Orthodox Church, *Church of Ethiopia*, 3.
5. Some Ethiopians believe that he is not Philip the Deacon, but Philip the

and was baptized. Ethiopian tradition holds that after returning to his home country, he propagated the gospel to his people. It is believed that Candace of Ethiopia was converted to Christianity due to the eunuch.[6] A coin with her name and a cross engraved on it, found in Aksum, is evidence of her Christian faith. This evidence indicates that she was the first Christian ruler in Ethiopia[7] and, furthermore, in Africa.

Historical evidence suggests that there had been many national and foreign Christians residing in Ethiopia, before the establishment of the EOTC as the official religion in AD 328. A number of Christian merchants from the Roman Empire settled in the region of Aksum and openly practiced their faith. Prayer houses are believed to have existed in important cities, such as Aksum and Adulis. This was another important route through which Christianity was introduced and established in Ethiopia.[8]

Emperor Ezana took the critical step of adopting and establishing Christianity as the official state religion of Ethiopia in the fourth century AD. Frumentius (Abuna Salama), the first bishop of the EOTC, played a critical role in this. He and other Syrian missionaries endowed the Aksumite Church with its earliest characteristics. Rufinus tells the story of Frumentius and the Christianization of the Aksumite kingdom as follows.

A philosopher of Tyre named Meropius was going to India for the investigation of the continent. He took with him two of his young relatives, Frumentius and Aedesius. On the return voyage, they stopped in a port to buy water and other necessaries. The ship was attacked by the locals and everyone except the two boys was killed. The locals brought them to the king. The king made Aedesius his cupbearer, and appointed Frumentius as his treasurer and secretary. After the death of the king, the queen asked them to participate in ruling the kingdom until her son, Ezana, grew up. Frumentius made every effort to spread Christianity among the people.

When Emperor Ezana was old enough to take over the responsibility of ruling the kingdom, Frumentius journeyed to Alexandria and his brother Aedesius went back to Tyre. Frumentius explained to the newly

Apostle, one of the twelve apostles of Jesus Christ (Belai, *Ethiopian Civilization*, 93).

6. Ibid.

7. Yesehaq, *Ethiopian Tewahedo Church*, 17.

8. The Ethiopian Orthodox Church, *Church of Ethiopia*, 3.

appointed Patriarch Athanasius what he had done in Ethiopia, and asked him to appoint a bishop to the Aksumite kingdom, where there were already numerous Christians and churches. The Patriarch summoned a council of priests and considered the request in the council. He spoke as follows regarding Frumentius in the council of priests: "What other man can we find like you, in whom is God's spirit as in you, and who could achieve such things as these?" Eventually, Frumentius was consecrated as the bishop of Aksum, and he returned to Ethiopia. A great number of people became Christians through his ministry in Ethiopia.[9]

The young Emperor Ezana became a Christian, and there is evidence that demonstrates his Christian faith. His inscriptions and coins refer to "the Lord of heaven and earth." A recently discovered inscription begins with the phrase, "In the faith of God and the power of the Father, the Son and the Holy Ghost." In addition, the later minted coins bear the sign of the cross.[10] He collaborated with Frumentius in spreading Christianity among the Ethiopians. Through their efforts, by the time of the emperor's death, Christianity became the official state religion of Ethiopia.

This sketch of early Ethiopian church history reveals that the pattern of the diffusion of Christianity in Ethiopia was significantly different from the pattern in the Greco-Roman world. Christianity was introduced first into the royal court and then from there gradually spread among the common people. Unlike the early history of Christianity in the Roman Empire, it was not confined to the lower classes of society, but the higher classes were receptive to Christianity and concerned with spreading the gospel to the people of the kingdom.[11]

The institution of the EOTC as the official religion of Ethiopia was a turning-point in Ethiopia's history. Since that time, the EOTC has had a profound influence on the course of Ethiopian history. Throughout most of its history until the Revolution of 1974, Ethiopia was ruled by Christians. The EOTC and the nation of Ethiopia have enjoyed a close relationship. At every important stage of Ethiopian history, the EOTC has taken a critical role in maintaining Ethiopian nationhood.

Thus, the EOTC is not simply a religious institution, but occupies a central place among the Ethiopian people. Sergew Hable Selassie notes that the EOTC "has for many centuries been the repository of the

9. Rufinus, *Church History*, 19–20.

10. The Ethiopian Orthodox Church, *Church of Ethiopia*, 4–5.

11. Ibid., 5.

cultural, political and social life of the people."[12] In the light of Ethiopian culture, it is "the most important cultural factor in the lives of the Ethiopian people."[13] The EOTC has provided many of the characteristic cultural traits of Ethiopia.

Moreover, the EOTC has played a critical role in forming the national identity of the Ethiopian people. In the midst of the ethnic, linguistic, and cultural diversity of the Ethiopians, the EOTC has been influential in all aspects of the Ethiopian people through its religious orientations. The EOTC has been considered to be "the most profound expression of [Ethiopia's] national existence."[14] The EOTC has also greatly contributed to the development of the civilization of the country, in areas such as education, literature, architecture, music, and visual art. Therefore, without knowledge of the EOTC, it is extremely difficult to properly understand the life and culture of the Ethiopian people.

The continued significance of the EOTC among Ethiopians is evidenced by its survival. It has endured despite repeated threats from both inside and outside of Ethiopia. Today, the EOTC has a central place in the lives of Ethiopian people. Regarding the relationship between the church and the nation of Ethiopia, Yesehaq appropriately states:

> The Ethiopian people have made the church the focal point of their lives, devoting much time to worship and prayers. The church stands for the people and shares their lives in times of happiness or sadness, in times of difficulties, in times of peace and war. The nation of Ethiopia cannot be defined without the church, nor can the church be defined without the government. In other words, the church and country are as soul and body.[15]

In sum, due to the central place of the EOTC in Ethiopia, Kessis Kefyalew Merahi asserts, "If you want to learn much about Ethiopia, the Ethiopian Orthodox [*Tewahido*] Church holds the key to the main gate."[16]

THE TRADITION OF THE EOTC

The EOTC has been influenced by many different traditions throughout its history. These traditions have become important elements of EOTC

12. Ibid.
13. Shenk, "Ethiopian Orthodox Church," 259.
14. Ibid.
15. Yesehaq, *Ethiopian Tewahedo Church*, xxii.
16. Kessis, *Contribution of the Orthodox Tewahedo Church*, 11.

faith and practice, and reside in the church as valuable heritages. Notably, the EOTC was not simply receptive to those traditions, but transformed them into its own unique tradition. Therefore, in order to understand the characteristics of the tradition of the EOTC, it is necessary to grasp the traditions, internal and external, that have influenced the church through various dynamic interactions.

Ethiopian Primal Tradition

It is important to recognize the underlying influence of the traditional primal culture of Ethiopia on the EOTC. Scholarly discussion on this topic to date has been lacking in several areas. In many cases, the discussion focuses exclusively on Semitic influence on the northern Ethiopian Aksumite kingdom, mostly composed of the Tigre and Amhara people. However, long before the immigration of Semitic peoples to Ethiopia, different ethnic groups were living there. Indigenous ethnic groups comprised the majority of the population, and exceeded the Semitic immigrants to Ethiopia in the number of people and the prevalence of language.

Donald N. Levine criticizes the prevailing traditional view regarding the first millennium BC Ethiopian demography, which sees Ethiopia as "a number of previously autonomous and distinct 'African' tribes subordinated under an alien Semitic minority." He argues that Ethiopia must be viewed "in the perspective of not three thousand years ago but six thousand years ago; not in Arabia but in Africa; not with the Semitic importations but with the Ethiopian peoples at home."[17] He proposes the idea of a "greater Ethiopia," which is "the image of a vast ecological area and historical arena in which kindred peoples have shared many traditions and interacted with one another for millennia."[18]

According to Levine, by 2000 BC there existed five core ethnic groups in Ethiopia with different languages and cultures: the Northern Cushites, the Central Cushites, the Eastern Cushites, the Semitic-speakers, and the Omotic-speaking peoples.[19] In his view, the present distribution of Ethiopian peoples, languages, and cultures had been brought about through "continuing internal differentiation within these five core

17. Levine, *Greater Ethiopia*, 26.

18. Ibid.

19. Levine, *Greater Ethiopia*, 28–29.

proto-Ethiopian stocks, and their differential interaction with a series of intruding influences."[20]

This image provides many different perspectives on the Ethiopian peoples and their cultures. It allows Ethiopia to be seen as it has been in its history, rather than through arbitrary scholarly inventions. Thus, while the people in Ethiopia have experienced different waves of influences of external traditions in their history, these traditions have always infiltrated in dynamic interaction with the Ethiopian primal cultures.

The Ethiopian peoples engaged in particular cultural and religious practices in their contexts. John T. Pawlikowski points out, "There is also in Ethiopian religion today, both in its Christian and its Jewish manifestations, a residue of native African rites and practices which predate the coming of Judaism to the country."[21] He continues, "Many of the native forms were taken into Judaism and then carried over into Christianity in the course of the nation's religious history."[22] Similarly, Smith notes, "Specific intrinsic African values and traditional practices were in existence long before the introduction of Judaism, *per se*, and Christianity in Ethiopia."[23]

The implications of this concept are important for rightly understanding the character of the EOTC. Certain remnants of primal religion have influenced the EOTC, and the ways of interaction between Christianity and primal religion are rather complex. A number of practices of the EOTC were derived from primal religion, and the church has undertaken to accommodate them. Thus, the meaning of the practices in primal religion has been transformed in a Christianized form. Calvin E. Shenk asserts:

> Though numerous practices of Ethiopian Christians are derived from primal religion, there have been attempts to bring them into harmony with the requirements of Christianity. There is not always a necessary correspondence between the original meaning and its significance in a Christianized form. One should not conclude that what has just been described is only primal religion with a Christian veneer. Whether the primal or Christian

20. Ibid.

21. Pawlikowski, "Judaic Spirit of the Ethiopian Orthodox Church," 196.

22. Ibid.

23. Smith, "Role of the Ethiopian Orthodox Church," 170.

> dominates varies from place to place, depending upon the quality of nurture.[24]

The primal religious beliefs in Ethiopia centered on the worship of the Serpent and the Sun gods. Ethiopians also believed in other gods, such as Mars, the Moon, the Sea, and the Land. Although the Ethiopian people worshiped many different gods, they believed in the High God, as well; one God, *Egzabier* ruled over other gods.[25] As Christianity developed in Ethiopia, these gods were assimilated into the beliefs and practices in the EOTC as good or evil spirits, and are presently "worshiped as minor deities or nature spirits" by some Christians.[26] Oromean Christians associate the goddess of fertility, *Atete*, with the Virgin Mary.[27]

Fetishes and charms are additional examples of practices from primal religion incorporated by Christians and established in Christian practice. The cross is "the most powerful amulet."[28] Many of the prayers "combine a primal stratum with a superimposed layer of divine invocation or references to the Virgin Mary and the saints."[29] Other examples that demonstrate the influence of Ethiopian primal values and practices on the EOTC include concern for the fertility of land and people, concern for power, mediums and mediation, concern for taboos and purification, pilgrimage to sacred places, and remembrance of and rites for the dead.[30]

There are cases in which the beliefs and practices of primal religion are officially condemned and prohibited by the EOTC, but they are still practiced by many Christians. Therefore, it appears that primal religious beliefs and practices form "a substratum that is part of the life of people who are members of the church but feel the need for additional resources to meet life's exigencies."[31] This is an important aspect for understanding the tradition of the EOTC, and the nature of its contextualization in Ethiopia.

24. Shenk, "Ethiopian Orthodox Church," 268.
25. Smith, "Role of the Ethiopian Orthodox Church," 177.
26. Shenk, "Ethiopian Orthodox Church," 266.
27. Ibid.
28. Ibid.
29. Ibid.
30. Ibid., 269–70.
31. Ibid., 265.

The Hebraic-Jewish Tradition

One of the most interesting aspects of the EOTC is its Hebraic-Jewish character. The EOTC is saturated with strong Hebraic and Semitic elements. Early Judaic influences and Old Testament practices and customs are deeply rooted in the EOTC. This phenomenon has been noted by many scholars of Ethiopian studies. Edward Ullendorff notes that the EOTC has signs of Hebraic-Jewish influence both in its religious and social customs. He states, "The whole cast of religious expression in Ethiopia" is "antique and ceremonial and imbued with an undercurrent of Judaic practice."[32] Shenk also asserts that this phenomenon is "one of the characteristics which distinguishes the Ethiopian Church from the many other Christian churches and even makes it unique among Oriental churches."[33]

It is not an easy task, however, to explain when and how the Hebraic-Jewish elements were introduced and established in the EOTC. There exists a great deal of uncertainty concerning the origin and development of the Hebraic-Jewish influence on the EOTC. Inevitably, therefore, there must be a considerable measure of surmise among scholars as to the way the EOTC developed its strikingly Hebraic-Jewish character.

This phenomenon cannot be explained away by the Judaizing character of the early church in the East. The influence is far greater than anything experienced in the other Oriental Orthodox churches. Notably, the Hebraic-Jewish customs and practices of the EOTC reveal "a distinctively pre-Christian character."[34] Accordingly, it seems reasonable to affirm that the Hebraic-Jewish elements were introduced and implanted in Ethiopia through its long history before the introduction of Christianity in Ethiopia and the formation of the EOTC.

The traditional Ethiopian explanation for this Hebraic-Jewish influence is found in *Kebra Nagast* (*The Glory of the Kings*). The present *Kebra Nagast* was translated from Arabic in the fourteenth century, but the tradition itself existed long before that period. According to Adrian Hastings, the substantial crux of the *Kebra Nagast* was probably formed from the sixth century at the latest and during the age of Emperor Caleb. Regarding the purpose of the *Kebra Nagast*, Hastings states that it "was originally composed in Coptic to glorify the Ethiopian monarchy of the

32. Ullendorff, *Ethiopia and the Bible*, 30.

33. Shenk, "Ethiopian Orthodox Church," 262.

34. Ullendorff, *Ethiopia and the Bible*, 113.

period, as heir to Solomon, superior in authority to the emperors of Byzantium and destined protector for the whole Monophysite world."[35]

The *Kebra Nagast* has a prominent position for the people of Ethiopia as the national epic. Ullendorff views it as "the truest and most genuine expression" of Ethiopian Christianity.[36] According to Pawlikowski, it is "the repository of the most important of Ethiopian national and religious feelings and aspirations."[37]

It has as its central theme the legend of Solomon and the Queen of Sheba, based on 1 Kings 10:1–13 in the Old Testament, with liberal amplification and embellishment. The Queen of Sheba went to visit King Solomon in Jerusalem. On her return to Ethiopia, she gave birth to the son whom she conceived with Solomon, Menelik. When he grew up, he visited his father in Jerusalem. He came back home accompanied by many Jews, especially the sons of the Levites. They brought with them the Ark of the Covenant (Ge'ez *tabot*), which they obtained by subterfuge. From that time on, the Ethiopians followed a form of Judaism, observing Jewish customs and practices. Some authorities believe that the Falasha tribe descended from the Jews at that time.[38]

With regard to the Hebraic-Jewish character of the EOTC, this national epic has very important implications. It indicates that Ethiopian Christians believe they had been Jews long before the introduction of Christianity into Ethiopia. It also explains partly the receptivity of the Ethiopian Christians to the Hebraic-Jewish tradition. However, the way in which the Hebraic-Jewish influence on Ethiopia came about is so complex that it defies any simple explanation. There are several other ways in which scholars have attempted to explain the Hebraic-Jewish character of the EOTC.

The first suggestion is the imitative influence of the Bible, especially the Old Testament (*imitation Veteris Testamenti*). In this view, the people of the EOTC desired to imitate the way of life revealed in the Bible, which reflects mostly Jewish culture. Ullendorff maintains that since the introduction of Christianity, the Bible has exercised "a strongly imitative impact in Ethiopia."[39] In support of this view, it is noted that the EOTC

35. Hastings, *Church in Africa 1450–1950*, 12–3.

36. Ullendorff, "Hebraic-Jewish Elements in Abyssinian Christianity," 226.

37. Pawlikowski, "Judaic Spirit of the Ethiopian Orthodox Church," 188.

38. The Ethiopian Orthodox Church, *Church of Ethiopia*, 2–3.

39. Ullendorff, *Ethiopia and the Bible*, 20.

was isolated for centuries from the rest of the Christian world by Islamic regions. In this situation, the Bible was the only source they depended on for their faith and life. That is the reason why the Hebraic-Jewish impact on the EOTC was much stronger than on other churches. Gradually, the EOTC reshaped itself in line with the Old Testament.[40]

This view sounds convincing, but it suffers important limitations. Above all, this view does not adequately recognize the power of culture. Desires to imitate the religious and social customs in the Bible are always expressed through the cultural forms of a people in their context. Thus, in my view, the historical reality was just the opposite. That is, because of the already existing Hebraic-Jewish elements of the Ethiopians and their self-identity as genuine Jews, they were more sympathetic with and receptive to the customs and practices of the Jewish people revealed in the Old Testament. They regarded this adherence as justifying their authenticity as the people of God. Therefore, the previously existing Hebraic-Jewish elements of the Ethiopian people were the main factor for the EOTC's receptivity to the Hebraic-Jewish tradition in the Bible.

Some scholars suggest that the Hebraic-Jewish tradition was introduced mainly under the influence of the Egyptian Coptic Church. As Hastings states, the Egyptian Coptic Church had developed "within a highly Jewish context."[41] Thus, the Egyptian Christian tradition was strongly mingled with Judaic characteristics. Given the close relationship between the two churches, it seems probable that the Hebraic-Jewish influence on the Coptic Church had a corresponding impact on the EOTC.

However, this view shares similar difficulties with the view just considered. The indirect influence of the Coptic Church cannot fully explain the pervasive Hebraic-Jewish elements of the EOTC. Even though the EOTC was in line with the theology of the Coptic Church, and followed some of its liturgical and ritual aspects, it is difficult to see this influence as having molded the whole character of the EOTC. The EOTC followed the Apostolic and Patristic traditions rather than the Jewish tradition of the Coptic Church.

Historically, it may seem more convincing that the Hebraic-Jewish character of the EOTC derives from "living contact and direct communication" between the two cultures.[42] Several scholars attempt to ex-

40. Hastings, *Church in Africa 1450–1950*, 11–12.

41. Ibid., 5.

42. Ullendorff, *Ethiopia and the Bible*, 20.

plain it in the light of the immigration of Jews. They assert that Jewish immigrants moved into Ethiopia from the direction of Egypt. However, a principal criticism of this view is that it has not been supported by historical evidence. Ullendorff rejects this view by arguing that there exists insufficient material to support the suggested Jewish migration from the north.[43] Similarly, Pawlikowski asserts that "a theory of northern Jewish migration appears to be nothing more than a conjecture lacking any solid documentation."[44]

Most probably, the influence of the Oriental Semites, especially in South Arabia, was the main conveyor of Hebraic-Jewish cultural elements into Ethiopia.[45] The Jewish impact on South Arabia was considerable. There was an extensive Jewish settlement in South Arabia. According to Arabic Jewish traditions, some Jews moved there around the period of the destruction of the First Temple. Later the massive migrations to the Arabian Peninsula took place immediately after the destruction of the Second Temple in AD 70.[46] Due to a series of Jewish migrations, Jewish religious and social customs and practices were strongly embedded in pre-Islamic Arabia.[47]

Subsequently, Jewish cultural elements in South Arabia were brought into Ethiopia. This was possible because cultural and historical affinities existed between South Arabia and Ethiopia. There had been "the South Arabian wave of migrations across the Red Sea into [Ethiopia]"[48] from ancient times. These immigrants carried their Hebraic-Jewish tradition to Ethiopia, and were accepted by the people there.

According to Ethiopian sources, the primitive population of the northern highlands of Ethiopia had been the Hamitic people. The Hamitic people had continually moved from Asia to northern Ethiopia, and this mass migration reached its peak around 3000 BC.[49] Later, in approximately 1000 BC, Semitic Arabs crossed the Red Sea from South Arabia to Ethiopia. During the second half of the first millennium BC, there was a good deal of interaction between northern Ethiopia and South Ara-

43. Ullendorff, "Hebraic-Jewish Elements in Abyssinian Christianity," 219.

44. Pawlikowski, "Judaic Spirit of the Ethiopian Orthodox Church," 183.

45. Levine, *Greater Ethiopia*, 32.

46. Ullendorff, "Hebraic-Jewish Elements in Abyssinian Christianity," 221–22.

47. Ullendorff, *Ethiopia and the Bible*, 20.

48. Pawlikowski, "Judaic Spirit of the Ethiopian Orthodox Church," 184.

49. Belai, *Ethiopian Civilization*, 18.

bia.[50] These Semitic peoples gradually occupied the northern part of the highlands and, during the subsequent centuries, the kingdom expanded.[51]

Geographically, Ethiopia and South Arabia are separated by the narrow Strait of Bab-El Mandeb, a waterline that is thirty kilometers wide. Thus, peoples on both sides had easy access to each other, and the transport of both peoples and commercial goods between the two regions must have been frequent[52] It had long been known in antiquity that there was intense commercial activity between South Arabia and Ethiopia across the Red Sea from ancient times. Some Jews must have been present among the immigrant traders.

In addition, on a few occasions, Ethiopian rulers reigned over a province of South Arabia. There had been several military interventions by the Ethiopian regime in Arabia, when "the Jewish impact on South Arabia was considerable."[53] Ullendorff suggests, therefore, that "Hebraic sediments, traditions, practices, and customs were subtly absorbed and, in due course, brought back—often in a much changed and adulterated form—across the Red Sea into Abyssinia"[54]

Queen Sheba, who introduced Judaism as the official religion into Ethiopia, was one of those rulers. She reigned over ancient Ethiopia and parts of Southern Arabia (Yemen) for thirty-one years.[55] Historians assert that there were two capital cities with the name of Sheba (Saba), one near Aksum and one in Yemen. She ruled both countries, living in her capital city, the Saba near Aksum. She is called "Queen Sheba (Saba)" for this reason.[56]

All of these support the assertion that Jewish cultural elements were introduced into Ethiopia through South Arabia. It seems most likely, therefore, that the Semitic culture in South Arabia was the major means by which Hebraic-Jewish elements penetrated Ethiopia.

Consequently, the EOTC continues to be strongly influenced by its historical interaction with Hebraic-Jewish traditions and practices. The Hebraic-Jewish elements in the EOTC are found in many different

50. Levine, *Greater Ethiopia*, 31.

51. Holy Trinity Theological College, "Introduction," 2.

52. Belai, *Ethiopian Civilization*, 18.

53. Ullendorff, "Hebraic-Jewish Elements in Abyssinian Christianity," 224.

54. Ullendorff, *Ethiopia and the Bible*, 21.

55. Belai, *Ethiopian Civilization*, 6.

56. Ibid.

areas of the church: the keeping of the Sabbath, dietary prescriptions, ritual purity, circumcision, the threefold arrangement of churches, forms of music, and the central liturgical importance of the Ark of the Covenant.[57] More importantly, the EOTC has a self-identity as genuine Jews and, therefore, the people of God. This notion permeates the belief and practices of the EOTC. Therefore, the Hebraic-Jewish tradition has significantly influenced the EOTC and comprises an important part of the church's character.

The Apostolic Tradition

As a member of the Oriental Orthodox churches, the EOTC officially states that their faith is based on the foundation of the apostolic tradition to which Scripture bears witness:

> A member of the Oriental Orthodox family of Churches, the Church of Ethiopia shares with them in essence a common faith. This faith, the Church believes, is derived from the apostolic heritage and borne witness to in the New Testament against the background of the Old Testament. It has been expounded by the fathers of the Church both in the ancient Councils and in their teaching. It continues as a living reality in the Church in its life of worship, preaching and discipline. In a word, then, the Church of Ethiopia is a community which has inherited and which holds to the historic Christian faith as it has been handed down through the centuries.[58]

The apostolic tradition was defined and interpreted in the teaching of the Patristic Fathers in the ancient Ecumenical Councils. The EOTC, with other Oriental Orthodox churches, recognizes only three Ecumenical Councils: the First Council of Nicaea (325), the Council of Constantinople (381), and the Council of Ephesus (431). They reject the dogma of the Council of Chalcedon (451), which officially approved the doctrine of the two natures of Christ. The EOTC claims Jesus Christ has one nature. For this reason, it is defined as *monophysite* (one nature), though the

57. Hastings, *Church in Africa 1450–1950*, 11.

58. The Ethiopian Orthodox Church, *Church of Ethiopia*, 43.

EOTC favors the term *tewahido* ("made one").[59] This is why the official name is the Ethiopian Orthodox *Tewahido* Church.[60]

Athanasius, in particular, had a significant impact on the EOTC. When the EOTC was established as the state religion in Ethiopia, the world church was confronted with the challenge of Arianism. Arius was condemned as a heretic by the First Council of Nicaea, and, shortly afterward, the EOTC was officially established. The EOTC stood by Athanasius in the fight against Arianism and accepted the Nicene Creed as binding.

Frumentius was consecrated as a bishop of Ethiopia by Athanasius; he stayed in Ethiopia and continued teaching in line with Athanasius.[61] For this reason, Athanasius is venerated in Ethiopia. His work, *The Life of Saint Anthony*, was translated into Ethiopic. One of the fourteen Anaphoras of the EOTC[62] is attributed to Athanasius. The Nicene Fathers of the First Ecumenical Council are also specially venerated. Another Anaphora of the Liturgy, the Three Hundred and Eighteen Fathers, is named after them.[63]

Thus, the EOTC was established on the foundation of the apostolic teaching and the Nicene faith, and has strictly adhered to the tradition "without change or subtraction."[64] Regarding theology, Harry Middleton Hyatt asserts, "The theology of the Abyssinian Church is the theology of the first three Ecumenical Councils and to this nothing has been added."[65] The EOTC claims that the apostolic and patristic tradition continues today as a living reality in the life of the EOTC. The tradition is still retained

59. Traditionally Oriental Orthodox churches, which rejected the Chalcedon formula, have been known as "monophysite," which means "one nature." However, the EOTC rejects the term in favor of "miaphysite," since "'mia' stands for a composite unity unlike 'mono' standing for an elemental unity." This doctrinal confession of Christ is clearly expressed in the name, the Ethiopian Orthodox *Tewahido* Church (Aymor and Motoyu, *Ethiopian Orthodox Church*, 98).

60. Shenk, "Ethiopian Orthodox Church," 260.

61. The Ethiopian Orthodox Church, *Church of Ethiopia*, 5–6.

62. The liturgy of the EOTC consists of two main parts. The first part is the Synaxis, which includes the reading of the Epistles and Gospels. The second is the Anaphora, which consists of the Canon of the church. The EOTC has fourteen Anaphoras, some of which are sung while others are read aloud by priests in the Mass (ibid., 78).

63. Ibid., 6.

64. The Ethiopian Orthodox Church, *Short History, Faith and Order*, 3.

65. Hyatt, *Church of Abyssinia*, 85.

in the beliefs, customs, and practices of the EOTC.[66] The believers in the church are proud that their faith has been inherited and is faithful to the tradition as it has been handed down through the centuries.

The Syriac Tradition

The impact of the Syriac tradition in the EOTC is also evident in several different areas. Most significantly, the people of the Aksumite kingdom in northern Ethiopia had a Semitic origin. It can be convincingly argued that Amhara and Tigray, the dominant ethnic groups of Ethiopia, were Semitic immigrants. They crossed the Red Sea into Ethiopia sometime before the establishment of the Christian kingdom in Aksum. Douglas notes, "Their language is Semitic. Their physiognomy is often Semitic. A large Semitic element is present in their customs."[67] The pre-Christian monuments found in Axum, the ancient capital of the kingdom, follow the general Semitic pattern of construction.[68]

The people in Ethiopia, especially Amhara and Tigray, self-identify as Semites. Douglas claims that Amhara, the dominant ethnic group of Ethiopia are "Semitic immigrants of a Syrian type."[69] In my experience in Ethiopia, the people share a consciousness of their ethnic identity as Semites, and they are proud of this identity. This may explain their receptivity to the Syrian influence at the beginning of the EOTC.

A direct Syriac influence was significant in Ethiopian Christianity from the fourth century to the sixth century. A small group of Syrian missionaries came to Ethiopia, and introduced Christianity to the Ge'ez (classical Ethiopic) speakers. Frumentius, the first bishop of Ethiopia, was a Syrian. He is venerated as Abba Salama, and one of the annual lectures of the Ethiopian Church today, the Frumentius Lecture, is named after him.

After Frumentius, the Nine Saints made a significant contribution to the EOTC. Among scholars, there is a general consensus that they were Syrians in their nationality.[70] They were nine Syrian monks, hailing from different parts of the Eastern Roman Empire. The Ethiopian tradition identifies them as Abba Pantelewon of Constantinople, Abba Likanos of

66. Yesehaq, *Ethiopian Tewahedo Church*, xxi.

67. Douglas, "Introduction," xxxiii.

68. Ibid.

69. Ibid.

70. For example, Levine calls the Nine Saints "Syrian missionaries" (1974, 109).

Constantinople, Abba Gerima of Constantinople, Abba Gubba of Chelsea or Cilicia, Abba Aragawi of Constantinople, Abba Afese of Asia Minor, Abba Tsehma of Antioch, Abba Alef of Caesarea, and Abba Yemata of Cosia or Cooz.[71]

All of them were adherents to the non-Chalcedon doctrine. They were persecuted because of their faith by the Roman Emperor, an enthusiastic supporter of the Chalcedonian doctrine. They fled persecution first to Egypt, where they stayed in monasteries for some years, and later proceeded to Ethiopia. They arrived in Aksum in approximately AD 480 during the reign of King Ala-Amida.[72] In Aksum, they studied the Ge'ez language and became familiar with the people and their customs. With the help of Ethiopian sovereigns, they set out in different directions to evangelize Ethiopia by preaching the gospel.

Smith notes that they played an instrumental role in "weaving the social fabric between the Church and State."[73] Levine also recognizes that they "profoundly altered the ethnic complex of northern Ethiopia." Under their influence, "Christianity soon became a central component of the ethnic identity of the Aksumites and their descendants the Tigreans."[74]

The Nine Saints introduced monastic institutions and established churches in the areas where they ministered. According to Hastings, the monasteries were "the most decisive institutions for the passing-on of the tradition and ministry of the Church, the copying of manuscripts, the cultivation of a minimum core of theological learning."[75] Importantly, the monasteries were "the advance guard of the Church."[76] Churches functioned as communal centers of worship, as well as important places of education for the spread of Christian values and culture.

The Syriac forms have become prominent in many different areas of the EOTC. Syrian elements are visible in the development of the Ge'ez language, liturgy and literature.[77] Furthermore, the Nine Saints translated books from Greek, Hebrew, Syrian, and other languages into Ge'ez.

71. Yesehaq, *Ethiopian Tewahedo Church*, 19.

72. The Ethiopian Orthodox Church, *Church of Ethiopia*, 7.

73. Smith, "Role of the Ethiopian Orthodox Church," 186.

74. Levine, *Greater Ethiopia*, 32.

75. Hastings, *Church in Africa 1450–1950*, 9.

76. Ibid., 23.

77. Pawlikowski, "Judaic Spirit of the Ethiopian Orthodox Church," 186.

The most important translation work was that of the Bible into Ge'ez. Frumentius began the translation of parts of the Bible. For example, a few passages of Psalms were translated for liturgical use. The Nine Saints ambitiously undertook the translation of the entire Bible by each taking on different portions of the Scripture.[78] The Ge'ez version is known as one of the earliest translations of the Bible. As such, it is valuable in textual criticism for the construction of the original text.[79]

The Nine Saints also translated a number of basic doctrinal and literary works into Ge'ez. Doctrinal treatises and homilies of the Patriarchs were translated. In particular, St. Cyril's *De Recta Fide*, which was translated under the title of *Qerlos*, laid a foundation for the teaching of the EOTC. *The Ascetic Rules* of Pachom still regulates the monastic life of today's Ethiopia. *The Life of Saint Anthony* by Athanasius remains popular among the people of Ethiopia.[80]

The influence of the Nine Saints extends beyond literature to the areas of music, art, and architecture. Under their influence, Ethiopian music and art flourished. Yared, the Aksumite scholar and musician, made a significant contribution to Ethiopian music. He inaugurated Ethiopian Church music and is believed to be a disciple of the Nine Saints, probably of Aragawi. He wrote music in three modes, which the EOTC still uses. His hymnody is inspirational and expressional. The EOTC proudly evaluates it as one of the best of its kind in the Orient.[81]

The Nine Saints were also influential in art and architecture. The style of church buildings found in the cities of Aksum, Adulis and Hawlti resembles that of Syriac churches. The Syriac influence is found in the church of Aragawi at Debre Damo, "the oldest existing example of Christian architecture in Ethiopia."[82]

As the EOTC recognizes, "the coming of the Nine Saints inaugurated a new era in the liturgical life of the Ethiopian Church and in cultural development in general."[83] The EOTC also acknowledges that Frumentius and the Nine Saints endowed the church with its earliest characteristics. They are venerated by the people of the EOTC, who celebrate their

78. The Ethiopian Orthodox Church, *Church of Ethiopia*, 8.

79. Ibid.

80. Ibid.

81. Ibid., 9.

82. Ibid.

83. Ibid., 8.

coming with legends about the places where they arrived. Under their influence, Syrian elements were introduced into the EOTC in various areas of the church's faith and life, and in Ethiopian culture as a whole. This influence is still strongly embedded in the EOTC today.

The Egyptian Coptic Tradition

The Egyptian Coptic Church also had a significant influence on the EOTC. In order to best understand this influence, a brief exploration of the Coptic Church is required. As discussed previously, the Coptic Church, along with the Syrian Church, was a representative of non-Greco-Latin Christian churches. The Coptic Church occupied a very important place in Christianity and played a significant role in shaping the contemporary and future church.

The beginning of the Coptic Church is obscure. There is little information about the existence of the church in Egypt during the first century and a half. For example, Hastings simply assumes that Christianity in Alexandria developed within a highly Jewish context. It appears that Christianity in Egypt reached the native Coptic-speaking people in the third century.[84]

Beginning in the fourth century, the Coptic Church became "paradigmatic for the African church of the future."[85] The Coptic Church was in full bloom during the period from St. Anthony to St. Cyril of Alexandria, due to its ability to access peoples across linguistic and cultural differences.[86] Coptic Christianity penetrated the African continent, bringing about mass conversion of the people. The early monastery movement led by Anthony and Pachom established a model for the monastery movement that followed. This movement attracted many people to Christianity. Hastings states that it was "one of the most truly decisive spiritual and institutional developments not only for the Egyptian Church, but also for the world Church."[87]

Historically, the EOTC has retained a special link with the Coptic Church. The EOTC was dependent both dogmatically and judicially on the Coptic Church from its foundation up to the twentieth century. The EOTC faithfully committed to the Council of Nicaea and the teaching of

84. Hastings, *Church in Africa 1450–1950*, 5–6.

85. Ibid., 7.

86. Ibid., 8.

87. Ibid., 7.

Athanasius and Cyril. The first Ethiopian bishop, Frumentius was consecrated by Athanasius, and spread the teaching of Athanasius in Ethiopia. The EOTC, with the Coptic Church, adheres to and advocates the doctrine of *monophysite*. The writings of the Coptic Fathers were translated into Ge'ez and have been embraced by many Ethiopian Christians.

In addition, it is believed that monasticism was introduced into Ethiopia from Egypt through the Nine Saints.[88] Tradition states that they stayed for some time in monasteries in Egypt before they arrived in Ethiopia. Abba Aragawi was conferred his habit by St. Pachom, and other Saints were monks of the Order of St. Anthony.[89] Eventually, they founded monasteries in Ethiopia, and established monastic orders. As noted previously, this has had a significant impact on the Ethiopian monasteries and the EOTC as a whole.

The EOTC had been "an integral province of the Coptic Church" and "subject to the ecclesiastical jurisdiction of the Egyptian Patriarch of Alexandria"[90] from the beginning of the fourth century until 1925.[91] According to the decision of the Council of Nicaea, the EOTC was not entitled to have a bishop on its own. At the time of the Council of Nicaea, the EOTC did not have any bishop who represented the church. Frumentius was consecrated only after the Council meeting.[92] The Bishop Minas, who succeeded Frumentius, was of Egyptian origin. This arrangement lasted for sixteen hundred years. During this period, the EOTC had Coptic elements, not only in theological tradition, but also in church practices such as the liturgy, rituals, the church calendar, and other customs.

However, the EOTC's relationship with the Coptic Church was not passive dependence, nor did it involve a sense of inferiority. The dependence of the EOTC on the Coptic Church was voluntary. There has been a prevalent belief among Ethiopian Christians that the decision of the

88. Hyatt, *Church of Abyssinia*, 65.

89. Ibid.

90. Douglas, "Introduction," xxxiv.

91. In 1926 Emperor Hailie Selassie negotiated with the leaders of the Coptic Church for the appointment of an Ethiopian bishop to be the head of the EOTC. In May 1929, five Ethiopian priests were consecrated as bishops in Ethiopia. The autonomy of the Church was made complete in 1959 when Abuna Basilios was installed as the first Patriarch of the Ethiopian Church (Yesehaq, *Ethiopian Tewahedo Church*, 85; The Ethiopian Orthodox Church, *Church of Ethiopia*, 38–39).

92. Yesehaq, *Ethiopian Tewahedo Church*, 84.

Council regarding the EOTC never actually happened.[93] Nevertheless, they willingly followed the decision and, moreover, accepted it as a glory to follow the Coptic Church.[94] When a bishop from Egypt came, the Ethiopian Christians celebrated jubilantly. They were willing to follow the way of the Egyptian bishops appointed by the Coptic Church.

Furthermore, the EOTC and the Ethiopian Emperor supported the Coptic Church in times of trouble. By faithfully standing with the Coptic Church in its struggle against the Greco-Roman Church, the EOTC materially and morally reinforced the Coptic Church.[95] In addition, in the Coptic Church's struggle for survival against Islam, the EOTC continued to endeavor to protect the Coptic Church. There have been several cases in which the Ethiopian Emperor threatened Egyptian Islamic powers in order to stop them from persecuting Christians in Egypt.[96] As Douglas states, "The secular misfortune and depression of its Coptic mother Church made Christian Abyssinia regard its dependence upon it as its national glory and the hope of redeeming it as its calling."[97] There is a special connection and mutual influence between the EOTC and the Coptic Church.

THE CONTEXTUALIZATION OF THE EOTC

The preceding discussion of the traditions of the EOTC addresses a significant missiological issue: contextualization. Various Christian traditions have been contextualized in the Ethiopian context, and this has produced and developed the unique tradition of the EOTC. Thus, the EOTC provides a compelling historical case of effective contextualization.

93. Yesehaq claims, based on several sources, that the statement of the Council of Nicaea that the EOTC cannot appoint a patriarch from their own people, but must be under the jurisdiction of the patriarch of Alexandria was not the decision of the Council, but was falsely attributed to the Council by the Arabic Canons, which are the work of "a more recent origin" (ibid.).

94. Douglas, "Introduction," xxxv.

95. Ibid.

96. This has happened several times. For example, when Emperor Yemrahanna heard that Egyptian Christians were being persecuted under Muslim rulers, he threatened to divert the waters of the Nile. Fearing this, the leaders of Egypt sent delegates and negotiated regarding the issue (1084–93) (Yesehaq *Ethiopian Tewahedo Church*, 37). Emperor Amde Tsion (1312–42) also threatened to deflect the course of the Blue Nile when the Church in Alexandria suffered persecution under the Mamluk Sultan (Holy Trinity Theological College, "Introduction," 50).

97. Douglas, "Introduction," xxxv.

The contextualization of the EOTC has several characteristic features. First, it was not carried out by foreign domination. Several foreign powers invaded Ethiopia over the course of its history, but the Ethiopians defeated them and remained independent. Therefore, Ethiopians never lost control over the contextualization process. This is rare, especially in the African context.

Second, it has taken place over a very long period of time. The EOTC has existed for nearly two millennia, with a history almost as lengthy as that of the broader Christian church. Throughout this long time span, the contextualization of the EOTC has happened through multiple processes.

Third, there is a great deal of complexity in the process of contextualization. As noted above, Christianity was introduced and established in Ethiopia in the milieu of both existing primal religions and Hebraic-Jewish traditions. Before the introduction of Christianity, the Judaism in Ethiopia absorbed primal religious traditions and attached new meanings to the forms of the traditions. These Hebraic-Jewish traditions and primal religious traditions were deeply embedded in the Ethiopian culture. Therefore, the contextualization of the EOTC has taken place in the dynamic interactions of Christianity, Hebraic-Jewish traditions, and primal religious traditions. In many cases, the three different strands reside together in the beliefs and practices of the EOTC.

The baptism of children is a good example of this. The EOTC practices paedo-baptism as a sign of the incorporation of the child into the community. The male child is baptized forty days after birth, and the female child is baptized eighty days after birth. This appears to follow the Jewish regulations for presentation at the temple.[98] However, the baptismal ceremony itself is derived from their "concern with demons both from the standpoint of the past and the desire to avoid potential demonic power over the child in the future through name magic."[99]

Another significant example is the Meskel holiday, which has been one of the most important holidays in the Ethiopian Church calendar. According to an Ethiopian tradition, it originated as the feast of the finding of the True Cross, and appears to have received its Christian endorsement at the end of the fourteenth century.[100] In the month of Meskerem (11 September—10 October), the Ethiopian people celebrate the New

98. Shenk, "Ethiopian Orthodox Church," 268.

99. Ibid.

100. Ullendorff, *Ethiopia and the Bible*, 114.

Year. A large number of people gather together to celebrate this festival with bright yellow flowers, the burning of a pole (*demera*) and many bonfires.

The Meskel festival marks the end of the rainy season in which bright yellow daisies bloom all across the country. People collect them in order to decorate stacked wood for the bonfires. Steven Kaplan notes, "Meskel's central symbols and the manner in which Christian and non-Christian elements have interacted in its celebration over time."[101] The origin of this ceremony is complex, but it definitely reveals a distinctively pre-Christian character, prominently associated with primal Ethiopian rites. For some, the burning pole symbolizes the prayers and success of Helena in finding the site of crucifixion. For others, this practice is related to the use of fire and incense in cult worship.[102] Ethiopian Christians adopted the primal rites and integrated them into a Christian practice by giving them new Christian symbolic meanings.

The fourth characteristic feature of Ethiopian contextualization is its ability of creative assimilation. Although the EOTC has been influenced by many different traditions, its response has never been a passive reception of those traditions. The different traditions have been woven together into the unique Ethiopian tradition.

Thus, Pawlikowski criticizes the view of fossilization of the Hebraic-Jewish tradition in the EOTC. This view is expressed by Ullendorff, who asserts that Ethiopian Christians are "stubborn adherents to fossilized Hebrew-Jewish beliefs, practices, and customs."[103] Pawlikowski argues that this view represents "primitive views of Ethiopian religion."[104] He articulates his understanding in terms of the Jewish spirit of assimilation, which refers to taking native forms from other religions and attaching new meanings to the forms without degradation. In this understanding, the EOTC became "the unique Semitic expression of Christianity" through the Jewish spirit of assimilation.[105]

In fact, Ethiopians have a special ability of weaving different traditions into a unique tradition of their own, which is not limited to Hebraic-Jewish influences. Historically, the Ethiopians have employed and

101. Kaplan, "Finding the True Cross," 448.

102. Shenk, "Ethiopian Orthodox Church," 267.

103. Ullendorff, "Hebraic-Jewish Elements in Abyssinian Christianity," 256.

104. Pawlikowski, "Judaic Spirit of the Ethiopian Orthodox Church," 179.

105. Ibid.

demonstrated the creative power of assimilation. Every tradition coming to Ethiopia has gone through the process of reinterpretation and transformation, according to the purposes and needs of the EOTC. Levine defines the Ethiopians' characteristic mode of relating external influences as "creative incorporation."[106] The Ethiopians are extremely receptive to foreign influences, but it is never passive borrowing. For example, in the area of literary writings, Enrico Cerulli states:

> [It] is precisely a typical Ethiopian tendency to collect the data of foreign cultural and literary experience and transform them, sooner or later, to such an extent that even translations in Ethiopia are not always translations, in our sense of the term; but they frequently contain additions, supplementary material, at times misrepresentations of the original, at other times simply the insertion of new materials in such quantity that the literal sense of the original is completely lost.[107]

He continues, "once these foreign inspirations have been absorbed and transformed, the resulting contents and styles are quickly canonized. They become part of a tenaciously conserved native tradition."[108] This is clearly demonstrated in the *andemta* commentary, an Ethiopian commentary tradition that will be discussed in the following chapter.

In this way, Ethiopians' receptivity to external traditions is always accompanied by a tendency to transform these foreign influences. Levine argues, "Whatever the stimuli, Ethiopian responses reveal a recurrent pattern that indicates neither nativistic rejection nor slavish adherence to imported forms, but a disposition to react to the stimulation of exogenous models by developing and rigidly preserving distinctive Ethiopian versions."[109] This tendency has been continually evidenced in Ethiopian history. The Ethiopians have been receptive to a series of external influences, such as Judaic, Syrian, Alexandrian, even Muslim Arab, but they have never lost their autonomy and sense of identity. Rather, they transformed the received traditions to suit their purposes and meet their needs. Through this process, they have produced the distinctive Ethiopian tradition.

106. Levine, *Greater Ethiopia*, 64.

107. Ibid., 65.

108. Ibid.

109. Ibid.

Smith calls this the process of "naturalization." The EOTC has worked diligently to assimilate internal and external traditions into their context and naturalize Christianity for the Ethiopian people. Smith argues, "Ethiopia's situation is unique in a world where most Christians of African descent have been shaped by a western interpretation . . . the history of the Ethiopian Orthodox Church [is that it] diligently worked towards the 'naturalization' of Christianity for her people."[110] Smith's remarks demonstrate the distinctive character of contextualization by the EOTC.

There might be a concern that the form of the EOTC's contextualization is an example of "over-contextualization," that is, one that is incapable of adapting to cultural changes and insufficiently evangelistic, especially outside of their own culture. This happens when religious practices lose the spirit of the gospel and become merely cultural activities. This could be a potential weakness in the EOTC's contextualization, even as the living tradition of the EOTC is a mostly positive example of effective contextualization.[111] Positive movement is found in the current emergence of "a serious interaction between Scripture and cultural realities"[112] in the EOTC. The church emphasizes the importance of the Bible and, based on the Bible, attempts to address the challenging cultural issues in the contemporary context of Ethiopia.

ETHIOPIAN NATIONALISM AS THE GUIDING PRINCIPLE OF CONTEXTUALIZATION

Ethiopian nationalism stands out as the guiding principle underlying Ethiopian contextualization. Levine argues, "However much divided by differences of region, dialect, custom, theology, and interest, they shared faint memories of ancient national glories and the symbols and practices of a national religion."[113] Out of this sense of nationalism, Ethiopians adopted and transformed foreign traditions "in a mode that upholds their sense of cultural autonomy, continuity, and creativity."[114]

This national sentiment is deeply rooted in the Ethiopian people. It most significantly engages in producing the unique Ethiopian tradition

110. Smith, "Role of the Ethiopian Orthodox Church," 169–70.

111. This discussion came from my conversation with Dr. Dyrness.

112. Dyrness, *Learning about Theology from the Third World*, 32.

113. Levine, "Ethiopia: Identity, Authority, and Realism," 247.

114. Levine, *Greater Ethiopia*, 68.

out of many different internal and external traditions. For example, the significance of biblical and historical figures is interpreted in light of their relationship to Ethiopia. EOTC Christians believe that Ethiopia is a fief given by Christ to his mother Mary. In Ethiopia St. George is especially venerated, because he is regarded as the patron saint of Ethiopia. In this way, the nation of Ethiopia as a community is highly valued by EOTC Christians.[115]

It is fair to say that all nations and peoples—not only Ethiopia—have a strong sense of national identity. What makes Ethiopian nationalism distinctive is the central place of the EOTC. The sense of nationalism has been sustained by the adherence of the Ethiopian people to the church. As the people of a historical Christendom, Ethiopians have a strong sense of national identity that is derived from their unique history.

Ethiopian nationalism is so strong that they believe they are superior to other peoples in the world, including Jews and Arabs. The strength of Ethiopian nationalism is exemplified in their response to the Jewish influence on Ethiopia. The most prominent feature of Ethiopians' self-identity is their belief that they are God's chosen people. The Ethiopian notion that they are the legitimate successors of Israel is woven deeply into the fabric of the nation's history and legend. Ethiopians used their claim of Jewish origins as a "means of ancestral ennoblement" to confirm the perceived superiority of the Ethiopians to the Jews.[116]

Kebra Nagast is the national epic of Ethiopia, and it clearly demonstrates Ethiopian nationalism. E. A. W. Budge states that Isaac, the Ethiopic translator, claimed: "1. That the lawful kings of Ethiopia were descended from Solomon, King of Israel. 2. That the Tabernacle of the Law of God (i.e., the Ark of the Covenant) had been brought from Jerusalem to Aksum by [Menelik], Solomon's firstborn son, according to Ethiopians. 3. That the God of Israel had transferred His place of abode on earth from Jerusalem to Aksum, the ecclesiastical and political capital of Ethiopia."[117] In these statements, Ethiopians' self-identification as the legitimate chosen people of God is clearly evident.

Thus, the Ethiopians contextualized the meaning of Zion. According to David Allan Hubbard, "To the Ethiopians Zion is not primarily a geographical location but is rather the name of God's dwelling place

115. Shenk, "Ethiopian Orthodox Church," 269.

116. Levine, *Greater Ethiopia*, 67.

117. Budge, *Kebra Nagast*, 6–7.

localized by them in terms of the Ark."[118] Therefore, the transfer of the Ark from Jerusalem to Aksum (as recounted in the *Kebra Nagast*) is the safeguard of Ethiopian Christians' self-identification as the true Israel, the chosen people of God.

The EOTC affirms that the original Ark of the Covenant resides in Aksum, and every Ethiopian church has its sacramental replicas (*tabot*). The Ark stands at the center of EOTC liturgical and national life. In the past, when an Ethiopian king marched forth with his armies, monks carried *tabot* in their midst. This is a symbol that shows the confidence of the Ethiopians in divine protection.[119] The presence of *tabot* is used by the EOTC to affirm their religious identity as the true Israel.

This sense of being God's chosen people is also found in the EOTC's observance of circumcision. Even though the EOTC does not officially recognize circumcision, it is still regarded by Ethiopians as a religious duty. According to Ullendorff, only Ethiopians, like Jews, practice circumcision on the eighth day after birth. This apparently originated from the Old Testament tradition prior to the introduction of Christianity into Ethiopia, and it is practiced today. In addition to being a religious duty, circumcision is regarded by Ethiopians as an indicator that they are the chosen people of God. It functions as "the symbol of their status as the new Zion."[120] This is further evidence of their consciousness that they are God's elect and therefore the authentic heirs of Israel.

This sense of being God's chosen people includes the notion that the EOTC is the only authentic church, and "the unique bearer of the Christian faith."[121] For the EOTC, *monophysite* Christianity is authentic Christianity, and it is believed that the EOTC represents *monophysite* Christianity as the custodian of the Christian faith; indeed, as noted previously, the church bears witness to this in its name: The Ethiopian Orthodox *Tewahido* (" made one") Church. The Nine Saints fled from persecution by the Roman Emperor for their *monophysite* faith, and their theology blossomed in the soil of Ethiopian Christianity.

Ethiopian nationalism has been strengthened through historical events. Although Ethiopians were receptive to foreign influences, they vehemently resisted any power that threatened their national and religious

118. Hubbard, "Literary Sources of the Kebra Nagast," 338.

119. Hastings, *Church in Africa 1450–1950*, 21.

120. Ullendorff, *Ethiopia and the Bible*, 108.

121. Levine, "Ethiopia: Identity, Authority, and Realism," 254.

identity. Most Ethiopians are "passionate nationalists" when faced with the challenge of being dominated by foreign powers.[122] The EOTC is the main contributor to this Ethiopian nationalism. Kessis states, "On many occasions when external aggressors threatened Ethiopia's national unity, peace and independence, the Mother Church had instilled a spirit of patriotism in Ethiopians, urging them to rise up in union; thus contributing a great deal to the effort to safeguard the country."[123]

This attitude was expressed in the EOTC's fight against Islamic power. The rise of Islam was a serious challenge to Christianity in Ethiopia. Ethiopia had been increasingly isolated from the global community by the growth in Islamic adherents in surrounding nations. Ethiopia became a "Christian island surrounded by Islam in the north and east and primal religion in the south."[124] This isolation from the outside world and the threat of Islamic power turned Ethiopia inward to depend on its own resources[125] and thereby strengthened Ethiopian nationalism. Ethiopian isolation also gave the EOTC "a conservative and nationalist spirit," and made it "deeply attached to the doctrines and customs of their ancient Church."[126] The EOTC kept the Christian faith intact against Islamic challenges, and played an important role as the protector of Ethiopian Christianity.

Later, in the sixteenth century, the Church and State of Ethiopia rejected Jesuit missionaries who attempted to Catholicize Ethiopia. The Jesuit mission threatened the stability of the nation by causing serious doctrinal controversies and bringing about divisions among the people. Shenk points out that the Jesuits made serious errors in their missionary enterprise, including sending a Latin Patriarch to the country, raising controversial doctrinal questions, and interfering with local customs (e.g., circumcision and Sabbath).[127] The Jesuit mission ignored "the Church's depth of contextualization in Ethiopian culture."[128] When the stability of their nation was in jeopardy, Ethiopians drove the Jesuit missionaries away.

122. Levine, *Wax and Gold*, 272.

123. Kessis, *Contribution of the Orthodox Tewahedo Church*, 5.

124. Shenk, "Ethiopian Orthodox Church," 261.

125. Ibid.

126. Shenk, "Reverse Contextualization," 98.

127. Ibid.

128. Ibid., 99.

Ethiopian nationalism was also apparent in the Ethiopian's fight against European imperialism. Ethiopia is the only nation in Africa that has defeated the invasion of a European imperialistic power, namely, Italy. They celebrate the victory of Adwa (1896), in which they defeated Italian forces, as a national holiday. The EOTC has stood in the forefront with the people of Ethiopia in the fight against external invasions. Ethiopians are "a proud Christian people who [have] defended and propagated their faith for centuries"[129] despite religious and military threats. In this way, Ethiopian nationalism has become a critical factor that determines the interaction between the EOTC and internal and external traditions.

TRADITION ON THE MOVE

By confusing traditionalism with tradition, many people fail to understand that tradition is dynamic. It continually interacts with and adapts to its changing context. The tradition of the EOTC is a good example of the dynamic nature of tradition. Throughout its history, EOTC tradition has evolved through reception, rejection, selection and negotiation of diverse inside and outside influences. In other words, the tradition of the EOTC has been continually contextualized through multiple processes.

Today, Ethiopia is confronted with many different challenges. One significant challenge is the encounter between tradition and modernity. Levine argues that "the conflict between the two sorts of orientation has produced acute forms of disorientation, on the one hand, and extraordinary challenges to creativity, on the other."[130] Based on my experience in Ethiopia, the two different orientations collide in many different areas of Ethiopian society such as family, local community, business, jobs, government offices, and church.

For example, the Ethiopian people are increasingly exposed to foreign influences, such as foreign diplomats, corporations, agencies (e.g., churches, missions, NGOs), and media culture. The influence of modern technologies (e.g., television, mobile phones, cinema, internet, and media) and their globalizing impact reach even remote areas in Ethiopia. Global market power compels change in the country as a whole. In order to survive and develop, the nation and church alike are compelled to accept modern values and systems. A major concern is how the Ethiopian people will integrate these outside influences into their tradition while

129. Ibid., 98.

130. Levine, *Wax and Gold*, 11.

maintaining their independent identity. Although Ethiopians desire to modernize, they do not want to lose their traditional values and customs.

The EOTC also faces internal challenges. It must address issues that are vital for the Ethiopian people, such as political instability, ethnic and religious conflicts, famine, poverty, endemic diseases, and economic inequality. The growth of Protestant (*pente*) churches presents another complex challenge for the EOTC. Although there has traditionally been enmity between Protestant and Orthodox believers, the challenge of Islam in the country has led the EOTC to recognize the importance of partnership with the Protestant churches. Therefore, the EOTC has become more receptive to Protestant churches, cautiously accepting some forms of Protestant theology and practice. However, building constructive relationships with the Protestant churches remains a significant challenge.

Historically, when challenges arose, Ethiopian nationalism asserted itself and became a guiding principle in response to these challenges. The EOTC has played a critical role in forming the national identity of the Ethiopian people. The EOTC has incorporated both inside and outside influences into its own tradition in ways that uphold its nationalistic and religious identity and autonomy. In the modern period the EOTC has been compelled to respond to changing religious demographics, modern values, and new cultural influences while maintaining the integrity of its tradition. The way in which the EOTC has responded to change over its long history can be instructive for the current Ethiopian nation and churches. It will be interesting to see how the EOTC, a church with a long history and tradition, copes with new challenges and maintains its distinctive tradition in the dynamic interaction of its local and global contexts.

SUMMARY

In this chapter, I have argued that the EOTC has developed a living tradition during its survival over nearly two millennia. I have demonstrated that it has been able to do so because of its ability to continually negotiate its way forward by accepting and rejecting internal and external influences in its historical and cultural context. Thus, the EOTC offers a compelling historical example of contextualization in which a church effectively forms and develops its unique tradition from various traditional stands.

The EOTC has drawn on traditional resources in ways that have enabled it to borrow and adapt materials from both internal and external traditions and successfully integrate them into its own dynamic tradition. These internal and external traditions include Ethiopian primal, Hebraic-Jewish, Apostolic, Syriac, and Egyptian Coptic. These traditions have been through the process of contextualization in Ethiopia, and have shaped the unique tradition of the EOTC.

The contextualization of the EOTC has several characteristic features. It was not carried out by foreign domination; Ethiopians never lost control over the contextualization process. It has taken place over a very long period of time and has happened through multiple processes. Accordingly, it involved a great deal of complexity. It also revealed the ability of the EOTC for creative assimilation. In addition, Ethiopian nationalism has functioned as the guiding principle underlying Ethiopian contextualization. The EOTC continues to exemplify how a church with a long history and tradition copes with new challenges and maintains its distinctive tradition in the dynamic interaction of its local and global contexts.

This chapter is significant for the overall argument of this monograph. The living tradition and context of the EOTC are the bases on which the biblical interpretation of the EOTC has been shaped and developed, and they continue to play a critical role in the EOTC's biblical interpretation. Therefore, it is essential to understand the tradition and context of the EOTC for an investigation of its biblical interpretation. This chapter has contributed to that understanding. In sum, the tradition and context of the EOTC are the most critical elements that characterize the biblical interpretation of the church. This will be discussed in the following chapters.

4

Interpretive Tradition of the EOTC

The *Andemta* Commentary

In the previous chapters, I have argued that biblical interpretation is contextual, and that tradition and context significantly influence biblical interpretation. I have also argued that the Ethiopian Orthodox *Tewahido* Church has developed a living tradition during its survival over nearly two millennia in the historical and cultural context of Ethiopia. In particular, the EOTC has developed its own interpretive tradition throughout its history. This interpretative tradition has substantially shaped the way the EOTC interprets the biblical texts.

This influence of context and tradition is manifest in the EOTC's commentary tradition, called the *andemta* commentary. There are only a few examples of this type of commentary in the history of the Christian church, especially in the African context.

The *andemta* commentary has been woven together from varied sources, which originated from both internal and external traditions, and has developed into a unique interpretive tradition of the EOTC. This development took place over centuries in the context of Ethiopia, particularly as the tradition was handed down through numerous generations from teacher to student in the context of traditional Ethiopian education. The *andemta* commentary, therefore, wonderfully exemplifies the dynamic relationship between tradition and context.

As the result of this dynamic interaction, the *andemta* commentary tradition contains the biblical interpretation of the EOTC. Therefore, this chapter will explore the EOTC's *andemta* commentary tradition. In this chapter, I will argue that the *andemta* commentary of the EOTC exemplifies the dynamic relationship between tradition and context, and thereby offers a fascinating case of contextual biblical interpretation.

The discussion of the *andemta* commentary in this chapter will contribute to the overall argument of this monograph in two interrelated ways. First, it will explore the *andemta* commentary as representative of the EOTC's tradition of biblical interpretation. Second, it will show that the *andemta* commentary is a living tradition that continues to substantially affect biblical interpretation within the EOTC. Thus, exploring the *andemta* commentary will help to illuminate the present interpretive practices within the EOTC.

I will begin this chapter with a description of the general features and history of the *andemta* commentary. Next, I will discuss various exegetical issues in order to clarify the interpretive character of the *andemta* commentary. This will be followed by an investigation of the internal and external sources of the *andemta* commentary. Finally, I will address the ways in which different interpretive traditions have been integrated in the context of Ethiopia to produce the unique interpretive tradition of the *andemta* commentary.

GENERAL FEATURES

The *andemta* commentary has several unique features, including its name, structure and form, intention, and contents.

Name

Andemta can be translated as "and [there is] one [who says]." The term *andemta* is derived from the repeated use of the Amharic word "*andem*" in the commentary corpus. According to M. A. Girma, "The etymological origin of the term *Andemta* is the Amharic word *Aand*—which literally means 'number one.' *Andem* means 'for one' with [the] obvious expectation of *lelam* which means 'for another.'"[1] This term suggests alternative interpretations of the Ge'ez biblical and patristic texts given by various teachers. The term occasionally introduces a chain of successive comments, which can number as many as ten or fifteen. It does

1. Girma, "Whose Meaning?," 184.

not give priority to any comment, but simply presents different interpretations of the text. By doing so, it provides the reader with a choice of interpretation.[2]

For example, in the introduction of the Book of Genesis, the word *andem* ("Another says") is repeatedly used in order to suggest alternative interpretations of the word *orit* (Torah):

> Orit (Torah) means "zéna" (narrative), for it narrates the story of the false Messiah, the second coming and the kingdom of Heaven.
>
> Another says, "It means 'testimony,'" for it says, "Testify, O Israel, the Lord thy God is one."
>
> Another says, "It means 'law,'" for having made a law, it says, "Let this be a law to you."
>
> Another says, "It means 'ordinance,'" for having made an ordinance it says, "Let this be an ordinance to you."
>
> Another says, "It means 'word,'" just as they interpret, "A holy 'ér came down' as 'a holy word.'"
>
> Another says, "It means 'light that was sent,'" just as Éremyas (Jeremiah) means 'light.'"
>
> Another says, "It means 'mirror'"; this is similar to saying that it means "light."
>
> Another says, "A mirror shows dirt on the teeth and grime on the head; the Orit reveals sin and righteousness, apostasy and faith."
>
> Also they liken it to a hill. A man on a hill sees stony ground and pasture, and people ascending and descending; the Orit shows what is done from the creation until the second coming.[3]

Structure and Form

The *andemta* commentary has a standard pattern of presentation. Most of the printed *andemta* commentaries begin with a preface in Amharic. The preface explains "the difficulty of obtaining books in Old Testament times, the activity of Ezra, the translation of the Septuagint, the translation of the Scriptures into Ge'ez and their [the Ge'ez texts'] interpretation

2. Liqä, "Interpretation of Books," 169.

3. Cowley, "Old Testament Introduction," 135–36.

into Amharic . . . preservation of the Christian faith in Ethiopia and the emperor's desire to have Christian books printed."[4]

Next, each biblical book in the *andemta* commentary has its own preface that addresses matters of authorship, background, content and canonicity. The preface of each book's commentary addresses certain issues, such as the author's name and its significance or reason for his name, the author's ancestry, the subjects discussed in the book, the sections of the book, important doctrines revealed to the author, the canonical authority of the book, and the usefulness of the writing. The preface concludes by saying "His [the author's] book was counted among the 81 which the apostles listed for Clement. It was not written in vain, but in order that we might be advised by it, Romans 15:4."[5]

The *andemta* commentary has a relatively consistent form and similar characteristics throughout both Old and New Testaments. For example, each Pauline epistle has an introduction, called a *Mekenyat*, which has the formal pattern: "a) Heading and introduction, b) A summary of the circumstances which prompted Paul to write, c) A listing of the subjects treated in the letter, and d) A note saying where the letter was written and by whose hand it was dispatched."[6] The *Mekenyat* to Romans demonstrates this pattern:

> The reason for his writing a letter to the Romans was because of many matters, for in Rome lived both Jews and Gentiles together, and both accepted belief in Christ; but afterwards they quarreled among themselves, and one would speak haughtily against the other. . . . When Paul heard of their quarrelling after this manner, he sent to them this letter, destroying the reason for dispute between the two of them, by saying, "Neither Jews nor Gentiles are sufficient by themselves for the salvation which bestows on them life, apart from the mercy of Christ." . . . Further, because apostles were teaching the Romans to observe the law and the gospel together, so Paul turned them from this error to belief in the true gospel . . . He wrote this letter while he was in Corinth, and he sent it by the hand of Phoebe, servant of the church of Cenchreae.[7]

4. Cowley, "New Testament Introduction," 10.
5. Cowley, "Preliminary Notes," 10.
6. Cowley, "New Testament Introduction," 144.
7. Ibid., 165–67.

Intention

The purpose of the material in the *andemta* commentary is to clarify and illustrate the meaning of the translated Ge'ez text and, by doing so, to instruct the community of believers. The writers of the *andemta* commentary believed that the meanings of the biblical texts are spiritual and profound, and are therefore beyond the understanding of readers. In other words, the Bible is full of mystery. The purpose of the *andemta* commentary is to illuminate those mysteries. Using the exegetical term "*andem*" indicates that different meanings of the text can be introduced without contention in order for the reader to grasp its deep spiritual meaning.[8] As Girma states, "Hence, hermeneutically, Andemta is an interpretive tradition . . . that opens the way for pluriformity of deeper meaning(s) by bypassing the material or literal meaning."[9]

This goal is articulated in the introduction of the *andemta* commentary: "It was not written in vain, but in order that we might be advised by it."[10] This is one of the most important statements in the *andemta* commentary for a proper understanding of its character. Cowley outlines the specific exegetical intentions of the *andemta* commentary as follows:

> (a) Justification of the interpretation of a word in a sense which is not its commonest meaning, by citing an authority;
>
> (b) Distinguishing between two words of similar meaning, or explaining a rare word;
>
> (c) Imparting of information illustrative of the text;
>
> (d) Illustration of a moral point with an appropriate story;
>
> (e) Illustration of origins or development, and search for reasons;
>
> (f) Demonstration of the agreement of diverse authorities;
>
> (g) Resolution of apparent disagreement between diverse authorities.[11]

In order to achieve this goal, the *andemta* commentary employs certain exegetical devices, which will be discussed later in this chapter.

8. Girma, "Whose Meaning?," 184.
9. Ibid.
10. Cowley, "Preliminary Notes," 10.
11. Cowley, *Traditional Interpretation*, 47.

Contents

The scope of the *andemta* commentary is quite extensive because it contains all eighty-one biblical books considered canonical by the EOTC, a number of patristic writings, and Ethiopian liturgical texts. According to the teaching tradition of the EOTC, the *andemta* commentary is composed of four parts: the Old Testament, the New Testament, the Books of the Scholars (the writings of John Chrysostom, Cyril of Alexandria, *Fitha Negest*, the fourteen worship books, etc.), and the Books of the Monks (the writings of Isaac of Nineveh, Philoxenus of Mabbug, and John Saba). It also includes the Arithmetical Books. In addition, there are other materials that are closely associated with the *andemta* commentary:

(a) Eusebian canons,

(b) Various notes on Ethiopian history and quotations from historical works in Ge'ez,

(c) Notes of the references of the most commonly quoted proof texts.[12]

HISTORY OF FORMATION AND DEVELOPMENT

The *andemta* commentary is the traditional Ethiopian commentary formed over the long history of the EOTC. It is an exegetical clarification in Amharic[13] of the Ge'ez (classical Ethiopic) biblical and patristic texts. It originated as an oral tradition and, at some point in Ethiopian history, it was written down. Recently, part of the commentary was published, but many of the books remain unpublished.

It is difficult to determine the precise geographical and chronological origin of the *andemta* commentary. There are a number of questions to be answered regarding its formation: Where did the *andem* type of interpretation begin? When did it start in Ethiopia? How was it introduced to Ethiopia? Many views have been presented, but they are mostly based on conjecture. Nonetheless, there are certain significant historical facts that provide important clues to understanding the formation of the *andemta* commentary.

Ethiopian tradition traces the origin of the *andemta* commentary back to Queen Sheba in the tenth century BC. According to the *Kebra*

12. Ibid., 14.

13. Amharic has been the official language of Ethiopia since the eighteenth century.

Nagast, when Menelik returned to Ethiopia, Jewish priests and nobles accompanied him (the *Kebra Nagast*, chapters 48–55). It is believed that they brought the Pentateuch and the oral commentary of the Pentateuch with them. The Pentateuch, along with its commentary, was translated from Hebrew into Ge'ez. This tradition indicates that the Pentateuch was interpreted by Ethiopians using a Jewish type of commentary.[14]

It is known that later in the Christian era, the books of the Old and New Testaments were translated directly from Greek to Ge'ez. At that time, the *andem* type of interpretation was introduced with the biblical books. In addition, the works of John Chrysostom, St. Basil, St. Ephraim, *Abu Faraji*, and other scholars were brought to Ethiopia and translated from Greek into Ge'ez. These books also contain the *andem* type of interpretation.[15]

Although it is difficult to identify the exact history of the formation of the *andemta* commentary, solid historical evidence indicates that its formation process started in the time of the Axumite kingdom (tenth century BC to ninth century AD). It reached the present definitive form in the time of the Gondar kingdom (sixteenth to eighteenth century AD).[16] According to Ralph Lee, this dating is demonstrated by "the language, references to rulers, other historical data, geography, and teachers named in the commentaries, along with their general outlook and manuscript evidence."[17] However, more research on the historical formation of the *andemta* commentary is required in order to suggest more precise dating.

Ethiopian scholars produced and developed the *andemta* commentary. They used the various commentary materials available to them and integrated these materials into the *andemta* commentary. Since its definitive form was established, Ethiopian scholars have continued to contribute to its refinement. One of the most prominent of these scholars was Mämher Esdros (eighteenth century AD), who refined the *andemta* commentary and sought to establish the definitive Ge'ez text. Some of his material is found in written and oral Ethiopian sources, and in the *andemta* commentary itself. His name is still remembered by those in

14. Liqä, "Interpretation of Books," 162–63.

15. Ibid., 163.

16. Ibid., 163–64.

17. Lee, "Symbolic Interpretations," 43.

contemporary commentary schools.[18] Cowley presents the story of Mämher Esdros as follows.[19]

Ethiopian tradition states that Esdros lived in Gondar. Though he was blind, he was a learned scholar who taught many students. After he retired to an island on Lake Tana, he conducted an extensive research, examining 300 books. Eventually he revised many existing interpretations of the time by correcting errors and supplying what had been lacking. This version is called the Mämher Esdros interpretation. His impact on the *andemta* commentary was so significant that his comments were preserved under his name in many places in the commentary.

Later, he invited his former students to learn from what he had studied. Some came and improved their exegetical approach, while others refused to come and continued in the previous way of interpreting texts. The former group was called "lower house" and the latter group was called "upper house." Thus, two different schools of interpretation were created. The names of these two schools are found in the *andemta* commentary. However, in Cowley's view, there is little significant difference between the two schools of interpretation.[20]

Two generations after Mämher Esdros, a prominent scholar named Aläqa Wäldä Ab also made a significant contribution to the refinement of the *andemta* commentary. He was a native of Shoa and a disciple of Senä Krestos, a student of Mämher Esdros. Aläqa Wäldä Ab further refined the style of the *andemta* commentary and, according to Liqä Selṭanat, he gave the *andemta* its definitive shape.[21]

Although the *andemta* commentary was shaped by Ethiopian scholars throughout the long history of the EOTC, it has not significantly changed since its definitive shape was established. It remains a strong exegetical tradition. Liqä states, "Because this *andem* commentary has been defined once and for all, and has remained until the present day incapable of improvement, alteration or addition, the student of it must remain within its confines, however much he may be devoted to research and inquiry."[22] This derives from the conviction that God directed the formulation of the *andemta* commentary in its final form. It is believed

18. Cowley, "Mämher Esdros and His Interpretations," 41.

19. Ibid., 41–45.

20. Cowley, *Traditional Interpretation*, 5.

21. Liqä, "Interpretation of Books," 165.

22. Ibid., 170.

by the EOTC that the *andemta* commentary presents the authentic interpretation of the biblical texts.[23]

EXEGETICAL ISSUES

The primary goal of the *andemta* commentary is to clarify and illustrate the meaning of the biblical texts for the community of believers. It does not show an interest in sophisticated exegetical theories, nor does it contain explicit interpretive rules. Rather, it reveals certain exegetical methods used by commentators in order to achieve their hermeneutical goals. Thus, the exegetical methods that are consistently evident throughout the *andemta* commentary reveal the interpretive approach of the commentators.

Typical Ordering

The *andemta* commentary contains a typical ordering in its comments on a particular passage throughout the commentary corpus. Cowley presents this ordering as follows:

1. The Ge'ez text. This is known as "the scholars' text," traditionally regarded as correct and authoritative. It sometimes differs from other Ge'ez Bible texts. This may also contain variant readings, notes from the margins of manuscript sources, alternative titles and headings, corrections to the text, and capitation. It has its own subdivisions of the text.
2. The Amharic translations of the text, which are either different ways of understanding or different expressions of the Ge'ez text.
3. The commentary proper. This includes more detailed explanations, illustrative stories, and quotations. It is often presented in a question and answer format. This part is sometimes omitted, or may be incorporated in more inclusive commentary on several associated verses.[24]

This typical ordering of the *andemta* commentary reveals some important interpretive commitments of the EOTC. First, it indicates that Ge'ez texts are regarded as correct and authoritative, consequently, texts

23. This discussion came from my conversation with scholars at the Theological College of the Holy Trinity.

24. Cowley, *Traditional Interpretation*, 3–5.

that depart from the Ge'ez texts are regarded as wrong.[25] The *andemta* commentary employs a systematic approach in order to remain faithful to the texts. Second, the *andemta* commentary is open to different interpretations of the same text. While the commentary is fixed in a final form, it contains within itself a variety of interpretations that are all considered valid. This exegetical method suggests an exploratory approach to the Bible. However, it is always carried out within the boundary of the EOTC's dogmatic intent. Finally, the goal of the *andemta* commentary is to elucidate the meaning of the text for the believers by adopting various interpretive methods.

Exegetical Terms

The *andemta* commentary includes a number of exegetical terms. Kirsten Stoffregen Pedersen lists several of those that appeared in the commentary:

abennät	"model, pattern" (introduces textual variant)
andem	"and one" . . . ("and there are those who say," "and there are those who interpret"). That is of course the word which has given this particular commentary its name.
and wägan	"one kind" (i.e., taking [them] together . . .)
aqna	"straighten" (the text)
ayläyyayemn	"is it not a contradiction?"
belo	"if someone says" (i.e., "if it is objected that . . . , then . . . ")
bilu. . .teluññ endähonä	"if they say . . . " (i.e., "if it is asked . . . ")
endil	"as it (he) says" (introduces a quotation)
endilu	"as they say" (introduces a proverb)
essär	"combining, reading in parallel"
hatäta	"comment(ary)"
kalä	"if it says . . . , then . . ."
messale	"example"
sil näw	"it means . . . " (i.e., "the text ought to read. . .")
tarik	(illustrative) "story"

25. Ibid., 3.

tergwame	"comment(ary)"
salläbat näw	". . . is implied, implicit in the text"
yelal	"it (i.e., a textual variant) says, reads . . ."[26]

By using these exegetical terms, the *andemta* commentary intends to clarify the meanings of the texts for the believers. This is its main concern.

Exegetical Techniques

Certain exegetical techniques are evident throughout the *andemta* commentary. These are exemplified by the introduction to the commentary on the Pauline Epistles. Cowley explains the exegetical techniques in this material as follows:

1. *zäyebe*, "that which it says," straightforward translation.
2. *yäzäyebe* awwäṭaṭ, alternative periphrases.
3. *yäzäyebe ṣäyyaf maqnat*, correction of grammatical error.
4. *gəṭəm*, "poetry" i.e., rearranging the text in parallel statements to make the meaning clearer.
5. *awwärarä́d*, "continuation," i.e., showing the similarity of parallel statements.
6. *are'əst*, "heads, title," i.e., pointing out with what reference a statement is made.
7. *weṭ(ṭ)en čarraš*, "completion of what was begun," i.e., filling in words implied, but not written in the text.
8. *anṣar*, "opposite, comparison," i.e., explaining the example (*säm*) first, and the truth it is used to illustrate (*wärq*) "afterwards."
9. *masmamat*, "bringing to agreement," i.e., quoting texts which express a similar idea.
10. *hatäta*, "examination" e.g., of distinctions in the meaning of words.
11. *tarik*, "story" especially retelling an Old Testament story briefly referred to in the New Testament.
12. *ərq*, "reconciliation," i.e., explanation of apparent discrepancy.

26. Pedersen, "Amharic *Andemta* Commentary," 255–56.

13. *məsṭir*, "meaning."[27]

Lee explains these techniques in a more detailed manner:

> The interpretation opens with a colloquial Amharic translation, often with alternatives that may reflect textual variants. Other techniques employed include: grammatical analysis including the discussion of alternative punctuation; clarification of ambiguous or unclear Ge'ez words; illustrate homophones or situations where germination of a consonant alters the meaning; elucidation of the meaning through poetical rearrangement; the supplying of words implied in the text; the identification of other biblical passages with similar meaning; the explanation of important details that might not be understood well by the listener; the retelling of related biblical stories; the reconciliation of the meaning with other apparently contradictory biblical passages often employing diverse authorities; and the explanation of the mystery or hidden meaning of the text, often utilizing the classical Ethiopic "wax and gold" method for conveying meaning. Although not articulated in the explanation in the Pauline Epistles the *andemta* interpretations frequently employ typology, and may utilize diverse authorities to show their agreement over particular matters. The corpus interprets prophecy as having significance in the historical period in which it was spoken, with true fulfillment in Christ, and may also give further meanings. These methods serve a much wider purpose, which is primarily to illustrate the "true," that is received, meaning of a text, and resolve any dispute over its meaning.[28]

Using these exegetical techniques is intended to clarify and illustrate the meaning of the text without introducing error. Contemporary readers outside of the Ethiopian context may be unfamiliar with this exegetical approach, and therefore may question this method of interpretation. However, as Cowley notes, "because they are expressed in a manner indigenous to Ethiopia, Ethiopians often find the explanations much more satisfactory than they would find an explanation that seemed 'clearer' to a foreigner."[29]

27. Cowley, "Preliminary Notes," 18.

28. Lee, "Symbolic Interpretation," 54–55.

29. Cowley, "Preliminary Notes," 18.

ANDEMTA SOURCES AND TRADITIONS

Ethiopian scholars used the various sources available to them to produce the *andemta* commentary. As diverse sources were available to Ethiopian scholars, several different interpretive traditions influenced the formation and development of the *andemta* commentary. These interpretive traditions include the Ge'ez Bible Translation, Jewish commentaries, apostolic and patristic materials, Syriac and Arabic traditions, and internal sources.

Ge'ez Bible Translation and Commentary Sources

The first important source for the *andemta* commentary is the Ge'ez translation of the Bible. The authors of the *andemta* commentary made comments on the Ge'ez Bible translation in the commentary. According to Ullendorff, the Ge'ez Bible was translated from Greek and Syriac, and revised primarily from Arabic.[30] Cowley recognizes three principal periods of translation: first, the translation of the Old Testament books from Hebrew into Ge'ez; second, the translation of the New Testament books from Greek into Ge'ez; and third, the translation of the whole Bible from Arabic into Ge'ez.[31]

Frumentius (Abuna Salama) and the Nine Saints made a significant contribution to the translation of the Bible. In their translation work, the Nine Saints used a Syrio-Greek text, since they knew both Syriac and Greek.[32] Later, in the fourteenth century, the translation of the whole Bible was revised from Arabic into Ge'ez.

In addition, there are Ge'ez commentaries on the Ge'ez text of all the biblical books as well as the patristic writings. They were translated from various foreign sources of diverse origins. These commentary materials in Ge'ez were employed as the sources for the *andemta* commentary. In fact, most of the commentary material used for the composition of the *andemta* commentary derived from Ge'ez texts.

Based on Cowley's three major groups of Ge'ez commentaries in the process of transmission, Miguel Angel Garcia discusses the major sources of the *andemta* commentary:

30. Ullendorff, *Ethiopia and the Bible*, 31–72.

31. Cowley, *Traditional Interpretation*, 17.

32. The Ethiopian Orthodox Church, *Church of Ethiopia*, 8.

> Biblical commentaries in Ge'ez are the result of a complex process of transmission of almost two millennia. They can be divided into three groups: a group made up of translations of exegetical commentaries which are Greek-Alexandrian in origin (fourth to seventh century); a later group, composed of translations to Syrian, Coptic and Arabic sources, that hold the ancient theological and exegetical tradition of Antioch (fourteenth century onwards); and, a group made up of original Ge'ez compositions that combine material of the first two groups and add material of their own.[33]

Cowley quotes the preface of printed editions of the *andemta* commentary, which itself presents the important exegetical traditions that influenced the *andemta* commentary tradition:

> In our country, in Ethiopia, all the scholars of former times were very learned and upright, and they wrote, translating into Ge'ez the Old and New testament commentary interpreted formerly by the apostles, then by the 318 scholars, then by Athanasius, John Chrysostom, Cyril, Gregory, and their fellows, which was written in the Greek, Hebrew, Coptic, Arabic, and Syriac languages; and then, in order that people should understand it, they translated it from the Ge'ez language into Amharic, putting the material in good order.[34]

As this statement indicates, important sources for the *andemta* commentary originated from various traditions. Ethiopian scholars used diverse commentary sources from different exegetical traditions and created the unique Ethiopian commentary. These various traditions are discussed below.

Jewish Sources

Some scholars have noted that there are similarities in exegetical methodology between the *andemta* commentary and Jewish rabbinic commentaries. This is true of both the Old and New Testaments. Cowley states that "it [the *andemta* commentary] does exhibit methodological and formulaic parallels with the Jewish material."[35] It might be assumed,

33. Garcia, "Ethiopian Traditional Biblical Interpretation," 3.
34. Cowley, *Traditional Interpretation*, 19.
35. Cowley, *Ethiopian Biblical Interpretation*, 374.

therefore, that the Ethiopian scholars of the *andemta* commentary drew heavily on the Jewish rabbinical exegetical approach.

However, some scholars argue that this is not the case. Cowley asserts that the link is not direct. The *andemta* commentary did not simply take material from Jewish rabbinic commentaries. Rather, it is more appropriate to see the similarity as an indication of a common source for both traditions.[36] There is evidence to support this view. First, it is most likely that a Hebrew text was consulted in the preparation of the *andemta* commentary and, therefore, the Ethiopian tradition inherited references from the Hebrew texts.

Second, the general similarities between the two commentary traditions are to be expected, given the Hebraic-Jewish character of the EOTC. As noted in the previous chapter, the EOTC has a strong historical link with Judaism. Thus, Lee states, "The style may, however, reflect a more general cultural approach to analyzing the Scriptures, perhaps arising out of Judaic influences on Ethiopian culture from an early date."[37] Therefore, it appears that the similarities between the two commentary traditions arose from the common cultural milieu that both traditions shared.

Apostolic and Patristic Links

The *andemta* commentary has clear and strong apostolic and patristic links. In the preface to Genesis, as quoted by Cowley, it states:

> This was written, and while it was being read and interpreted, it was handed down from the prophets to the apostles. The apostles (MSS read "the 300") gave it to Clement, calling it the eight divisions of the *Orit*. If you ask which they are, they are Genesis, Exodus, Leviticus, Numbers and Deuteronomy, five; Joshua, Judges and Ruth, eight.[38]

Pedersen recognizes the apostolic and patristic links found in the *andemta* commentary in the Book of Psalms. He asserts that the scholars who produced the *andemta* commentary had either direct or indirect access to patristic commentaries and other writings. This is evident in the names of the church fathers cited in the commentary of the Psalms. The introductory *tarik* (illustrative story) explains how the Book of Psalms

36. Ibid., 66.

37. Lee, "Symbolic Interpretations," 56.

38. Cowley, "Old Testament Introduction," 137–38.

was handed down from the prophets to the apostles together with the rest of the eighty-one biblical books.[39]

The patristic tradition is also clearly evident in the comments made regarding various biblical verses. The *andemta* commentary cites primary sources by name, including St. Cyril, John Chrysostom, St. Basil, and St. Ephrem. They are frequently mentioned, either by direct attribution, or by clear quotation.

For example, St. Cyril (ca. 376–444) is said to have interpreted the verse, "The Lord will give strength unto His people; the Lord will bless His people with peace" (Ps 28:11), as a prophecy concerning "the 200 bishops," who condemned Nestorius at the Council of Ephesus in 431. St. Chrysostom is mentioned in the comments on Ps 44:7, which state that he sees the meaning of the verse as follows: "with that which was different having been united, you have united 'the oil of gladness' with the different one with which prophets and priests were anointed (Acts 10:38)."[40] The *andemta* commentary states that St. Basil incorporated Ps 46:1 ("Clap your hands, all ye people") into the sĕr'atä qĕddase (the Eucharistic liturgy). St. Pachom's interpretation of Ps 67:23 ("That thy foot may be dipped in the blood of thine enemies, and the tongue of thy dogs in the same") is also found in the *andemta* commentary.[41]

In addition, the commentary on the Book of Revelation cites primary sources by name, including John Chrysostom, St. Basil, and St. Ephrem. The commentary on Rev 20:4 states, "Behold, John Chrysostom commented in his homily which is read on the day of Palm Sunday that he sat on clothes which were upon the ass and her foal without being helped by a strap or binding." The commentary on Rev 19:16 contains the statement, "as Basil pillar of the faith said, 'By the coming of your unique one, you have abolished death, which entered first into the world by the jealousy of Satan.'" The commentary on the Veneration of Mary states that "the 'tree of life' has been interpreted by Severus and by John of the resurrection, by Mar Yesehaq of love, and by Ephraim of the eucharist."[42]

39. Pedersen, *Traditional Ethiopian Exegesis*, 57.

40. Ibid.

41. Ibid., 57–58

42. Lee, "Symbolic Interpretations," 42.

Syriac, and Arabic Traditions

A number of Ge'ez translations from Syriac and Arabic sources are used in the *andemta* commentary. Scholars from the Church of the East, both the East and the West Syriac traditions, had a significant influence on the *andemta* commentary. In particular, the influence of the Antiochene tradition stands out. Two of these scholars, Theodore of Mopsuestia and ibn aṭ-Ṭayyib, were particularly influential.

Theodore of Mopsuestia is representative of the influence of the Antiochene tradition that is especially prevalent in the *andemta* commentary. His influence is evident in the commentary on the Psalms,[43] even though his name is not directly mentioned. This is not surprising, since his writing were condemned as heretical at the Council of Constantinople.

In his own commentary on the Psalms, Theodore of Mopsuestia sought to find the historical context of the Psalms. He emphasized the primacy of history while rejecting allegorical and exaggerated Christological exegesis. Notably, the *andemta* commentary on the Psalms employs his way of interpretation as its basic method.[44] In addition, the titles of the Psalms in the commentary are taken from his commentary.[45] Thus, as Pedersen states, "the Antiochene exegesis" is "fundamental to traditional Ethiopian Bible clarification."[46] Cowley also argues that the *andemta* commentary stands firmly in line with the Antiochene tradition.[47]

However, the effect of Theodore of Mopsuestia on the *andemta* commentary was indirect. It came through his "seminal influence on the East Syriac tradition," and particularly through prominent Arab Christian scholars, such as ibn aṭ-Ṭayyib (d. 1043).[48] ibn aṭ-Ṭayyib depended significantly on Theodore of Mopsuestia. He is known as "'one of the major figures in Christian Arabic literature' and his Commentary on the Gospels 'is the most influential work of Gospel exegesis in Arabic.'"[49] He exerted a significant influence on the *andemta* commentary through

43. Pedersen, *Traditional Ethiopian Exegesis*, 294.

44. Ibid., 59.

45. Ibid., 294.

46. Ibid., 293.

47. Cowley, *Ethiopian Biblical Interpretation*, 375–76.

48. Lee, "Symbolic Interpretations," 43.

49. Ibid., 49.

his commentaries on the Pentateuch, and on the Gospels. His commentaries were translated into Ge'ez, and they were used in the *andemta* commentary.

Internal and Additional Sources

The *andemta* commentary has its own unique style and shape. Ethiopian scholars themselves made significant contributions to the *andemta* commentary. Cowley introduces original Ge'ez compositions used in the *andemta* commentary. These include comments on the Octateuch, the Pentateuch, comments on excerpts from Isaiah, Job, Daniel, Proverbs, Hosea, Jeremiah, a prophecy against Pashhur, Wisdom, Zechariah, a commentary on Revelation, comments on parts of the Octateuch, Enoch, Kings, Job, Ezra, Maccabees, Song of Solomon, the major and minor prophets, the Gospels, Revelation, and Sinodos. They also include explanations of difficult words, various Ge'ez introductions (notably to New Testament books), and fragments from commentaries in Ge'ez (notably on Genesis and Kings).[50]

Finally, other sources of varied kinds are included in the *andemta* commentary. Lee enumerates these sources as follows:

> hagiographies from the Ethiopian Synaarium, the Miracles of Jesus, and the Miracles of Mary; secular historical works of either Ethiopian origin or sometimes from outside; some other theological works in Ge'ez translation including unspecified works of Jacob of Serugh translated into Ge'ez; Ge'ez prayers and chants; natural history derived principally from a book called *Fisalogos*; grammatical comments from traditional Ethiopian works; philosophical sayings from Mäṣḥafä *fälasfa*; unattributed sources on astronomy and medicine; and writings of Cyril *ibn Laqlaq* a thirteenth century patriarch of Alexandria. There are also some rabbinic sources, found only in the commentary on Ezekiel, whose compiler may have added material after a visit to Jerusalem between 1882 and 1912 AD.[51]

In sum, the *andemta* commentary was woven out of diverse internal and external sources from various interpretive traditions. However, these sources have been creatively incorporated into a unique Ethiopian interpretive tradition by Ethiopian scholars. In other words, they have

50. Cowley, *Traditional Interpretation*, 38–40.

51. Lee, "Symbolic Interpretation," 47.

been contextualized in the Ethiopian context. This will be discussed later in this chapter.

GENERAL INTERPRETATIVE CHARACTERISTICS

Thus far, I have explored the basic aspects of the *andemta* commentary, including its history, general features, exegetical techniques, and sources. Now, I will address general interpretive characteristics of the *andemta* commentary. The *andemta* commentary is both traditional and theological. It follows the interpretive traditions of the early Christian church, and has been influenced by the theological tradition of the EOTC. The *andemta* commentary is also systematic and practical. It employs a systematic approach in its interpretive work, and aims at helping the community of believers understand the text for their life.

Traditional and Theological

First, the *andemta* commentary is a traditional commentary in the sense that it recognizes and follows the exegetical traditions of the early Christian church. It draws on the richly varied traditions of the Christian church in a holistic way. It has treasured and followed the apostolic and patristic interpretive traditions. It has also adopted Greek, Syrian, and Arabic traditions in its biblical interpretation. In contrast to the writings of historical criticism, which attempt to exclude traditions in the interpretation of the biblical texts, the *andemta* commentary has maintained traditional biblical interpretations as living traditions in their exegetical practices.

Second, the *andemta* commentary is a theological commentary in its biblical and confessional presuppositions. Most importantly, it declares that the Bible is the divine revelation of God. The Bible is also declared to be the sacred Scripture of the church. The preface of the *Mäqdemä* Wängēl expresses the confession on God as the Author of Scripture:

> In the name of the Father and the Son and the Holy Spirit, one God for ever, we begin with the help of God . . . to write the preface of the four holy gospels and the ten tables, in the peace of God the Father, Amen. . . . After this, it is good to write the preface to a joyful matter, in which is revealed an equitable proclamation, glory be to God, who conceals and who covers,

> who speaks and can perform what he has spoken, who is alive and gives life and who conquers, who arouses our hearts to his remembrance and guides our tongues to his glorification and praise . . . let us sanctify his honored name with fitting sanctification, because he has revealed to us some of the mysteries of faith concerning his own unity of nature and trinity of his persons.[52]

It is expressed in the *andemta* commentary that the Bible, as the word of God, is the life-giving book. Thus, the *andemta* commentary states that "man should obtain in it life, eternal life for the children of men and their drawing near to their creator, by word and by deed."[53]

The *andemta* commentary evidences strong theological presuppositions. Important doctrinal confessions are held as basic theological assumptions in the interpretive work it contains. The authors of the *andemta* commentary were aware of the theological issues of the EOTC, and their teachings in the *andemta* commentary form a significant part of the theological tradition of the EOTC.

For example, the commentary expresses a strong non-Chalcedonian theological position, specifically a *miaphysite* Christology. Pedersen notes that the comments in the *andemta* commentary on several verses in the Psalms commentary employ aspects of Christological exegesis that differ from Chalcedonian Christology. This includes commentary on the Incarnation, the union in Christ of the divine and the human natures, Jesus as the Good Shepherd, the Passion, the Resurrection, and the Ascension.[54] The commentary addresses other aspects of Christian theology as well: the Trinity, the Transfiguration, the revelation that took place in connection with the baptism of Jesus, the Apostles and their successors, the bishops, various leaders and teachers of the Church, the conversion of St. Paul, the election of St. Matthias, the Sacraments, Transubstantiation, confession and absolution.[55]

Pedersen argues that, although the *andemta* commentary shows "little tendency of theological dispute"[56] and substantial doctrinal discussion is not prevalent, it still shows an awareness of theological controversies. For example, the writings of certain authors are consistently noted as

52. Cowley, "New Testament Introduction," 146.

53. Ibid., 147.

54. Pedersen, *Traditional Ethiopian Exegesis*, 296.

55. Ibid.

56. Ibid., 4.

being rejected for heresy on theological grounds. Origen is referred to as a heretic, which explains why his works were not accepted.

In addition, the *andemta* commentary frequently mentions the outcomes of the controversies in the early church, which reflects the sources the *andemta* commentary originally used. Moreover, the Ethiopian scholars added significant issues from within the Ethiopian context. Lee offers an example of this theological awareness in the commentary on John 15:2:

> ANDM: "And every branch which does not bear fruit" if you answer: Everyone who having believed in me and does not do good work the Trinity will separate his soul from his flesh. "And to every branch which bears fruit": to he who does good work, to the faithful, but the heretics after being excommunicated they will [also] be separated: the 300 [bishops at Nicea] [excommunicated] Arius, the 150 [Bishops at Constantinople] [excommunicated] Macedonius, the 200 [Bishops at Ephesus] [excommunicated] Nestorius.[57]

Thus, the biblical and theological presuppositions of the EOTC are evident in the *andemta* commentary. In addition, the *andemta* commentary follows the theological traditions of the early Christian church. In this sense, the *andemta* commentary is both traditional and theological.

Systematic and Practical

The *andemta* commentary is systematic in its approach to the interpretation of biblical texts. It employs relatively regulated methodological devices in order to elucidate the text's meaning. Garcia notes that the *andemta* commentary "methodically records variant readings, amendments to the biblical text and different scholarly opinions on a given verse, phrase or word." He also notes that the *andemta* commentary "makes semantic remarks and cross-references."[58] The *andemta* commentary also includes marginal glosses, alternative titles, and headings.[59] These methodological devices are intended to illumine the meaning of the text without introducing errors.

The primary goal of employing such methodological devices is to clarify and illustrate the meaning of the text in order to help believers

57. Lee, "Symbolic Interpretations," 56.

58. Garcia, "Ethiopian Traditional Biblical Interpretation," 2.

59. Cowley, *Traditional Interpretation*, 3.

bear good fruit in their lives. In this sense, the *andemta* commentary is a practical commentary. It does not express interest in a purely theoretical exegesis of the biblical text, but is rather practically oriented. The *andemta* commentary deals with the real life of the faith community and, therefore, is related to the Christian experience in all its dimensions. This is clearly articulated in the introduction of the *andemta* commentary: "These were not written for nothing, but in order to be counsel, advice and instruction for us, as it says, 'All that was written was written for our instruction, that by our patience and through confidence in the writings we may obtain our hope' (Rom 15:4)."[60]

The *andemta* commentary aims at helping the community of believers understand the text for their lives. It addresses the communal life of the church in its interpretive context. This practical and communitarian dimension of the *andemta* commentary is opposed to the current theoretical and individualistic commentary traditions. As Garcia states, "At the heart of this Ethiopian tradition, Scriptural interpretation appears to be more experimental and less theoretical; more communitarian and less individualistic." He continues, "In a direct, austere formulation, these commentaries reveal a deep spiritual wisdom that communicates the message of the biblical text to a community that celebrates the word."[61]

It is important to note that in the life and faith of the EOTC, it is hard to make a clear distinction between theology and the life of believers. Theology is most properly contained and exhibited in the practices of the church, such as liturgy and the lifestyles of the faith community. Girma asserts that "liturgy (which is based on careful precision) and the lifestyle of the believers (i.e., prayers, fasting, helping, etc.) were and are the main theological documentations." He continues, "Liturgy and lifestyle are indeed two prominent media that have maintained the theology of the EO[T]C for over one and a half millennia with very little alteration, if any."[62]

HERMENEUTICAL CONSIDERATIONS

Now, I will address certain hermeneutical considerations regarding the *andemta* commentary. These considerations include its interpretive

60. Cowley, "Preliminary Notes," 10.

61. Garcia, "Ethiopian Traditional Biblical Interpretation," 1.

62. Girma, "Whose Meaning?," 183.

characteristics, its interactions with Alexandrian and, Antiochene traditions, and the influence of Syriac traditions.

Alexandrian or Antiochene?

The *andemta* commentary has been influenced by other earlier interpretative traditions and represents a continuous link with earlier commentaries. Scholars have debated which interpretative traditions have had the greatest influence on the *andemta* commentary. This debate has focused especially on the Alexandrian and the Antiochene traditions. Some argue that the Alexandrian interpretive tradition is the most significant influence, given the close association of the EOTC with the church in Alexandria. Others claim that the influence of the Antiochene tradition is more prominent. Thus, the following discussion regarding these two traditions will help clarify the character of the *andemta* commentary.

Based on his investigation into the *andemta* commentary tradition, Cowley asserts that the commentary "stands in fundamental continuity with earlier commentaries, especially those of the Antiochene tradition."[63]

Girma, who favors the Alexandrian influence, criticizes Cowley for his "blatant denial of the presence of allegory" in the *andemta* commentary.[64] He argues that the *andemta* commentary uses thoroughly allegorical exegesis, and offers an example from the interpretation of Isaac's story:

> Isaac is a likeness of this world; the sheep is a likeness of the Lord. Isaac is the likeness of the godhead, the sheep is a likeness of the manhood, the knife is a likeness of the authority of God, and the blade is a likeness of suffering and the deaths. The thought of Abraham is a likeness of the grave. Isaac is a likeness of the Lord. The fire is a likeness of the Holy Spirit, the wood is a likeness of the cross, and the two servants are likenesses of the two brigands.[65]

Cowley uses the same interpretation as "examples of homiletic application, not allegory proper."[66] Girma states that this is not homiletic application but rather "thoroughly allegorical exegesis," since "application . . . has to do with relating ethical and religious principles (of the

63. Cowley, *Ethiopian Biblical Interpretation*, 375.

64. Girma, "Whose Meaning?," 184.

65. Ibid.

66. Cowley, *Ethiopian Biblical Interpretation*, 376.

Scriptures) to the daily life of the readers."[67] In his view, the presence of allegory in the *andemta* commentary demonstrates the Alexandrian influence on the commentary. He argues that "the influence of the Alexandrian tradition on the EO[T]C's allegorical interpretative philosophy seems to be incontestable."[68]

Garcia takes a mediating position. He argues that the *andemta* commentary interweaves the two different exegetical methods of the two Eastern traditions. In his view, the Alexandrian school adopted allegorical interpretation of the biblical text and the *andemta* commentary followed this methodology. In contrast, the biblical interpretation of the Antiochene School, as represented by Theodore of Mopsuestia, is more conceptual and more interested in explaining the historical context of the text, which is also evident in the *andemta* commentary.[69]

Here, Garcia views the use of allegory as the criterion to distinguish between the Alexandrian and Antiochene traditions. Similarly, Pedersen characterizes the Alexandrian school as having a "strongly allegorical approach," and the school of Antioch as having "the purifying and rationalizing urge," using "scientific, critical, philological and historical methods."[70]

Recent scholarly discussion, however, has noted that this distinction between Alexandrian and Antiochene approaches is too simplistic and does not consider historical realities. The use of allegory itself is not a critical standard by which to distinguish between Alexandrian and Antiochene interpretation. Both schools used allegorical interpretation. In other words, both Alexandrians and Antiochenes used figurative language in their interpretation of the biblical text. Therefore, simply discerning whether allegory is used in an interpretation is not a criterion that distinguishes between these exegetical traditions.

The actual differences between the two schools are found in other significant areas. The first is their differences in theology, which influenced their interpretive traditions and, therefore, their exegesis of the biblical texts. One important point of theological difference lies in how the character of the text was understood and how the text was treated. For Alexandrians, according to D. S. Wallace-Hadrill, "The text was a

67. Girma, "Whose Meaning?," 184.

68. Ibid., 183.

69. Garcia, "Ethiopian Traditional Biblical Interpretation," 2.

70. Pedersen, *Traditional Ethiopian Exegesis*, 8.

code to be deciphered, a riddle to be solved" for congregations present and future.[71] Therefore, the text was used as "a jumping-off ground for spiritual exhortation."[72] On this basis, they developed biblical interpretation using their imaginations and philosophical understandings, particularly Platonic concepts that were foreign to the Bible.

In contrast, for the Antiochenes, the history of the biblical narrative was the foundation of biblical interpretation. Wallace-Hadrill states, "The written text was a convenient vehicle to convey the details of an historical event to later generations."[73] This is evident in the Antiochene concept of *theoria*. *Theoria* is a higher vision of the historical account of a text. The interpreter can expound the higher sense of a text, but it must be always done "according to the historical substance (*historia*) and the plain literal sense (*lexis*)."[74] *Theoria* never abrogates history, but rather develops it into a higher sense, especially "other but similar events in addition.[75]"

Another difference is found in their respective understandings of the goal of biblical interpretation. The Alexandrians were concerned with the spiritual formation of believers. Human life was a spiritual journey to God. Their understanding of anagogy is "the movement upward from the bodily level to a spiritual sense." Here the Bible is "a means to an end, a guide for the soul on its way upward."[76] In particular, the spiritual senses of the biblical texts guided the way to God.

In contrast, the Antiochenes had a strong moral, ethical orientation. The anagogy of Antiochene *theoria* was to lead people into "a truly moral life which continued into eternity as an existence free of sin."[77] The Bible provided a map of the battle for the salvation of humans, and a guideline for human education.[78] The narratives of the Bible were interpreted as exemplary for moral life. This anagogy regulated their interpretation of the scriptural texts.

Lastly, the two traditions used allegory in different manners. Manlio Simonetti defines allegory as follows: "to say one thing in order to signify

71. Wallace-Hadrill, *Christian Antioch*, 31.

72. Ibid., 35.

73. Ibid.

74. Diodore, "Commentary on Psalms, Prologue," 85.

75. Diodore, "Preface to the Commentary on Psalm 118," 88.

76. Froelich, *Biblical Interpretation in the Early Church*, 18.

77. Ibid., 23.

78. Ibid., 63.

another."[79] In this sense, the Alexandrian *allegoria* and the Antiochene *theoria* are similar. The difference is found in their understanding of the location of signification. For the Alexandrians, meaning existed outside of the text. In other words, the letters of the text referred to the spiritual truth that existed outside of the text. They attempted to find this truth by way of allegory. Thus, they readily left the literal and historical account of the text in order to find deeper spiritual meaning.

The Antiochenes used allegory as representation, and endeavored to maintain the historical ground of both the text itself and that which the text signified. The most distinctive feature of Antiochene biblical interpretation is that it undertook to find the meaning of a text that was coherent with its narrative. Frances M. Young stresses that "the Antiochenes cared more about the narrative logic of the whole biblical text than about historicity or literalism."[80] In the Antiochenes' view, Alexandrian allegorical interpretation was arbitrary and piecemeal, since it did not consider, but rather destroyed the narrative coherence of the Bible.

Therefore, the traditional account of two different exegetical traditions, Alexandrian and Antiochene, seems flawed. Moreover, this dichotomous understanding of the two exegetical schools fails to explain appropriately the influence of each school on the *andemta* commentary. It is apparent that the *andemta* commentary was significantly influenced by both Antiochene and Alexandrian traditions. However, it was not the exegetical theory *per se*, but rather the outcomes of interpretation that influenced the *andemta* commentary. That is, the EOTC did not import specific exegetical rules *per se*, which is demonstrated by the fact that any notable discussions of Antiochene and Alexandrine schools are absent in the *andemta* commentary.

Although Cowley emphasizes the significant influence of the Antiochene tradition, he properly asserts that "the exegetical fruit has been transmitted, but the root of its theoretical basis has been detached and lost."[81] He continues, "Antiochene theory has generated Antiochene exegesis, and . . . this has been transmitted to Ethiopia."[82]

However, this does not imply that the *andemta* commentary is thoroughly in line with the school of Antioch. Although Cowley states that in

79. Simonetti, *Biblical Interpretation in the Early Church*, 5.

80. Young, "Fourth Century Reaction against Allegory," 124–25.

81. Cowley, *Ethiopian Biblical Interpretation*, 376.

82. Ibid.

the *andemta* commentary itself there is no clear link between it and theologians from Alexandria (such as Origen and Clement of Alexandria), this is not evidence that the *andemta* commentary was not influenced by the Alexandrian tradition. The EOTC has a close historical and ecclesiastical link with the Alexandrian church and, therefore, the influence of the church in Alexandria is significant in the faith and life of the EOTC, including its biblical interpretation.

The Influence of Syriac Symbolic Interpretation

Recently, scholars have drawn attention to the influence of the Syriac tradition, and St. Ephrem in particular, on Ethiopian biblical interpretation, including the *andemta* commentary. Syriac Christianity had a unique ecclesiastical tradition in the Semitic and Asian context. Syriac Christians developed theology using primarily Syrian (a dialect of the Aramaic language, which was probably Jesus' primary language), not Greek, in their particular historical and cultural context. According to Lucas Van Rompay, the Aramaic language functioned as a main unifying factor in Syriac Christianity and contributed to its rapid expansion.[83]

In addition, Syriac Christianity expresses theology in symbolic and poetic form. This symbolic interpretation of the Bible is distinct from Alexandrian and Antiochene interpretive traditions. Syriac symbolic interpretation has considerably influenced the EOTC's interpretation of biblical texts, and has become part of the core theological understanding of the EOTC.

Ephrem's Symbolic Theology

Ephrem the Syrian (ca. 306–73) is the most prominent representative of early Syriac theology, and was highly esteemed by Syriac Christians.[84] Ephrem's theology is most properly described as symbolic theology. The mode of Ephrem's symbolic theology, which is "essentially Biblical and Semitic," is quite different from Hellenistic philosophical and systematic theology. Although Hellenistic theology employs a dogmatizing approach by using definitions or boundaries, Ephrem uses symbols to speak of God.[85]

83. Van Rompay, "Christian Syriac Tradition of Interpretation," 613.

84. Ibid., 622.

85. Brock, *St. Ephrem the Syrian*, 40.

The starting point of Ephrem's theology is the recognition of an impassible ontological chasm between God the Creator and his creation. The chasm is so profound that no created beings can know God. Ephrem emphasizes "the hiddenness of God."[86] God is hidden, so that human beings cannot interpret God, nor make any statement about him. Only God can interpret himself. Therefore, the only way humans can interpret God is through God's interpretation of himself to humans. Regarding this understanding, Shinichi Muto states, "Therefore, any possible interpretation by humans is necessarily to be an interpretation of an interpretation. What humans interpret is what God has already interpreted Himself [sic]."[87]

God took the initiative and bridged the chasm in his love for his creation to reveal something of himself. Because of God's revelation, humans can gain knowledge of God. Ephrem eloquently articulates this truth:

> For, behold, he (The Lord) is hidden from all in all things.
> And unless he willed to explain Himself to us,
> there would not be anyone in creation who is able to interpret Him.
> (Hymns on Faith 44, 7)

Significantly, God reveals and interprets himself to his creation by using symbols. Thus, the term *raza* (plural: *raze*) holds a central place in Ephrem's theology. Even though it is generally rendered as "symbol," it has a quite different connotation from the modern use of that term. In the modern use of the term, "symbol" is essentially different from what it symbolizes. In contrast, for Ephrem, the term "symbol" has a strong sense, in that it has "an ontological link with what is symbolized."[88] Symbols actually participate in some sense with what they symbolize, and function as "a means of expressing relationship and connections."[89] In this way, symbols connect two different modes of reality: physical and spiritual.

Thus, symbols disclose to humans aspects of the hidden reality of God, which Ephrem identifies with "truth."[90] This shows the nature of Ephrem's theology. According to Kees den Biesen, "The basic principle

86. Ibid., 44.

87. Muto, "Early Syriac Hermeneutics," 46.

88. Brock, "St Ephrem the Syrian on Reading Scripture," 39–40.

89. Brock, *St. Ephrem the Syrian*, 42.

90. Griffith, '*Faith Adoring the Mystery*,' 30.

of Ephrem's theology consists in his understanding that all of creation is symbolical or sacramental in nature."[91] God has bestowed "hidden meaning" (*hayla kasya*) upon the entire creation. Symbols (*raze*) reside hidden everywhere in both the Bible and Nature.

Thus, for Ephrem, Nature and the Bible are two witnesses to God. Van Rompay states, "This symbolic vision is not restricted to the Bible, but holds true for the whole world."[92] Both the Bible and the natural world provide "an immense spider's web (as it were) of interconnections between the created world and divine reality."[93] Ephrem states:

> Lord, Your symbols are everywhere,
> Yet, You are hidden from everywhere!
> (Hymns on Faith 4, 9)

Therefore, it is essential to perceive symbols in the Bible and Nature in order to gain knowledge of God. In addition, God's self-revelation through symbols in the Bible and Nature is an integral part of the divine plan for the salvation of human beings.[94] Ephrem expresses it in this way:

> In his book Moses described
> the creation of the natural world,
> so that both Nature and Scripture
> might bear witness to the Creator:
> Nature, through man's use of it;
> Scripture, through his reading of it;
> they are the witnesses
> which reach everywhere,
> they are to be found at all times,
> present at every hour,
> confuting the unbeliever
> who defames the Creator.
> (Hymns on Paradise 5, 2)

The Bible, in particular, is the primary source of the knowledge of God. Symbols in the Bible must be perceived for the understanding of

91. Den Biesen, *Simple and Bold*, 48.

92. Van Rompay, "Christian Syriac Tradition of Interpretation," 626.

93. Brock, "St. Ephrem the Syrian on Reading Scripture," 39–40.

94. Ibid., 40.

God's revelation. Notably, only the believing eye can discover the revelatory symbols that lie hidden everywhere.[95] As Ephrem states:

> The Scriptures are laid out like a mirror,
> And the person whose eye is luminous
> Sees therein the image of Divine Reality.
> (Hymns on Faith 67, 8)

Only the eye of faith can see the hidden things of God in Nature and the Bible. Sebastian Brock states, "Just as the physical eye functions by means of light, so the interior eye functions by means of faith, and the greater the faith, the more *raze*, or symbols, hidden in both Nature and Scripture is it capable of perceiving." He continues, "Conversely, if this inner eye is clouded by sin or by lack of faith, it will either fail to see these *raze* altogether, or it will perceive them only very faintly."[96] According to Ephrem, only illuminated eyes of faith can perceive divine symbols hidden in Nature and the Bible.

Ephrem affirms that the supreme mode of God's self-revelation is Jesus Christ in his Incarnation.[97] He is the perfect image of God and manifests God's hiddenness to his creation. Jesus Christ is also the interpreter of God's symbols. The Son interprets the symbols that God the Father created. Furthermore, he "fulfills the symbols through his interpretation."[98] As Ephrem expresses it:

> This Jesus has multiplied symbols for us.
> I have fallen into the waves of His symbols . . .
> (Nisibene Hymns 39, 17)

The understanding of God's self-revelation through symbols that reside in his creation comprises the core feature of Ephrem's theology. According to Griffith, for Ephrem, it is theology.[99]

Multivalence of Spiritual Meanings in Syriac Symbolic Interpretation

According to Ephrem, there are many different spiritual meanings of the same biblical text among interpreters. Although spiritual reality

95. Van Rompay, "Christian Syriac Tradition of Interpretation," 626.
96. Brock, "St. Ephrem the Syrian on Reading Scripture," 45.
97. Brock, *St. Ephrem the Syrian*, 41.
98. Muto, "Early Syriac Hermeneutics," 47.
99. Griffith, *'Faith Adoring the Mystery,'* 29.

objectively exists, its perception is unavoidably subjective. The interpreters have multiple perspectives, and thus multiple understandings of the same text. Therefore, the interpretation of the text differs from one interpreter to another. Even the same interpreter can read the same text differently with time and situation. The level of understanding also leads to different understandings of the text. In this sense, Ephrem's hermeneutics is multivalent rather than univalent. Brock explains this with an analogy:

> The surface biblical text corresponds to a pictorial stained glass window, but on the stained glass there are innumerable pin-pricks (as it were) of clear glass. These pin-pricks of clear glass correspond to Ephrem's *raze*, or symbols, and what lies beyond the stained glass window is Ephrem's "Truth," or divine reality, allowing the biblical text (the surface picture) to be seen in relationship to different aspects of the salvation that has been brought by Christ . . . so too the *raze* can only point to particular facets of "Truth"; however, just as changing the angle of vision will allow for the possibility of seeing many different things through the same pin-prick, so too a single *raza* can have many different meanings.[100]

The multivalent interpretation of the text derives from the plurality of images in a single word. Muto states, "A word in the Bible has many images that are God-fashioned beautiful forms just as nature has many images created by God. Being the images of a word, they are not the word itself but truly represent something of it . . . he [Ephrem] does not offer the fixed 'meaning' of the word interpreted, but searches for as many possibilities as he can."[101] Therefore, "there is no single proper interpretation valid for everyone at the same time," but multiple interpretations of the biblical texts.[102]

The interpreter sees an image of a word in the Bible, which reveals an aspect of the spiritual reality. All images reflect the spiritual reality, and they are related to one another. If one finds more images in the biblical text, one can know God more clearly.[103] The task of biblical interpretation is, therefore, to find relationships between the images in the Bible.

In addition, Ephrem attempts to fill gaps in the biblical narrative in his interpretation of the text and thereby develops his own theological

100. Brock, "St. Ephrem the Syrian on Reading Scripture," 47–48.

101. Muto, "Early Syriac Hermeneutics," 52.

102. Ibid., 53.

103. Ibid.

discussion. The purpose of his interpretive approach was to refute the heretical teachings of his day. In this sense, Ephrem's biblical interpretation is theological: it is "the work of a defender of orthodox theological schemes and an opponent of unorthodox views, rather than that of an unbiased exegete."[104] Thus, Syriac symbolic interpretation is in line with other interpretive traditions of the early church.

Influence of Syriac Symbolic Interpretation on the Andemta Commentary

Syriac symbolic interpretation has significantly influenced Ethiopian biblical interpretation. This effect is noticeable in Ethiopian literature, including the *andemta* commentary. The Ark of the Covenant, in particular, holds a central place in Syriac symbolic interpretation and, consequently, in Ethiopian biblical interpretation. The theological concepts expressed in the symbolism of the Ark (*tabot* in Ethiopic) play a critical role in the theology and practice of the EOTC.

For Ephrem, the Ark is interconnected with Paradise and the Cross imparting significant symbolic meanings that help believers understand aspects of God and the salvation of human beings. The Ark expresses eschatological hope, since it is symbolically associated with the heavenly Jerusalem or Zion, and with Paradise.[105] For Ephrem, "the Law or Torah as revealed to Moses during the Sinai Theophany, particularly the Paradise and Ark narratives, were key revelations of the Creator, which were to be interpreted in the light of Christological doctrine."[106]

For Ephrem, the Ark of the Covenant symbolizes "divine indwelling and immanence."[107] This link is also found in Ethiopic literature. Importantly, this notion has uniquely developed in the Ethiopian context. As discussed previously, Ethiopians view Zion as the name of God's dwelling place localized in terms of the Ark, rather than a geographical location. For Ethiopians, the Ark itself is Zion and, since the Ark was transferred to Ethiopia, God's place of abode also moved from Jerusalem to Ethiopia. Thus, the symbolic meaning of the Ark is extended to the nation of Ethiopia and, politically, it is the most important extension of the Ark. This is a sign that the nation of Ethiopia is the true Israel, the chosen

104. Van Rompay, "Christian Syriac Tradition of Interpretation," 624.

105. Lee, "Symbolic Interpretation," 84.

106. Ibid.

107. Ibid.

people of God. This is one of the most significant examples of symbolic interpretation employed and expanded by the EOTC.

In addition, in the theology of the EOTC, the Ark of the Covenant is another name for Mary. The Ark (*tabot*) also stands at the center of the liturgy of the EOTC. *Tabot* is located in the church, and it is always kept in ornate coverings in the Sanctuary. The liturgy of the EOTC is celebrated always with the presence of *tabot* in the church.[108] Without *tabot*, liturgy cannot be held. Thus, the Ark, Zion, Mary, liturgy, and Ethiopia are united, and guarantee the divine selection and protection of Ethiopia, and the authenticity of the EOTC.[109]

There are several other symbols that signify the divine presence for Ephrem and in Ethiopic biblical interpretation. For example, Noah's Ark is symbolically interpreted in the *andemta* commentary. It stands for the presence and immanence of the divine, as does the Ark of the Covenant. The *andemta* comments for Genesis 6–8 presents diverse symbolic interpretations of the narrative of Noah's Ark with various New Testament themes:

> The Ark as Mary, Noah as Christ;
> The Ark as the Cross, Noah as Christ;
> The Ark as baptism, Noah as the baptized;
> The Ark as the Church, Noah as the believers;
> The Ark as the resurrection, Noah as the dead who are raised.[110]

Lee notes several additional examples of symbolic interpretation of various biblical texts:

> The *andemta* on Zechariah 4:3 explains, "the lampstand [is a symbol of] Our Lady, the gold of her purity and her holiness, the bowl for the wick of her womb, the cover of her virginity, the fire of divinity, the wick of the Incarnation, the oil of the Holy Spirit . . . "
>
> The *andemta* on Ezekiel 44:2 interprets "The closed East [Door]" contained in the Ezekiel 44 vision of the temple, stating, 'having become pregnant without a seed, [it is a symbol] that he be born with sealed virginity, it proves that his mother will live without [the signs of virginity] being opened after his birth.'

108. Aymro and Joachim, *Ethiopian Orthodox Church*, 53.

109. Hastings, *Church in Africa*, 21.

110. Lee, "Symbolic Interpretations," 108.

> The *andemta* on Psalm 72:6 (71:6) explains the reference to the "fleece of David" in Judges 6:36–40, where Gideon lays out a white fleece which collects dew, and also to the LXX version of the Psalm, "He shall come down as rain upon a fleece; and as drops falling upon the earth" (hence the Lord will dwell in Mary's womb. ANDM the dew being His symbol, and the fleece her symbol in Our Lady's womb he will dwell. The fleece means that of Gideon (Judges 6).'

> The *andemta* on 2 Kings 19:22 states, "As Elisha said, starting from that day until today the water was changed from bitterness to sweetness. For the time it was said like this, but for later it is a symbol. The new pitcher of Our Lady, meaning it is the handiwork of Elisha; the salt [is a symbol] of the Lord, meaning the salt which makes sweet the insipid; the water [is a symbol] of baptism; the bitterness is a symbol of wages of sin, of the curse on Adam and Eve; the bitterness comes from outside, rather than from the water; the wages of sin, and the curse of Adam are not from baptism; that the water became sweet because of the pitcher and the salt is a symbol that it is because of the Lord, because of Our Lady that sonship is to be gained."[111]

These examples show the multiplicity of a referent in symbolic interpretation of biblical texts. They do not collide with each other, but together clarify the diverse aspects of symbols in the Bible. They also demonstrate the significant influence of Syriac symbolic interpretation on the *andemta* commentary.

Alexandria, Antiochene, and Syriac Traditions Contrasted

The Syriac interpretive tradition is distinct from both the Alexandrian and Antiochene traditions. In the Alexandrian tradition the words of the text refer to the spiritual truth outside of the text. Alexandrians attempt to find the truth by way of allegory. They use the text as a launching point for spiritual exhortation. Alexandrian allegorism rejects the literal interpretation of many texts.

Although Ephrem uses symbolism expressed in poetic images, he differs from the Alexandrians in the way he uses allegory. In Syriac symbolic interpretation, the plain historical meaning of the text is not overlooked, but it stands parallel to the symbolic interpretation. Ephrem's symbolism is also much narrower in its outlook. Almost all of his

111. Ibid., 107–8.

symbolic interpretations of the Old Testament relate in some way to the incarnation, whereas Alexandrian allegorism allegorized in almost every direction. Ephrem's symbolism is much more constrained by the bigger picture of the Bible, and by the plan of salvation.

Ephrem's exegesis is based on the historical narrative of the biblical text. In other words, for Ephrem, "the historical framework of the Bible constitutes the starting-point of the interpretation."[112] A word in the Bible has multiple images that reveal different aspects of spiritual reality. Muto gives the example of Noah:

> The word "Noah" means no other than Noah himself in the Bible, but at the same time has many perspectives in relation to many other things because Noah himself has many things in relation to himself. Noah himself who is meant by word "Noah" is to be compared and connected, and related to as many other figures (persons and things) both in the Bible and in nature as possible. And they altogether lead to better understanding of Noah.[113]

Thus, while Alexandrian interpretation seeks a uniform allegorical interpretation of the text, Syriac interpretation has multiple senses (images) of the text.

Scholars have recognized many similarities between the Syriac and Antiochene interpretive traditions. Van Rompay notes points of similarity between them: for example, both are mainly non-allegorical and based in the plain meaning of the text.[114] In addition, both traditions emphasize the importance of the historicity of the text. The Antiochenes viewed the text as conveying the details of an historical event. Antiochene *theoria* theorized regarding underlying prior history and presented a higher vision of other, but similar, events. It was firmly grounded in history. In this sense, Lee asserts, "Syriac symbolism could be taken as a particular kind of typological interpretation. Perhaps it would be more correct to consider it a subcategory than a completely separate method of interpretation."[115]

However, the Syriac tradition is rather distinct from the Antiochene tradition. Antiochenes understood the text to have a single sense, which referred to one historical event. Subsequently, it points forward to another

112. Van Rompay, "Christian Syriac Tradition of Interpretation," 624.

113. Muto, "Early Syriac Hermeneutics," 53.

114. Van Rompay, "Christian Syriac Tradition of Interpretation," 627.

115. Ralph Lee, e-mail message to author, June 10, 2012.

historical event that occurred later. In contrast, the Syriac tradition holds that the text refers to one thing, but has many figures. Muto states, "In Antiochene *theória*, a word has one sense and two referents, whereas in Syriac '*theória*,' it has one sense and many referents."[116]

Therefore, while Antiochene interpretation is characterized by "the virtual duplicity [sic] of referent," Syriac tradition is characterized by "the multiplicity of referent."[117] Therefore, Syriac symbolic interpretation is beyond "the limited range of applicability in Antiochene *theoria*."[118] Lee states that Ephrem is critical of the Antiochenes for their rigid and literal exegesis.[119] Van Rompay asserts that "the idea of the 'textual plurality' of the Bible" is "a characteristic of the whole Syriac interpretation."[120]

In this regard, it is important to understand the philosophical framework that leads to Ephrem's symbolism. Lee highlights that Ephrem's symbolism is essentially non-Hellenized, and more "Semitic" in its outlook. He asserts, "The important thing is not only the language, Syriac, which is quite distinct, and has distinct ways of interpreting things. The more important aspect of this tradition, particularly for Ephrem is that Ephrem was not strongly influenced by Hellenism, which the Antiochenes were. In the city of Antioch Greek was the lingua franca, and Syriac was more typical of those living outside the city. The roots of this form of Christianity are believed to have been in Edessa."[121]

In sum, the Syriac interpretative tradition is distinguishable from both Antiochene and Alexandrian traditions. Thus, it is more appropriate to state that there were three distinctive interpretive traditions, rather than two, in early Eastern Christianity. The *andemta* commentary was influenced by these three interpretive traditions. However, it is not simply the product of passive reception of these influences, but of creative incorporation of these influences into the commentary corpus. In order to elucidate the meanings of the biblical texts, the authors of the *andemta* commentary absorbed other theological and exegetical traditions and developed their own tradition in the Ethiopian context.

116. Muto, "Early Syriac Hermeneutics," 58.

117. Ibid., 57.

118. Griffith, '*Faith Adoring the Mystery*,' 29.

119. Lee, "Symbolic Interpretations," 76.

120. Van Rompay, "Christian Syriac Tradition of Interpretation," 614–15.

121. Ralph Lee, e-mail message to author, June 10, 2012.

THE ANDEMTA COMMENTARY AND CONTEXTUALIZATION

The *andemta* commentary is a contextualized commentary that was formed and developed in a particular historical and cultural context throughout the long history of the EOTC. It would, therefore, be incorrect to regard the *andemta* commentary as a simple Ethiopian version, or a periphrastic rendering, of other commentary traditions. Though the *andemta* commentary follows the general mode of traditional interpretations, the authors of the *andemta* commentary have formed a distinctively Ethiopian commentary. As Cowley notes:

> The exegetical content of the *andemta* commentary is largely dependent on sources external to the corpus, but the shaping and ordering of the material is not, and must be attributed to the Ethiopian scholars who are recorded as having formed and developed the andemta commentary tradition. It is they who digested the sources, and formed a body of material which was then further shaped by the processes of transmission by tradents.[122]

In other words, the biblical interpretation of the EOTC has been contextualized in the Ethiopian context by creative Ethiopian scholars. Garcia notes that "the Ethiopian exegesis has partially broken away from its original context in order to assimilate a new setting in life . . . it has been revised (contextualized) and enriched with subsequent experiences."[123]

This exegetical contextualization is clearly evident in the *andemta* commentary, and can be seen in its method, interests, and outlook.[124] Exegetical contextualization is evident in the selection of materials by the authors of the commentary. They went through the process of selection over a long period of time, and did not incorporate all the available materials from foreign traditions. This selection process took place partly by accident and partly by intention. The Ethiopian scholars chose some materials and excluded others "for a variety of ecclesiastical, geographical, and accidental reasons."[125] For example, the *andemta* commentary consistently refers to Origen as heretic, so that his works were excluded.[126]

122. Cowley, *Ethiopian Biblical Interpretation*, 379–80.

123. Garcia, "Ethiopian Traditional Biblical Interpretation," 1–2.

124. Pedersen, *Traditional Ethiopian Exegesis*, 61–62.

125. Cowley, *Ethiopian Biblical Interpretation*, 378.

126. Ibid.

Cowley presents certain principal factors that influenced the selection of sources included in the *andemta* commentary:

(a) The date of translation into Ge'ez—traditions accepted early were not dislodged, though they might be supplemented, by those arriving later;

(b) Congruity with already accepted tradition;

(c) Effective availability of MSS;

(d) Association with celebrated teachers;

(e) Memorability;

(f) Church use of the non-Biblical texts drawn on as sources of commentary;

(g) Discontinuities caused by historical disturbances.[127]

In addition, the Ethiopian scholars did not simply transmit or translate the traditional sources. Rather, they incorporated the sources in order to produce a body of material that was further shaped by the processes of communication from generation to generation. Thus, the judgment and creativity of Ethiopian scholars was engaged in the formation of the *andemta* commentary.

In this formation, the relevance of the material became an important criterion for inclusion. As noted above, the *andemta* commentary is not merely theoretical or individualistic, rather, it is a practical and communitarian commentary intended to meet the ecclesiastical needs of the EOTC. Therefore, relevance for the faith community functioned as a controlling interpretive factor in the selection of material from the diverse traditions available.[128]

The contextualization of the *andemta* commentary is also found in the addition of traditional Ethiopian materials to the commentary. These additions are frequently related to significant doctrinal issues in the Ethiopian context. The doctrinal issues are addressed along with reflections on the original materials. The eighteenth century "unctionist" controversy in Ethiopia is a good example. In the comments on Matthew 1:16, the *andemta* commentary extensively discusses the timing and nature of the anointing of the Messiah.[129]

127. Ibid., 379.

128. Cowley, "Blood of Zechariah," 297.

129. Lee, "Symbolic Interpretation," 56.

Another characteristic of contextualization in the *andemta* commentary is the unique perspective given to the *andemta* commentary by Ethiopian scholars. Pedersen notes some prominent features of the Ethiopian influence in the *andemta* commentary, the most prevalent of which is the use of the *tarik* (illustrative stories). The commentary frequently presents stories from the Ethiopic biblical canon itself in order to illustrate the meaning of the text. These biblical stories are not in the form of literal quotation, but "in the form of paraphrasic rendering," a strong Ethiopian influence.[130]

Ethiopian contextualization is also evident in examples in the *andemta* commentary taken from the Ethiopian cultural context. Ethiopian scholars used examples "from daily life, the natural environment, the folk customs and the national history known to the Ethiopian student of traditional Bible exegesis."[131] Pedersen presents some of the significant Ethiopian examples used in the *andemta* commentary: military customs, Ethiopian geography and topography, Ethiopian court customs, strong drinks, *gareda* and *täjj*, sociological interest, the customs and life of the Ethiopian Church, popular superstitious practice, the monastic life and ascetical practices, school life, Ethiopian tools, clothing, food and drink, Ethiopian agricultural life, the use of proverbs, very frequent use of the ĕndil (as it says), grammatical and linguistic observations, and the field of science.[132]

Lee offers an example of highly contextualized explanations of a biblical text that clearly point to their origin in Ethiopia. The *andemta* for Exod 27:21 gives the following explanation of the hooks and rings used to suspend the curtains of the Tabernacle:

> ANDM: The hooks are like the fastening of a däbälo,[133] and the rings are like the leather strap, spread out [along the hem] they hold [the curtain].
>
> ANDM: The hooks and rings are like [on] a ṣäḥafi korägo,[134] sown in several places from the top to the bottom they catch

130. Pedersen, *Traditional Ethiopian Exegesis of the Book of Psalms*, 62.

131. Ibid., 65.

132. Ibid., 65–73.

133. A "cloak made of tanned sheep or goatskin with the hair left on. Formerly part of the standard attire of a traditional religious student" (Lee, "Symbolic Interpretations," 54).

134. "The small goatskin bag in which writing materials are kept" (ibid.).

> each other. When you hang them up people call them curtains. The breadth of the cloth is forty cubits.[135]

These specific examples taken from the historical and cultural context of Ethiopia reveal the unique contextualization of the *andemta* commentary.

In sum, although the *andemta* commentary is a traditional commentary that used materials from other exegetical traditions, Ethiopian scholars creatively incorporated these materials and produced a unique Ethiopian commentary. Thus, the *andemta* commentary is a wonderful example of contextualized commentary. Regarding the process of contextualization of the *andemta* commentary, Garcia states:

> Hence, the Ethiopian exegesis has partially broken away from its original context in order to assimilate a new setting in life. This exegesis is traditional in the sense that it has been carefully received and reflected upon. Then it has been revised (contextualized) and enriched with subsequent experiences. Ultimately, it has been responsibly handed down over the centuries, through masters and disciples, until today.[136]

It is important to note that this happened in order to elucidate the meaning of the text for believers in the Ethiopian historical and cultural context. Thus, the *andemta* commentary itself became a valued exegetical tradition of the EOTC. Once established, it has carried on as a living tradition, which continues to influence the interpretive practice of the church.

SUMMARY

In this chapter, I have proposed that the EOTC has a unique tradition of biblical interpretation, which is contained in the *andemta* commentary. This tradition continues to influence the interpretive work of the EOTC. It is also an illustrative example of contextualization.

The *andemta* commentary was formed and developed under the influence of various theological and exegetical traditions, which were both external and internal. However, these traditions were assimilated into the *andemta* commentary by scholars in the Ethiopian historical and cultural context. Thus, these Ethiopian scholars created a unique exegetical

135. Ibid.

136. Garcia, "Ethiopian Traditional Biblical Interpretation," 1–2.

tradition that passed on from generation to generation. This tradition continues to be the most significant exegetical tradition of the EOTC.

The *andemta* commentary is a traditional and theological commentary. It employs traditional exegetical methods to address biblical and doctrinal issues significant to the EOTC. It draws on the richly varied early traditions of the Christian church in a holistic way. It is also a systematic and practical commentary. It employs a systematic approach in order to elucidate the meaning of the text for the community of believers.

The discussion of the *andemta* commentary in this chapter is significant for the overall argument of this monograph. First, the *andemta* commentary is representative of the EOTC's tradition of biblical interpretation. Second, the *andemta* commentary is a living tradition that continues to substantially affect biblical interpretation within the EOTC. Thus, exploring the *andemta* commentary helps to illuminate the present interpretive practices within the EOTC.

Having addressed the contextual biblical interpretation of the EOTC exemplified in the *andemta* commentary, I will now turn to the contextual biblical interpretation of the EOTC exemplified in its preaching. The sermons of the EOTC will most practically reveal the characteristics of the EOTC's biblical interpretation. Thus, the following chapter will investigate the sermons of EOTC preachers in order to identify how they interpret biblical texts for the believers in the context of the EOTC.

5

Biblical Interpretation in the Preaching of the EOTC

In the previous chapter, I demonstrated that the *andemta* commentary represents the tradition of the biblical interpretation of the Ethiopian Orthodox *Tewahido* Church, and discovered distinctive characteristics of the EOTC's traditional biblical interpretation found in the *andemta* commentary. This commentary tradition, as part of the EOTC's tradition, continues to influence the contemporary interpretive work of the EOTC.

I propose that the biblical interpretation of the EOTC is most practically revealed in the preaching of the EOTC. It addresses particular theological and practical issues in the context and tradition of the EOTC. Thus, in this chapter, I will investigate the interpretive characteristics of the preaching of the EOTC.

This exploration will contribute to the argument of this monograph that the EOTC provides a compelling historical example of contextual reading of the Bible, which has been shaped and developed under the substantial influence of the EOTC's tradition in the historical and cultural context of Ethiopia. First, it will demonstrate the distinctive characteristics of the biblical interpretation of the EOTC. Second, it will disclose important interpretive elements that significantly influence the biblical interpretation of the EOTC.

Throughout its history, preaching has been important in the EOTC. It has been significant in the strong teaching tradition of the church. In the traditional educational system of the EOTC, students had to invest over thirty years of full-time study under their teachers in order to be considered biblical scholars. Then, these scholars served as priests, as teachers, and/or as preachers in the church.[1] In the EOTC today, those priests with this traditional training have tremendous biblical knowledge and are very skillful in their preaching. Through their teaching and preaching, these EOTC priests have a significant influence on believers.

In addition, preaching is one of the most significant parts of the liturgy in the EOTC. In recent years, the importance of preaching has been increasingly emphasized. Currently, the EOTC has two worship services, morning and afternoon, in which preaching is delivered in contemporary Amharic. Typically, extensive biblical teaching is offered in the afternoon worship service, and these services are well attended by many Orthodox Christians. In some churches, preaching is recorded on cassette tapes and made available for circulation; these tapes are popular among believers. Thus, in its representation of church tradition and its practical impact, the preaching of the EOTC priests well represents the contextual biblical interpretation of the EOTC.

Therefore, in this chapter, I will analyze the sermons of various EOTC preachers and then discuss the characteristics of the EOTC's biblical interpretation that are revealed in them. The main source materials for this study are the eighty sermons in my personal collection (listed in Chart 1 below). The sermons in this collection were gathered from 2008 to 2009, in several different ways: most of them were presented in local churches; some of them were obtained as cassette tapes made by the EOTC for circulation; some of them were written in EOTC documents. They were translated from Amharic into English. My ETC students helped with the collection and translation of these sermons.

From this collection, I selected nine sermons for analysis. I believe these sermons exemplify the interpretive characteristics of the EOTC sermons as a whole. In addition, I sought a balance in selection, choosing five sermons based on Old Testament texts, three sermons based on New Testament texts, and one topical sermon without any specific biblical text. I refer to other sermons as well in the interpretive discussion.

Table 1: List of Sermons

	Text	Title or Topic
1	Gen 1–4	Creation of God and God's Greatness

1. Alaka, *Traditional Ethiopian Church Education*, 32.

	Text	Title or Topic
2	Gen 6:14—8:19	The Ark of Noah
3	Gen 15:5	Look Up at the Heavens
4	Gen 35:1–5	Get Rid of the Foreign Gods and Let's Go Up to Bethel
5	Gen 37	The Middle Is Not to Be Told
6	Exod 23:20–22	Do Not Rebel against Him
7	Exod 25:22	The Ark of the Covenant*
8	Num 35:9–15	The City of Refuge
9	Deut 19:1–21	Cities of Refuge
10	Judg 6:13	Is God Really with Us?
11	Judg. 6:23	Do Not Be Afraid. You Will Not Die*
12	2 Kgs 18:1–4	*Nehushtan**
13	2 Kgs 25:22	*Gedaliah**
14	2 Chr 25:9	God Is Able
15	Ps 18:25–26	Who Is Your Friend?
16	Ps 48:12	Go around Zion
17	Ps 65:3	Praise to Our God
18	Ps 65:11	You Crown the Year with Your Bounty
19	Ps 91:11	God Sends His Angel for Us
20	Prov 3:27	Do Not Withhold Good from Those Who Deserve It
21	Song 5	Christ and His Bride, the Church
22	Isa 49:23–26	They Shall Bow Down before You with Their Face to the Ground
23	Isa 52:11	Depart, Depart, Go Out from There!
24	Isa 53:1–8	From the Descendants Who Understand These?
25	Isa 53:8	Who Can Speak of His Descendants?*

	Text	Title or Topic
26	Jer 6:16	We Will Not Walk in It
27	Jer 39:18	You Will Not Fall, Because You Trust in Me
28	Ezek 37:3	You Alone Know
29	Ezek 37:13	You Will Know That I Am the Lord, When I Open Your Graves
30	Dan 5	Mene, Mene, Tekel, Parsin
31	Joel 1:14	Declare a Holy Fast; Call a Sacred Assembly
32	Joel 2:12	Return to Me with Fasting
33	Matt 7:15–23	Watch Out for False Teachers
34	Matt 9:14–15	Fasting
35	Matt 25:13	Keep Watch, Because You Do Not Know the Day or the Hour
36	Matt 25:14–30	The Parable of the Talents
37	Matt 26:6–16	Convenient Time*
38	Luke 6:21	Blessed Are You Who Weep Now
39	Luke 11:29–32	A Wicked Generation Asks for a Miraculous Sign
40	Luke 12:15–20	How We Evaluate Our Life
41	Luke 15:8–10	The Parable of the Lost Coin
42	Luke 21:34	Your Hearts Will Be Weighed Down with Marriage
43	John 1:44–50	To Follow the Lord
44	John 2:1–11	They Have No More Wine
45	John 4:7–9	Jesus' Earthly Ministry: Preaching Good News for All Nations
46	John 4:7–10	The Gift of God
47	John 4:7–19	Holy Communion (Lord's Supper)
48	John 5:1–17	Do You Want to Get Well?
49	John 15:4	Remain in Me

	Text	Title or Topic
50	John 16:14	Eternal Counselor*
51	Acts 3	Look at Us
52	Rom 3:1	What Advantage, Then, Is There in Being A Jew?*
53	1 Cor 3:16	Put on Your New Self
54	1 Cor 14:33	God Is Not a God of Disorder But of Peace
55	1 Cor 15:3–4	The Work of Christ
56	1 Tim 1:12–17	The Life of Paul
57	2 Pet 1:17	The Sacred Mountain
58	Rev 2:1–5	You Have Forsaken Your First Love
59	Rev 13:1	What Is the Beast? What Is 666?
60		Salvation of the World in Christ*
61		Concepts of Trinity, Worshipping Angels, Mary and Saints
62		Sin
63		Evil Deed of Satan
64		Identity of Heresy
65		Enemies against Our Church
66		St. Mary's Death and Ascension to Heaven
67		St. Mary in the Bible
68		Our Lady Mary Should Be Praised!
69		St. Mary
70		About St. Mary, Fasting and, Charity
71		The Perpetuation of the Lord's Ark
72		The Necessity of Fasting and Prayer
73		On Fasting
74		Fasting and the Blessing of Fasting

	Text	Title or Topic
75		Teaching on Fasting
76		God's Good Will for Each of Us
77		Doctrine of Our Service
78		Living for God
79		Avoid Temptations and Sins
80		Life Is Like a Mirror

* Sample sermons discussed below.

ANALYSIS OF SAMPLE SERMONS

The selected sermons will be analyzed in the following section. First, an abstract of each sermon will be given. This will be followed by a discussion of the major interpretive characteristics revealed in each sermon.

Sermon 1—Text: Exodus 25:22; Title: The Ark of the Covenant

Abstract

In Amharic, Ark is *tabot*, which comes from the Ge'ez word, *Tehadere,* meaning "be present." In the Old Testament, the Ark symbolically represents the presence of God among his people. In the New Testament, the Ark signifies the seat of the glorification of Jesus' flesh and blood. Moses came down from Mount Sinai with the Ark. This is a symbol that Jesus Christ came down from heaven to save us. The Ark was thrown onto the idol, which was crushed and broken. This is a symbol that Jesus Christ died on the cross and crushed the devil. Jesus overcame death by his resurrection on the third day.

It was God who first gave the Ark to humans. Therefore, the Ark is not an idol. God gave saints the authority to make the Ark, as he told Moses to make the tablets. Moses made a replica of the previous tablets, and God wrote the Law on them. In addition, he commanded Moses to choose Bezalel and Oholiab to make the Ark. We can make many Arks today on this basis. Just as there are many copies of the Bible, there are many Arks in order to facilitate ministry and meet the needs of humankind.

God's Ark has a place only in God's temple. In Malachi, God gave the prophecy that the temples would be many and that ministries would increase. The Corban will be offered where there is God's temple, and where there is Corban, there is the Ark of the Covenant. Now, the temple is everywhere since God is near.

Major Interpretive Characteristics

This sermon focuses primarily on the theological importance of the Ark of the Covenant for the EOTC. The preacher promotes the significance of the Ark for the church and for its associated religious practices. In this message, he employs symbolic interpretation of the text with regard to its objects and figures.

This sermon reveals two major characteristics of biblical interpretation in the EOTC. First, it advocates for the particular religious practices of the EOTC. Second, it employs symbolic interpretation, specifically with regard to the Ark of the Covenant.

Religious Practices of the EOTC

This sermon is highly apologetic. The doctrine and religious practices of the EOTC are defended against challenges from other Christians, especially Protestants in Ethiopia. Specifically, the preacher emphasizes the significant place of the Ark in the church. He highlights the divine origin of the Ark, while strongly refuting the claim that the Ark is an idol. He states, "They say the Ark is an idol. May the Lord give them understanding! Look, if we say the Ark is an idol, what does it mean? Who first gave the Ark to humans? It is God. If we say the Ark is an idol, then we are saying that God first made an idol and gave it to humans. However, God had not given an idol to humans in the beginning. The Ark and an idol are different entities. An idol is the work of Satan."

Notably, the preacher identifies items related to the Ark with the Ark itself. For example, the tablets that were placed in the Ark of the Covenant are identified as the Ark. He states, "In Exodus 31:18, when God finished talking with Moses, he gave him the two tablets carrying God's commands written with God's fingers on them. The tablets were the work of God's fingers. Thus, what does opposing the work of God mean? It means opposing God himself. My friends, the Ark is not an idol."

In order to support this point, the preacher draws on a theological interpretation of a text in the New Testament. He states, "The New Testament apostles are talking about the difference between the Ark and idols. St. Paul says in 2 Corinthians 6:16: ' . . . What agreement is there between the temple of God and idols?'" Here he identifies the Ark with the temple of God in order to make his case that "the Ark is not an idol."

He also addresses other concerns regarding the Ark. He asks the rhetorical question: "How can we make a *tabot* [a replica of the Ark of the Covenant]?" He frames this question as a matter of authority: "On what basis can we make a *tabot*, and that many *tabots*?" He answers the question by proposing two bases of authority. The first is derived from Exodus 32–34. He states, "Originally it was God who made the Ark. But now the passage talks about the authority of saints to make the Ark. God told Moses to make the tablets and bring them to him. Moses made the same replica of the previous ones and God wrote on them. Our opponents say the Ark was broken and none is left. What they read is only Exodus 32. However, if they could read a little further in chapter 34, they would get the point." This expresses the belief that the EOTC has the authority to make *tabots* because the Ark was not lost, but currently resides in Ethiopia.

The second base of authority is also derived from Exodus. He states, "After that God commanded Moses to have the Ark made by chosen and inspired saints. Exodus 31:1–11 tells us that Bezalel from the tribe of Judah and Oholiab from the tribe of Dan were given the wisdom of making the Ark. This is God-given command and no one can oppose what God has given. Bezalel, chosen from the tribe of Judah, made the Ark." He continues, "According to Exodus 37:1, Bezalel made the Ark and brought it to Moses. Who gave him the authority? It is God . . . " Thus, the preacher uses the example of Bezalel's God-given authority to make the Ark to affirm the God-given authority of the EOTC to make many *tabots*.

He continues his discussion of the Ark in relationship to the EOTC by identifying the church, which includes the church building and its compound, with the temple. For him, God's Ark has a place only in God's temple. Because the church is God's temple, the Ark is located in the church.

This raises a significant question: "Why are there many temples?" He offers two reasons. First, he explains that there are many temples based on the prophetic promise that the ministries of God would increase. He bases his argument on a theological interpretation of Mal 1:11. He asserts, "Our God gave the prophets the prophecy that the temples would be many and that ministries would increase. . . . We are now here in a certain part of the city. We have a temple of God right here. And when we go to the other part of the city, we can find another temple. For this word of prophecy to be fulfilled, the temples are being built everywhere in the world. The Corban will be offered where there is God's temple. Where there is Corban, there is the Ark of the Covenant. Where there is the Ark of the Covenant there is the incense."

The second reason he offers for many temples is the nearness of God. He states, "Why is the temple everywhere? Because in the New Testament God is near. In the Old Testament time, there was only one temple and it was in Jerusalem. The people of the world went to Jerusalem to worship where the Ark of the Covenant was found. In the New Testament God is not distant. In Jeremiah 23:23 it is written, 'I am a God who is near,' declares the Lord.'" Thus, the preacher affirms that God is present in the many churches of the EOTC.

Throughout his sermon, the preacher's method of biblical interpretation provides a theological justification for the religious practices of the EOTC. In particular, he defends the making many of *tabots* with theological interpretation of biblical texts regarding the Ark of the Covenant. His symbolic interpretation of the Ark is discussed below.

Symbolic Meaning of the Ark

In order to make a theological case for the belief and practices of the EOTC, the preacher employs symbolic interpretation of biblical texts throughout his sermon. This is especially evident with regard to the place and significance of the Ark of the Covenant. The preacher attributes several significant symbolic meanings to the Ark.

First, in the Old Testament, the Ark signifies the presence of God among his people. The preacher states, "The benefit of the Ark is symbolically representing the presence of God among his people. . . . We are separated from God for 5,500 years because of our sins. Though we are separated from God, God through grace is not separated from us. He says to us, 'Though you are separated from me due to sins, I am not separated from you due to grace and have manifested to you this in the symbol of the Ark.' Thus this was the Old Testament purpose of the Ark. God's presence with his people was signified by it."

In addition, the preacher discusses the significance of the Ark in New Testament texts. In the New Testament, the Ark represents the seat of glorification of Jesus Christ. He expresses this understanding by stating, "My friends, this Old Testament history is a shadow for the New Testament teaching. Moses coming down from Mount Sinai with the Ark is a symbol of Jesus Christ coming down from heaven to save us. Then the Ark was thrown onto the idol, crushing the idol and itself being broken. This is a symbol of Jesus Christ dying on the cross to save us." He continues, "Take this to heart that he died on the cross and crushed the devil. He overcame the devil through his death. He crushed the devil by his cross and killed him. After killing the devil he himself died. Then overcoming death he resurrected on the third day." The Ark in the Old Testament is symbolically connected to the events of Jesus Christ.

He further explores the symbolic meaning of the Ark in the New Testament by describing it as the "seat of glorification" of the flesh and blood of Jesus. He states, "Now look at John 6:54. To have life, it is necessary to eat Jesus' flesh and drink Jesus' blood. His flesh we eat and his blood we drink requires a throne of residence. You know a king is revealed by sitting on his throne. Similarly therefore, the seat of glorification of Jesus' flesh and blood is the Ark of the Covenant. That is the New Testament purpose for the Ark. Those who have not understood this secret, simply go on opposing us." In other words, the Ark symbolizes the residence of the resurrected Jesus in the Eucharistic elements of bread and wine. Those who oppose the EOTC in this belief and practice do so because they "have not understood this secret."

Thus, the preacher employs a symbolic approach in interpreting biblical texts in order to advocate for the theology and religious practice of the EOTC, particularly concerning the Ark of the Covenant. Similar approaches are employed by EOTC preachers in order to defend the doctrines of the EOTC. This approach is evident in the sermon below.

Sermon 2—Text: Judges 6:23; Title: Do Not Be Afraid. You Will Not Die.

Abstract

Even though God warned the Israelites regarding their sin, they continued to do evil in front of God. Therefore, he allowed them to be held as slaves of Midian for seven years. The Midianites were very oppressive and took everything from Israel. The Israelites cried out to God for salvation, and God reminded them of their history in order for them to understand the source of their problems. Then God appeared to Gideon, who was afraid when he realized he was seeing the angel of the Lord face to face. God said to him, "Peace! Do not be afraid. You are not going to die." Then God sent Gideon and saved the Israelites from the hand of the Midianites.

When we face many troubles, we are weak and helpless, so our spirits are down. However, even though we are weak, we will be preserved, since the devil has been conquered by Jesus on the cross. God gives us his power to win our victory. Remember the word of God in times of trouble, "Don't be afraid; you will not die."

Main Interpretive Characteristics

In this sermon, the preacher's theological assumptions and view of the biblical texts are evident. It represents the theological assumptions of EOTC preachers regarding the biblical texts: the biblical texts are the inspired word of God. Most of the text is literally interpreted. He applies this theological assumption to the entire Bible. He refers to several different biblical texts without any reservation, and without any serious consideration of the historical context. He assumes all biblical texts are the authentic word of God.

In addition, this sermon reveals three major characteristics of biblical interpretation in the EOTC. First, the preacher employs traditional doctrinal formulas. This reveals the influence of EOTC tradition on EOTC preaching. Second, the preacher contextualizes the text by applying it to the current situation in Ethiopia. Third, in order to advocate for significant doctrines of the EOTC, the preacher employs a diversity of interpretive techniques, including allegorical and symbolic interpretation of the text.

Doctrinal Formulas

The preacher begins the sermon with a greeting that has a traditional structure and articulates traditional doctrines of the EOTC, particularly doctrines regarding the Trinity, Jesus Christ, and the Holy Spirit. He concludes the introduction of the sermon with a doxology. He states, "In the name of God the Father, the Son and the Holy Spirit. Amen! Oh, God, you sit on cherub and cover all with the glory cloud. Your clothes fill the temple. You are the owner of the praises. Oh, our God, you added your goodness, protection, and blessing in our life. By your mercy and forgiveness you blessed us. Your Fatherly love and great forgiveness have been revealed on us. . . . Let glory and praises be unto you. May the worship and adoration from the earth to the heavens be for your name!"

Contextualization

The interpretation of the biblical text in this sermon reveals strong contextual characteristics. It demonstrates the preacher's belief in the immediacy of God's word, and the preacher's application of the biblical message to present circumstances. At many points during his preaching, he directly connects the story of Israel to the situation of Ethiopia. He states, "We are facing problems. We do not live a happy life, or walk freely. Why is it that we sow but do not produce? It is said that eighty percent of Ethiopians are farmers, but we have empty stomachs. We are poor. We are watching distraction. Even the white people are teasing us about our problem by saying, 'the green famine.' 'The land is green, but you do not work. You are in famine because you do not work.' They say, 'They could be satisfied but they are lazy.' We forgot God, our God, and what he did for us. That is why the enemy is laughing at us."

He continues:

> We say we have a long history as Ethiopia, and that is true. The country is said to be the beginning of civilization. That is true. Then why is the country behind now? Why did we lose our beauty? It is because we forgot our God and are not faithful. We are told in the Bible that "Ethiopia stretches her hand to the Lord." But we forgot our God and Savior. When we turn our face from him, he warns us. God said that "I will take off your glory and you will not eat what you sow, because I will send the enemy to destroy your land. And you will return being ashamed." To be known as an Ethiopian became shame in some areas. Today it is shame to say that "I am an Ethiopian."

Contextualization is evident in the preacher's alignment of the story of Israel with the story of Ethiopia. It is also evident in the preacher's use of Ethiopian parables to deliver his message. He states, "Our fathers had a parable, saying, 'If one give birth to fifty children there will be fifty problems.' . . . What is the use of our multitude?" Victory does not come from the number, but from God. The preacher encourages believers to remember the word of God in times of trouble in their life situation, "Don't be afraid; you will not die."

Interpretive Strategies

Throughout the sermon, it appears that the preacher does not pay much attention to the textual context in which the main verse (Judg 6:23) is located. In its narrative context, Judg 6:23 may mean that even though Gideon saw the angel of God (i.e., God himself), he will not die, which is against the general notion of the time among the Israelites that the one who saw God would die. However, the preacher picks up the verse, "Do not be afraid. You will not die," and applies it to various difficult situations with which believers are confronted in their lives. He employs allegorical and symbolic interpretation of the text in order to speak to contemporary believers and to clarify important doctrines of the EOTC.

Allegorical Interpretation

The preacher employs an allegorical interpretation of some objects and events in order to find a relevant message for his audience. For example, the story of Gideon is applied to the current Ethiopian context. The preacher identifies "the hole" in which Gideon hid himself with various problems in contemporary life. He states, "When Gideon got out of the hole, the salvation came. Let God make us get out of our hole. Now let God make us get out of death hole, suffering hole, problem hole, and sorrow hole. God wants it and he is calling us. Even though we are surrounded by death clouds, 'Do not fear. You will not die,' says the Lord. God sends this voice for us who are slaves of the fear of death. We need to look up to God from our fear hole." Then he exhorts the believers by saying, "This is a decisive moment for us to get up and get out of what we have feared and to listen to the calling of God and give him response. We are at a time of decision."

Another example is found in the way in which the preacher interprets the choosing of the soldiers. Each step is interpreted allegorically. The manner in which the soldiers drink water is given significant spiritual meaning in this interpretation. The preacher states, " . . . God gave Gideon a remark to separate the soldiers, those who lap the water and drink water with their tongues like a dog from those who kneel down to drink." He continues, "The majority knelt down to drink . . . God said, 'I will not fight with these men. Let each of them go to his place.'"

The preacher then gives the spiritual meaning of this behavior:

> What is the secret behind this? What does God teach us from this? Those who got down on their knees to the place, which is not right, and who submit themselves to sin could not fight for the Lord. Those who are governed by the world and kneel down to the worldly things, those who kneel down to adultery, idols, and those who kneel down to self-centeredness, genocide, ethnicity . . . those who kneel down to the fruits of the flesh could not fight God's fight. We never see the victory that God is doing by the life of kneeling down to evil. If our knees need to kneel down, it must be only at the feet of God. A Christian does not have a knee which kneels down everywhere. He knows where he should kneel down. He does not submit himself to the things of this world and flesh. May God be our Strength!

Another allegorical interpretation is evident in the preacher's discussion of the phrase: "to enter the middle." He states, "God instructed them to enter the middle of the enemy. A spiritual person is not the one who is at the edge or far from the middle. Spiritual fight is not like watching a soccer game, sitting on a seat in a stadium. It is not like clapping for others. Spiritual fight is to witness to God's work in the middle. Jesus said, 'I will send you in the middle of wolves like a sheep . . .'"

In addition, the preacher draws spiritual meaning from the "empty jar." He states:

> Gideon's men did not hold any weapon but an empty jar. We praise God who uses empty jars for his mighty deeds. We are empty. Surely we have nothing. We are poor. We are not educated. We do not have knowledge. We do not have anything to depend upon in our flesh. We do not have anything to hope for in this world. But we are victorious. We know one truth that God is with us. God who can do everything is with us and in us. These men went to fight holding jars while their enemies were holding weapons. This is the way how God does things. . . . We do not have weapon but God is our protection. We Christians should not depend on the weapons of the flesh.

Symbolic Interpretation

The preacher also employs symbolic interpretation throughout the sermon. For example, Mount Gilead symbolizes the church. He states, ". . . God's children, if you are frightened and if your heart is filled with fear, you will not pass from Mount Gilead. The Mount Gilead is the holy church. We all are gathered at Mount Gilead. We are here to fight. We accompany God who is the fighter."

In addition, the jar and the fire are given significant symbolic meaning as St. Mary and Jesus. The preacher states, "Look, the men of Gideon have the jars and fire in it. This is the secret of the jar. They were having the jars in their hands, surrounded by their enemies. . . . But our Light Jesus Christ is with us. . . . There is no problem we cannot overcome. Our enemy Satan that darkens the heart of the people will be kicked out." He continues, "The light is Jesus Christ. He is the glory of the world, and the beauty of the world. The jar is the holy Mariam who brought Jesus to the world. Mariam is the mother of Jesus."

These allegorical and symbolic interpretations demonstrate that the preacher interprets the text according to the doctrinal tradition of the EOTC. Specifically, the preacher in this sermon asserts significant doctrines for the EOTC, including those regarding Jesus Christ, St. Mary, and the church.

Sermon 3—Text: 2 Kings 18:1–4; Title: Nehushtan

Abstract

From the beginning of humankind, sin entered the town of human community through disobedience to God and, as a result, there is a yoke of sin upon the people. God called his people to break the yoke of sin from the town in order to be free. Those who believe and trust in God, and have a good relationship with God by faith and good work, can break the yoke of sin from the town. In order to do this, the people must do three specific things: know God and give the first place to Him; learn from God; and follow the direction of God. Hezekiah set a good example by giving his life to God, coming to Jerusalem, and obeying his mother. God's people can win the town for God by breaking different yokes of sin from their lives and from the church.

Major Interpretive Characteristics

This sermon reveals several major characteristics of biblical interpretation in the EOTC. First, the preacher contextualizes the text by applying it to the current situation in Ethiopia. Second, he explores the historical background of the text. Third, he employs a diversity of interpretive techniques, including figural, allegorical, and symbolic interpretation in order to provide foundations for the faith and life of believers.

Contextualization

The preacher begins his sermon by stating his ethical concerns for the believers in Ethiopia through a comparison between the biblical town and their own town: "The main point is to win the town by breaking sin from the town. God called his people to break the yoke of sin. Wherever you see there is the town of sin. From the very beginning, sin entered the town though disobedience. Because of man's disobedience to God, there is a yoke upon people. In order to become free from the bondage of sin, you should break the sin of yoke from the town."

He continues by emphasizing the importance of right relationship with God in order to break the sin from the town. He asserts, "Those who believe and trust in God will have a good relationship with God by faith and good work. To break sin from the town, there are three important things in relation with God: first, knowing the Lord God and giving the first place for him; second, learning from God; third, following the directions of God. You should follow God's directions to break the town of sin." He then directly applies this message to the contemporary Ethiopian situation: "Today many towns are full of sin because of the lack of people who follow God's directions. People do not want to follow God's direction. Because of this there are unbroken sins everywhere."

Describing the Historical Background.

In his sermon, the preacher describes the historical context of the biblical text, which centers on the reign and action of King Hezekiah. He states, "In 2 Kings 18:1, Hezekiah son of Ahaz king of Judah began to reign. He was twenty-five years old when he became king, and he reigned in Jerusalem twenty-nine years." The preacher also traces the original background of the events in the text. He states, "In Numbers 21:4–9, we see the wickedness of Israel and the punishment of God. God ordered Moses to make a bronze snake as the solution to the problem. Later, the bronze snake was brought to the temple, and then people began to worship the bronze snake." He connects this story to the present text: "Hezekiah cleared the idol from the temple."

He then seeks the spiritual meaning for his audience from the historical event in the text. He states, "The passage shows us the broken relationship of Israel with God. They were against God and against Moses. . . . Today the people in the church do the same thing as the Israelites. We should stand firm and break sin from the church and our life as Hezekiah did. Then we can see the glory of God in our life." Thus, he explores the historical background of the biblical text. Yet, his purpose is not merely to find the original meaning of the text, but to find a direct application of the text to his contemporary audience.

Use of a Biblical Figure as a Model

The preacher uses Hezekiah as a model of faith and life for believers. He states, "We have seen from the king Hezekiah three important things to learn. First, he gave his young life to God and obeyed God and His directions. Because of this God brought him to a good position. You young people should give first time, place, energy, power for God. Not only this, but also you should follow his instruction and direction. Then he will give you a good position . . . " He continues, "Second, he came to Jerusalem. Jerusalem is the holy place, holy town and kings' town. There is God and His throne in Jerusalem. You young people should come to Jerusalem. Third, he obeyed his mother. In the Old Testament time, all mothers indicated our true spiritual mother *emabetachen* who is St. Mary. That's why he obeyed his mother.

Filling in the Gap in the Biblical Narrative

The preacher's assertion that Hezekiah obeyed his mother is not found in the biblical text on which his sermon is based. Nor is it found in the biblical canon. The preacher inserts this story into the biblical narrative in order to make his point. It is not original to him, however, but derives from the tradition of the EOTC. "Filling the gaps" in the biblical narrative with traditional material is a frequent interpretive practice in patristic biblical interpretation. Thus, in this case, the preacher is following the interpretive tradition of the church.

Adopting a Word as an Interpretive Key

The preacher continues by focusing on a single word in the biblical text. He states, "Hezekiah smashed and cut down bad things and ungodly worship, especially he broke the bronze snake. The change and restoration of faith is called *Nehushtan*, which means breaking down ungodly things among the nations and town. *Nehushtan* is more important today for our church. That is very significant to reforming the church and to bringing change to our society."

In the text, the word *Nehushtan* refers to the bronze snake itself. However, the preacher states that it means "breaking down ungodly things," which included the bronze snake. It is not clear whether the preacher offers this definition based on a misunderstanding or an intentional distortion. In either case, the preacher uses this word as a spiritual and ethical motto for believers. Thus, it functions as the interpretive key in his preaching. It seems that this is not the preacher's creative coinage, but a theologically fixed interpretation of the text in the EOTC. This demonstrates the significance of tradition in the biblical interpretation of the EOTC.

Here the preacher interprets the word *Nehushtan* allegorically. *Nehushtan* stands for "breaking anything that leads to sin." In this case, the preacher employs an allegorical interpretation in order to find ethical implications for believers.

Symbolic Interpretation

The preacher adopts symbolic interpretations of important words in the text at crucial points of his preaching. For example, he identifies the church building with Jerusalem, stating that both are the place of the presence of God. He asserts that Hezekiah came to "Jerusalem, which is the holy place, holy town, and kings' town. There is God. God's throne is in Jerusalem. You young people should come to Jerusalem. Today's Jerusalem is our church, our compound. This compound building is very unique because God is living here. This place is the presence of God. So come to worship here in Jerusalem to be a king in this generation."

He continues with another symbolic interpretation: "The name of Jerusalem is the name of female, *emabetachen* (our mother). Mary is *emabetachen*. All blessing for us is given through *emabetachen*." He states that all mothers indicate *emabetachen* (Mary). Then, he returns to the third lesson from the example of Hezekiah:

> The third truth that we learn from Hezekiah is that he obeyed his mother. All mothers in Old Testament time indicate our true spiritual mother, Mary (*emabetachen*). He obeyed his mother because of this. He became king and was blessed with God's gifts in every situation. Today many false teachers oppose our mother [*emabetachen*]. They do not have knowledge about our mother. Our mother [*emabetachen*] indicates their mothers by the will of God in the Spirit . . . Mary is the mother of the people in the whole world. So we should follow her way, instruction and character in order to receive blessing, to be king.

This sermon is primarily a moral exhortation for the faith and life of believers. The preacher gives this exhortation by using different interpretive strategies, such as describing the historical background, filling in the gap in the biblical narrative, using a biblical figure as a model, adopting a word as an interpretive key, and employing allegorical and symbolic interpretation.

Sermon 4—Text: 2 Kings 25:22; Title: Gedaliah

Abstract

God is *Gedaliah*, which means "God is great." God is always present with his mighty hand with his covenant people. God never forsakes, but protects, those who wait for him. When we are faced with obstacles, we should understand God's presence in our daily life. In the Babylonian captivity, the Israelites believed and confessed, *Gedaliah*. In an uncomfortable situation we should proclaim *Gedaliah*, as Paul and Silas did. In our time of great suffering and sorrow, as in Habakkuk's time, our great God (*Gedaliah*) comforts us in a way the world cannot.

The way God selected David as king shows God's greatness (*Gedaliah*). God rejects those who are proud, but exalts those who are humble. David went to fight against Goliath without any fear because he believed in the great God. Our forefathers fought against their enemies to bring great honor to Ethiopia. They were martyred for the sake of God and proclaimed God's greatness. Jesus Christ came and healed the man who was invalid for thirty-eight years. God Almighty never forsakes those whom the world has forsaken, but exalts them. We should proclaim *Gedaliah* in our lives by taking care of the forsaken, the poor, and the sick.

Major Characteristics

This preacher's sermon fully focuses on the greatness of God (*Gedaliah*). Here, the word *Gedaliah* is the interpretive key and primary message of his entire sermon.

This sermon reveals four major characteristics of biblical interpretation in the EOTC. First, it employs the use of a single word as an interpretive key. Second, it conveys the message through both biblical and extra-biblical stories. Third, it advocates for the particular religious practices of the EOTC. Fourth, it places an emphasis on the practice of faith.

Adopting a Word as an Interpretive Key

The topic of this sermon was chosen from 2 Kings 25:22. The preacher states, "When Jerusalem was captured, its gate was destroyed by fire. Nebuchadnezzar, king of Babylon, made *Gedaliah* governor of the Israelites in 597 BC. At that time, *Gedaliah* worked with Jeremiah." The preacher does not focus on the person named *Gedaliah*, but on the meaning of his name, which is "God is great." By doing so, he delivers a message regarding God's greatness. As shown in the abstract, *Gedaliah* also functions as an interpretive key for the sermon. The preacher applies *Gedaliah* to stories found both in the Bible and in Ethiopian history.

Use of Biblical and Extra-Biblical Stories

The sermon is composed of a series of stories, which are biblical and extra-biblical. Thus, it is very narrative oriented. By using stories, the preacher supports the main message of *Gedaliah*: "God is always present with his mighty hand with his covenant people . . . God never forsakes, but protects those who wait for him. When we are faced with obstacles, we should understand God's presence in our daily life."

He continues, "God is not always with only those who are successful, but also with the unsuccessful. The Israelites did not forsake their

Creator even when they were captive to Babylonians. Outsiders raised a question, 'Who is the owner of the destroyed city.' The Israelites response was 'God is great' (*Gedaliah*)."

He then applies this to a story from the New Testament: "Christians should demonstrate their love for others not only in the time of success, but also in suffering and persecution. In Acts 16:25–26 . . . Paul and Silas were in prison. They worshiped God with prayer and singing in an uncomfortable situation. It brought about the tremendous sign from heaven . . . In an uncomfortable situation we should proclaim *Gedaliah* (God is great)."

The preacher continues with another application from the Old Testament to contemporary life: "As the prophet says in Habakkuk 3:17 . . . even though our salary is not enough for our life, we should shout, '*Gedaliah* [God is great].' In our great suffering and sorrow, our great God [*Gedaliah*] comforts us more than the world can do . . . If a man glorifies God in his life, God will respect him in the sight of others . . . If we say God is great, we will get things we want, peace and heart desire, since God is the Giver of holy and good things."

He presents David as a good model of this. He states, "David was just a shepherd, tending sheep in the wilderness. Even his family rejected him. But God always respects those who are rejected . . . From Jesse's house, David the youngest one was anointed . . . God chose only those who faithfully obeyed him . . . The method of selecting David proclaims on God's greatness (*Gedaliah*) . . . God rejects those who are proud but exalts those who are humble."

He continues, "Even though our enemies come to our town to destroy our temple and burn it, the God Almighty is with us and no one can oppose us . . . David stood to fight against Goliath on behalf of the Israelites . . . David went to fight against Goliath without any fear because he believed in God (1 Sam 17:45) . . . Saul wanted to dress David with his own tunic, but David took it off . . . David's dress was the instrument of God's spiritual armor. Revelation 16:15 says, ' . . . Blessed is he who stays awake and keeps his clothes with him . . . ' The clothes are Jesus Christ our Savior." The preacher applies the text to the Ethiopian context. He aligns the Old Testament with the New Testament in discussing David's physical and spiritual clothes. He also uses symbolic interpretation in comparing the clothes of David to Jesus Christ.

The preacher also uses stories from the history and traditions of Ethiopia to deliver the message of God's greatness (*Gedaliah*). He gives an illustration from Ethiopian history: "Our forefathers fought against their enemies to bring great respect to this country Ethiopia. They were martyred for the sake of God and proclaimed God's greatness. The Bible says Ethiopia seeks the face of the Lord for her development and prosperity (Ps 68:31). Our forefathers kept Ethiopian boundaries and protected them from foreign colony by carrying the Ark. They planted trees to protect from natural disaster and land nakedness . . . "

He also employs stories from Ethiopian mythology: "One day Birtawiz's family gave her to a dragon as a sacrifice and forgot her. In a miraculous way, Giyorgis[2] intervened to save her from the teeth of the dragon and gave her back to her family. Tekele haymanot[3] stays still in this era. God wants to delegate other elders on behalf of Tekele haymanot to follow his footstep. Today all youth are Giyorgis . . . and all the elders are Tekele haymanot." The Word of God says, "Do not forget the poor, and remember the forsaken. God healed the thirty-eight year invalid man. We should always say in our life, *Gedaliah* (God is great). He is our Peace. He is our Savior. May God bless us!"

Religious Practices of the EOTC

Another important characteristic evident in this sermon is the justification of the religious customs of the EOTC. At an important juncture, the preacher advocates for different religious customs of the church. For example, he states, "The first hospital for the patient is sprinkling *tsebal* in the church. The next one is our neck cross. When Satan comes to you and sees your neck cross, he will flee from you. For example, suppose you go to a cinema or football field and sit on a chair. If you want to go outside for a while, you will put your T-shirt on the chair. Then people will see the T-shirt and know the place is taken by somebody. Just like this, when Satan comes to you and sees your neck cross, he will say the person belongs to God."

Tsebal is holy water, which is used to seek God's blessing and protection from evil powers. Sprinkling *tsebal* is part of many EOTC ceremonies. The EOTC believes the cross symbolizes the redemption through

2. Giyorgis (St. George) is an Ethiopian Murrish knight and patron saint. This story is drawn on an Ethiopian icon of St. George.

3. Tekle Haymanot is an Ethiopian patron saint and popular both within and outside Ethiopia. He founded a major monastery in his native town Shewa. He is believed to perform many miracles daily for the believers.

the death of Jesus Christ. The EOTC believers wear neck crosses all of their lives. The preacher advocates these practices in his sermon.

Emphasis on the Practice of Faith

The preacher applies his sermon directly to the current situation of the people in Ethiopia, and calls on believers to practice the faith in their life situation. His aim in this message is to encourage believers in difficulties. He states, "God Almighty never forsakes the poor but exalts them. In John 5:1–9, John talks about the one who had been invalid for thirty-eight years . . . During the whole thirty-eight years all his friends had forsaken him, but God did not desert him. The Friend and Healer Jesus Christ came and healed him. . . . Therefore, we Christians do not fear. Our Savior Jesus Christ is always with us."

Then, he commands believers to care for the forsaken, the poor and the sick in their own context. He states, "The High Priest, our Church Father John Afework said, 'If you want to know God, please go visit the poor people who are living on their mats on the street.' Who is forsaken in our village? Who is excluded because of sickness? Go visit those poor and sick people, and you will have a great crown. Today the people in high positions do injustice, because of that the poor people are crying out to the Lord. God hears the cry of the poor. He healed the invalid person for thirty eight years from his suffering."

The preacher then demonstrates a traditional understanding of a specific Psalm. He states, "In Psalms 12:1 David prays, 'Help, Lord, for the godly are no more; the faithful have vanished from among men.' This Psalm is known as the eighth thousand era song. In this eighth thousand era, people live an ungodly life. David prays to the Lord, 'Save us from this bad era.'"

The primary message of this sermon is the greatness of God (*Gedaliah*). It functions as the interpretive key throughout this sermon. The preacher employs several interpretive methods, including story-telling, in order to achieve his goals. He also advocates particular religious practices of the EOTC and emphasizes the practice of faith for believers.

Sermon 5—Text: Isaiah 53:8; Title: Who Can Speak of His Descendants?

Abstract

"Who can speak of his descendants?" (Isa 53:8) is a word of proclamation regarding Jesus Christ. In Isaiah 53, the prophet Isaiah prophesied about the Messiah, including his nature, emptiness, suffering, and death. In 2 Corinthians 8:9, Paul writes that Jesus' sacrifice is all for our sake. After his resurrection, Jesus returned to his glory. Now he reigns in all his power and authority. Jesus Christ is not a man, nor a prophet, nor a mediator. John 1:1–3 declares that he was the Word, who was with God and was God. He was with God. He created the world. He was God. This Word dramatically became flesh. He became man through the Virgin Mary. The prophecy in Isaiah 7:14 was fulfilled in Matthew 1:21.

Isaiah 53 is also significant in the story of the Ethiopian eunuch (Acts 8:26–38). He was the financial minister of Queen Candace of Ethiopia, who went to Jerusalem to worship God. On the way back to Ethiopia, he was reading Isaiah 53. Philip explained to him the meaning of the passage and he received Jesus Christ. He was then baptized. He was the very next person to be baptized after the baptism of Jesus' disciples. Thus, Ethiopia was the first country to receive baptism and to read the Bible. Ethiopia took the first initiative to seek God. Later, the Ethiopian Orthodox Church became the *Tewahido* church and, therefore, the true church. In this way, Ethiopia laid the foundation for Christianity.

Major Characteristics

The preacher interprets the biblical passage as having two historical references: the first is Jesus Christ and the second is the event regarding the Ethiopian eunuch. Here, the prophecy and fulfillment schema is employed as the key interpretive approach. In this way, the preacher highlights the salvation of Jesus Christ, and the historical significance of the EOTC.

This sermon reveals four major characteristics of biblical interpretation in the EOTC. First, it is Christ-centered. Second, it employs a prophecy and fulfillment schema. Third, it seeks to connect the biblical text with the Ethiopian context. Fourth, it places an emphasis on the practice of faith.

Christ-Centered Interpretation

Christ is the center in the preacher's sermon, and the text is christologically interpreted. He states, "'Who can speak of his descendants?' (Isa 53:8). This verse is the word which exclaims on Jesus Christ." He continues, "This was delivered by the prophet Isaiah. He lived in 700 BC. However, he spoke about Jesus, his very nature, suffering, death, emptiness, and so on, in Isaiah 53." Then, the preacher seeks the specific implications of the text in the New Testament. He states, "'Who can speak of his descendants?' The story is about Jesus Christ. Paul, in 2 Corinthians 8:9, tells us that Jesus' submissions are all for our sake. The rich Christ became poor for us. The Lord sat on a donkey. He was buried in a human tomb. In order to make us free, he received suffering which we were supposed to take. Then he returned to his glory. Now he is in all his power and authority."

This preaching demonstrates the traditional view of the EOTC on Christ. For example, the preacher states, "He is not the one who many people assume to be. He is not man. He is not prophet. He is not mediator. Then who is Jesus? In order to know him we need to listen to John's teaching. According to John 1:1–3, he was the Word. He was in the beginning. He was with God. He created the world. He was God. This Word dramatically became flesh. He became man. Let me ask you a question. Please, answer me. Who is Jesus? Jesus was the Word. What happened to him? He became man. How did he become man? Through Virgin Mary. This was prophesied by the prophet Isaiah. Glory be to his mighty name!" This demonstrates that the EOTC reflects the traditional teachings on Christ of the early church.

Prophecy and Fulfillment in Christ Schema

The preacher's interpretation of the biblical text follows the traditional prophecy and fulfillment schema between the Old and the New Testaments. In this schema, the prophecies in the Old Testament are accomplished in the New Testament. He states, "Isaiah 7:14 says, 'Therefore, the Lord himself will give you a sign: The virgin will be with child and will give birth to a son, and will call him Immanuel.' Matthew 1:21 says, 'She will give birth to a son, and you are to give him the name Jesus, because he will save his people from their sins.' Isaiah told that 'She will be with child and will give birth to a son.' And the gospel writer said that she gave birth to a son, and named him Jesus. The prophecy was fulfilled."

Seeking the Ethiopian Connection

In this sermon, the text is interpreted in light of a special Ethiopian connection. For the preacher, the verse refers to the circumstances of the Ethiopian eunuch. He asserts, "Especially, the verse 'Who can speak of his descendants?' (Isa 53:8) talks about an Ethiopian person. This verse refers to a particular situation he was in. He was the Ethiopian eunuch . . . Let me read you the verse which records this truth in the Book of Acts 8:26–38. The Ethiopian eunuch, whose name was Barosh, was the head of the finance ordained by Candace, queen of Ethiopia. . . . The man was reading Isaiah 53. Then he was baptized by Philip."

The preacher then seeks the implications of this event for the contemporary Ethiopian context: "Jesus told his disciples to get baptized after his baptism. The Ethiopian eunuch was the very next one who was baptized after that. . . . The Ethiopian Orthodox Church shared his baptism early before. . . . Therefore, Ethiopia was the first country to receive the baptism. Ethiopia laid the foundation of Christianity. . . . This country still lives by faith and will stay forever and ever. Amen!"

The preacher continues, "He accepted Jesus Christ before the Apostle Paul came to Christ. He knew Jesus before the Roman Empire and Greece. Praise be to his holy name! Through this man Christianity came to Ethiopia. Then later the Ethiopian Orthodox Church became the true church and *Tewahido* church. This is the way our faith came. This is our religion. . . . I am telling you that Ethiopia became the first Bible reading country. I am telling you that Ethiopia took the first initiative to seek God."

Emphasis on the Practice of Faith

Throughout his sermon, the preacher is concerned with the faith and life of contemporary believers. He consistently repeats the phrase, "Who can speak of his descendants?" (Isa 53:8) and applies it to contemporary Christians. This verse is the word which exclaims on Jesus Christ. Among the generations, God saved those who spoke of him. However, those who did not speak of him perished. Even today, those of us who speak of him will be saved, but those of us who do not speak of him will be perished. Nevertheless, the will of God is to save all. May God help us to speak of him and be saved!"

He continues to advocate for the traditional Christology of the EOTC, while bringing this Christology into the contemporary context. He states, "Today many believe that Jesus is man, prophet, and intercessor. They do not know him yet. They seem to worship him but they are not with him . . . " He repeats this affirmation and adds an exhortation for his own generation: "Today many people say that Jesus is prophet, man and mediator as the Pharisees say. We know Jesus by his teaching, not by the teaching of Pharisees. He is God the Creator. We do not doubt him as Philip did. We believe in Jesus as written in the Bible, not by assumption . . . As the disciples were with Jesus, they did not know him. It obviously happens today in our generation. May God give a chance of repentance for those who went away from his presence!"

The central message of this sermon is the person and salvific work of Jesus Christ. The preacher employs a christological interpretation of the Old Testament text (Isa 53:8). The preacher also interprets the text as having another historical reference: the event regarding the Ethiopian eunuch. The preacher in this sermon seeks to highlight the salvation of Jesus Christ, and the historical significance of the EOTC.

Sermon 6—Text: Matthew 26:6–11; Title: Convenient Time

Abstract

We must use convenient time to come to God rather than to commit sin. Simon the leper invited Jesus Christ to his house in convenient time. While he was there, a woman came to Jesus and poured perfume on his feet in convenient time. This was preparation for the burial of Jesus. A hospitable man did not make use of the time to bear with an old man who refused to read the Bible. Judas sold out Jesus for thirty silver coins in convenient time. Amnon defiled his sister in convenient time, and Absalom killed Amnon as revenge for his sister in convenient time. A married woman tried to carry on committing adultery with three men in convenient time, but her husband revealed her sin in convenient time. Cain killed his brother in convenient time.

The wage of sin is death. Judas committed sin in convenient time, and died. Cain committed sin in convenient time, and died. Amnon committed sin in convenient time, and died. But the woman expressed her love for Jesus in convenient time by pouring perfume on Jesus. She wanted Jesus to break the yoke of her sinful life and to change her life into the aroma of the perfume. God will break all of our burdens in convenient time. Therefore, use convenient time to come to God, not to sin.

Major Characteristics

This preaching shows the importance of narrative in the EOTC. The main point of this sermon is using convenient time to come to God, not to sin. In order to deliver this message, the preacher uses biblical and extra-biblical stories of different kinds. All of these stories are consecutively woven together to become part of the main narrative. Here, as in previous sermons, the preacher uses traditional storylines to fill narrative gaps in the biblical story. It seems that the preacher does so in order to make the biblical story more plausible to the people in his culture.

This sermon reveals three major characteristics of biblical interpretation in the EOTC. First, it employs an idea as an interpretive key for the entire sermon. Second, it conveys the message through both biblical and extra-biblical stories. Third, through these stories, it reveals strong ethical concerns for contemporary Ethiopian society.

Employing an Idea as the Interpretive Key

The idea of "convenient time" is the interpretive key in this sermon. In other words, all the biblical and extra-biblical stories in this sermon are interpreted in the light of "convenient time." As defined by the preacher, "convenient time" means "proper" time. The stories are used as positive and negative examples in order to deliver his message to use the time for glorifying God rather than for committing sin. For this purpose, he employs both literal and allegorical interpretations of the texts. This demonstrates that historicity is not the main concern of the preacher. His main concern is how to deliver the message effectively. This drives his interpretation of the biblical texts.

Use of Biblical and Extra-biblical Stories

The preacher starts his sermon by mentioning Simon's invitation of Jesus to his house at the "convenient time." He states, "In Bethany there was a rich and respected person. He was a leper which was the sign of being a sinner in the ancient time. His sin was recognized by all people because of his leprosy. If our sin is manifested in the form of leprosy like in the ancient time, all of us will have leprosy. But this does not happen because of God's mercy. When he came to know that Jesus was coming to Bethany, he invited him to have a meal in his house at the "convenient time." We should also invite God to our life. There is nothing greater than inviting God in our life. And Jesus accepted the invitation of Simon without considering him as a sinner or leper."

Then, the preacher introduces the story of the unnamed woman. The story he delivers is not found in the biblical text. It seems that he follows the tradition of the EOTC, which fills in details in the story so that it might be more resonant with contemporary believers. He states, "While Jesus was in the house of Simon, in the neighborhood there was a woman, looking at herself in the mirror. The Bible tells us that she was very beautiful, but under a great burden. She said to herself, 'I am beautiful but a sinner.' She decided to repent, and went to the house of Simon. When Simon saw her, he was very much disappointed. Look, Jesus accepted Simon with his sin, but Simon did not accept the woman with her sin."

He uses another traditional Ethiopian story to make a similar point:

> There was a man who is well known for his entertaining guests in his house. When a guest came to his house, he washed his feet, prepared a meal for him, and gave him the Bible to read. One day, a sixty-year-old man came to his house. After washing his feet, he invited the old man to read the Bible, but he became angry and refused to read the Bible, saying, "I do not know God." Soon the owner ousted the guest from his house in the middle of the night. Then he asked God, "God, what kind of man did you bring in my house?" God answered him back, "How old was the man you had expelled tonight?" He replied, "Sixty years old." Then God said to him. "How could you not spare him for one night, while I have carried him for sixty years?" Christians, God is the God of mercy who carries us to the end of our ages.

Then, the preacher gives the story of Judas as another negative example of using "convenient time." He states, "Then the woman poured the perfume on Jesus' feet. But the disciples murmured about the woman's good deed. Judas complained, considering it as waste, but Jesus admired her deeds, for she did it for his burial. Then Judas began to look for convenient time to betray Jesus. Judas was a treasurer and got ten percent out of the hundred ministry income. To compensate his loss of ten percent from the perfume he agreed to sell Jesus with thirty silver coins. His final destiny was death."

Emphasis on the Practice of Faith

Another example is drawn from the story of David's children in the Old Testament. This is one of many stories given as a message directed to the moral issues in contemporary Ethiopian society. The preacher states, "David had children he begot from two different wives, whose names were Amnon, Absalom, and Timar. Amnon fell in love with Timar and became sick. His evil friend advised him to bring her to his home and defile her. Amnon waited for convenient time and raped his own sister. After two years, he was killed by Absalom. It was the result of his sin. Today there are a number of Amnons who snare women to defile. Many young people commit premarital sex, but they finally fall in bed in severe pain and sickness."

He continues with a contemporary fable:

> Today there are also married couples who are not faithful for their marriage. There was a married woman in one village. She had three informal male partners. Her husband was informed by his neighbors about her unfaithfulness, but he did not believe what he heard. Eventually he wanted to confirm the rumor. Waiting for convenient time, he pretended to go to the field for work. As he left his house, the three men came one by one. The woman hid the men in different places. Suddenly the husband appeared, and the woman was surprised. Her husband offered her a present, and the woman asked, "Where did you get the money to buy this?" Her husband answered, "I borrowed some money." She asked again, "Who is going to pay back?" Pointing to the roof, her husband said, "He will pay it." Soon the man who was hiding up on the roof quickly said, "Not only me but the man under the bed should also pay." Then the man under the bed quickly said, "Not only me but the man in the inner house should also pay." All her secrets were revealed. But when her husband pointed to the roof, what he meant was "God will pay it." But each of the three men who were hidden thought that he was pointing to himself. So use convenient time to come to God not to sin.

The preacher also uses the Old Testament story of Cain and Abel, "filled in" with traditional material. He states, "After Cain killed his brother he built a house of stone. The house fell upon him and he was killed. A man reaps what he sows. Judas committed sin in convenient time and died. Cain committed sin in convenient time and died. Amnon committed sin in convenient time and died. Therefore, the wage of sin is death."

It is after presenting these negative examples that the preacher interprets the meaning of the woman's story. He states, "Now let us go back to the first story about the woman. She preferred to offer perfume than any other offering because she wanted Jesus to change her life into the aroma of the perfume. She also broke the jar of perfume, beseeching Jesus to break the yoke of her sinful life. We know that we all have burdens, and God will break it in convenient time."

This sermon reveals important characteristics of the EOTC's biblical interpretation. In order to give an ethical exhortation, the preacher uses stories of different kinds woven together to become part of the main narrative. The preacher also uses traditional story-lines to fill narrative gaps in the biblical story.

Sermon 7—Text: John 14:16; Title: Eternal Counselor

Abstract

On the day of Pentecost the Holy Spirit came upon the disciples of Jesus Christ. Jesus Christ promised the disciples in John 14:16, "And I will ask the Father, and he will give you another Counselor to be with you forever." The Holy Spirit is the Counselor. He comforted and counseled the disciples. He gave them power to proclaim the gospel boldly. Their life was changed by the Holy Spirit. The Holy Spirit is also the Guide. John 16:13 states, "When he, the Spirit of truth comes, he will guide you into all truth." He guides our life and helps us get to good things. He teaches us truth so that we may know the truth. It was this Counselor Spirit who guided Philip to meet the Ethiopian eunuch, and who helped the Ethiopian to be converted and become a messenger to Ethiopia. By dwelling within our fathers, the Holy Spirit established the church.

In order to receive the power of the Holy Spirit, we must stay in Jerusalem, which the holy church has replaced. The church transfers grace and blessing. The fathers succeeded the apostles, and the priests and deacons have succeeded the fathers. Today, the Holy Spirit guides and blesses our ministry. But there are many ministers who work without the Holy Spirit. Only the ministries of those who are possessed by the Holy Spirit will be blessed. They will not scatter the flock, but gather new converts.

Major Characteristics

The main topic of this sermon is the Holy Spirit. This preaching is solidly based on the Bible, and clarifies the traditional teaching of the EOTC on the Holy Spirit. Thus, the preacher endeavors to elucidate the spiritual meaning of text in relation to the life and faith of the audience and the ministry of the church.

This sermon reveals three major characteristics of biblical interpretation in the EOTC. First, it exemplifies the EOTC's traditional teaching on the Holy Spirit. Second, it discusses the work of the Holy Spirit in the contemporary context. Third, it advocates for the religious beliefs and practices of the EOTC.

Traditional Teaching on the Holy Spirit

The preacher begins by depicting the day of Pentecost as the background of the text. He states, "Today is the day of the Holy Spirit. When the Holy Spirit came upon the disciples, they received his grace abundantly. And it is the day when the church was born. On the day the church was established." Then he explains the implication of the empowerment of the Holy Spirit upon the disciples on that day. He states, "Christ, whom you and I believe, was proclaimed through Asia Minor to the world. To make this happen the Holy Spirit gave power, wisdom and knowledge to our fathers on this day."

He uses John 14:16 as the frame of reference for the whole sermon: "The Spirit of truth, the world cannot accept him because it neither sees nor knows him. But you know him because he lives with you." He continues, "Counselor in Greek is *paracletos*. . . . The word Counselor is the special nick name for the Holy Spirit. This special name reveals the nature and work of the Holy Spirit, and his relationship with us. . . . At that time, Jesus Christ was the only Counselor for the disciples who had left their home, property and relatives in order to follow him. But when he was about to depart from them to the cross, he promised the disciples, 'You will be given another Counselor, eternal Counselor.'"

He continues, "The Counselor was not meant to live somewhere else and contact them on and off. He lived within them, comforting and counseling. When we see the disciples, their life was different between before and after they received the Counselor. The Counselor in them was their Comforter. The Counselor in them was their hope. A man who has hope will work. A man who has hope has purpose. A man who has hope also has vision. A man who has hope also has destiny. Eternal Counselor!" This concept of the Holy Spirit as eternal Counselor reflects the view of the EOTC about the Holy Spirit. It is officially confessed, "He [Jesus Christ] sent us the Paraclete."

He continues, "The Counselor is the Guide. He was given to guide them (John 16:13) . . . He guides our life. He leads our life by comforting. He leads our life and helps us get to good things. He teaches us truth through comforting so that we may know the truth. Because our fathers accepted him and were guided by him, they did what was impossible, what was unthinkable and what was beyond the men of flesh. They preached the good news which is joy and peace for us today. What was their life became our life today. Why? Because it was this Spirit of truth who guided, supported and counseled them. It was this Counselor Spirit who guided Paul and Lydia to meet together."

He then connects the guidance of the Holy Spirit to the history of Ethiopia. He points out, "It was this Counselor Spirit who guided Philip to meet the Ethiopian eunuch. When this African was on his way back home from Jerusalem, something happened. . . . The Holy Spirit opened his heart so that he may hear the good news. It was this Counselor Spirit who guided all to meet together, brought them agreement, and harmonized their language. And he helped the Ethiopian to be a new convert and messenger to Ethiopia."

The preacher then speaks of the power of the Holy Spirit: "The work of God cannot be done by the power of men. . . . In Acts 2, we read, those weak disciples, who shut the door during the resurrection for fear, began to proclaim after receiving the power. They began to speak in other tongues. They began to speak boldly." This reflects the view of the EOTC that the Holy Spirit is powerful.

He continues:

> By dwelling on our fathers, the Holy Spirit established the church. And the good news has been brought to us. Today we need the Comforter in the world which is full of sorrow. In the world which is full of confusion, we need the Guide who leads us to the truth. The Holy Spirit is the Guide not only for the ministers of God but also for all the people in the world. . . . The Holy Spirit guides us in different ways. Those who are demonized have no option except the power from above. We can give them the things we can make with our hands. But we cannot obtain power from artificial sources. Food is a source of energy for human beings. Of course, man will be strengthened when he gets food and drink. But sometimes notwithstanding the presence of food, drink, and all kinds of luxury, we lose strength. You know why? It is because our power is not from the world, but from above.

The Holy Spirit at Work Today

The preacher applies the work of the Holy Spirit to the ministry of the contemporary church. He states:

> The grace belongs to the Holy Spirit. He will bless all. He will guide all. When the Holy Spirit anoints one, when the Holy Spirit blesses one, when the Holy Spirit selects one, he will submit to the Holy Spirit. His work will be the work of the Holy Spirit. What he says will touch the heart of people. What he speaks will captivate the people's heart. What he speaks will not go back to him in vain. It will be back after making captures. He will be the one who can make agreement between those who are not in comfort. He will be able to gather those who are scattered. He will be able to hold up those who are far down. He will be able to restore the dead. Whose words? The words of the man, who is elected by the Holy Spirit. Whether deacons, priests or Pope, whoever possesses the Holy Spirit, his ministry will be blessed. He will not scatter the flock, but gather new converts.

EOTC Doctrines and Ministries

The preacher continues by pointing out the problems of the contemporary church:

> Our problem today is this: There are a lot of ministries on earth. We thank God for this. The Holy Bible is everywhere. There is no place where there is no spiritual song being heard. There is no place where the Bible is absent. The Bible is there in the bus. The Bible is there on radio. The Bible is there on television. The Bible is there available in magazines. The Bible is there in newspapers. It is everywhere. Our Holy Bible enters even the mosques. Our planet is full of ministries. But the question here is this: Who is the guide? Who is behind the ministry? If the answer is the Holy Spirit, it will be a blessed ministry. The fruits will be the Holy Spirit's. Do you understand me? Who is guiding your ministry? May the Holy Spirit guide and bless our ministry. Glory and praise be to God who has been counseling and teaching us. Amen!

The preacher then discusses how to gain the power of the Holy Spirit. He states, "The Bible says, 'In order to get power, stay in Jerusalem.' . . . What they needed was to wait until they received the Holy Spirit. They did not get out of the city and the Holy Spirit descended upon them." He continues, "The place where we gather now, the holy church, replaces Jerusalem. We are not supposed to go to Jerusalem now. Therefore, the holy church transfers blessings and grace. Fathers who replaced apostles will arise, and the deacons who replace the apostles will arise . . . "

This exemplifies the EOTC's understanding of the church and its offices. Here the preacher identifies Jerusalem with the church. The church replaces Jerusalem as the place where the Holy Spirit comes upon the disciples. In other words, the church symbolically signifies Jerusalem. As previously discussed, this is a significant example of symbolic interpretation of the biblical text in the EOTC.

The preacher also articulates the EOTC's understanding of apostolic succession. The fathers succeeded the apostles, and the deacons and priests succeeded the fathers. The doctrine of ministerial succession is significant in the EOTC.

This sermon also shows deep concern for contemporary ministry of the church. The preacher is concerned that today's ministry is carried out without the power of the Holy Spirit. The preacher maintains that this lack of power is reason for the lack of fruit in the ministry of the church. He exhorts believers to gather at the church in order to receive the power of the Holy Spirit.

This sermon articulates the traditional teaching of the EOTC regarding the Holy Spirit. The Holy Spirit is the Counselor who continues to do the ministry of Jesus Christ. He is the Guide who leads the believers. He is the Spirit of Truth who leads the people into the truth. The Holy Spirit gives power to the ministers of the church. In order to receive the power of the Holy Spirit, believers must come to the church.

Sermon 8—Text: Romans 3:1; Title: "What Advantage, Then, Is There in Being a Jew?"

Abstract

Jews were, physically, the sons of Abraham. However, the genuine sons of Abraham are those who act as Abraham did. Jews claimed that they were sons of Abraham, but their life style was different from that of Abraham. God gave Abraham the promise: "His offspring will be like stars in heaven, but also they will be like the dust of the earth." Abraham's sons in faith are like stars in heaven. They inherit the nature of Abraham. But those who are sons of Abraham only physically are like the dust of the earth. Dust is dry, hard, and cold. Likewise, they are stiff-necked, disobedient, hardened, and cold people. They do not do in their life what Abraham did.

Today many Christians live a hypocritical life. Their behavior inside the church is quite different from their behavior outside the church. They commit idolatry, sexual immorality, division, drunkenness, and other sins. God wants our purity rather than our numbers. We all will die, and then we will stand before the throne of the Trinity. If we want to live a life that is right before the Lord, we must confess our sin and submit ourselves to our heavenly God. Christianity is life. We are called to live such a life.

Major Characteristics

The main purpose of this sermon is to define the genuine descendants of Abraham, who live a godly life, in contrast to the physical descendants of Abraham, who do not. This sermon reveals five major characteristics of biblical interpretation of the EOTC. First, it employs traditional doctrinal formulas. Second, it explores the historical background of the text. Third, it employs allegorical interpretation. Fourth, it identifies circumcision with baptism. Fifth, it demonstrates a concern for genuine Christian life.

Doctrinal Formulas

The preacher begins with greetings to the congregation, which contain the doctrinal formulas on Trinity, the salvation of Jesus Christ, and St. Mary. It also contains doxology and thanksgiving, and expresses the preacher's concern for the spiritual wellbeing of the congregation: "In the name of God the Father, God the Son, and God the Holy Spirit, One God. Amen! Unchangeable God who sits on the white throne and rules over all, the God of saints and our fathers, thank you for the peace you have given us. Thank you for the mercy on our sinful age and giving us the wonderful time to hear you. Let honor, praise, thanksgiving be accepted by you."

He continues, "Dear sons and daughters of God, who love our mother St. Mary. I greet you in the name of our God who loved us through his Son Jesus Christ who died on behalf of us. May God be praised for the time that he has given us to open our mouth with praise and the opportunity to listen to his word!"

Describing the Historical Background

The preacher then seeks to clarify the historical background of the text in order to locate the message in the right context. He states, "The letter was written by Paul to the Christians who lived in Rome." He continues, "The purpose of my message is showing the uniqueness of Christianity and the benefits of being Christians, so that we can worship God with all our spirits and without sin." Then he comes to the title and main focus of his preaching: "Paul asks, 'What advantage, then, is there in being a Jew? What value is there in circumcision?' (Rom 3:1)."

He sets up the background as follows: "As all of you know, those who believe in the good news are in light and God has brought them from darkness. They have passed from death to life. Because of this, the New Testament ministry was that of love and righteousness. This had many Gentiles convert from idol worship to the worship of God. They moved from the law to the gospel. After Jesus' ascension, his followers were commissioned to preach the gospel and to bring people to bearing righteous fruits."

Then, he presents the main issue in his preaching: "One of these followers is Paul. He was working hard to bring believers in Rome to the heavenly glory. Yet others were working in the opposite way . . . they taught, 'If you do not become Jews, you will never have peace . . . If you are not circumcised, your faith is in vain.' They disturbed Christians with this teaching. 'If you are not Jews, and not born of Abraham, you do not have life.'"

He then moves to the present circumstances of his listeners: "How many times have you heard similar teachings like this? Some philosophers say, 'Christianity is the gathering of fearful people, and born of stress.' Others say, 'The Scripture is a fiction, and there is no God.' But we clearly understand that there is God, who created this world, who created the sun. He has given this fresh air for us to breathe. He is our God and our Lord. Christianity is not the product of human meetings. It is the product of blood. It is life . . . " The preacher states that those people, like Jews, would pull people away from genuine faith.

Allegorical Interpretation

The preacher employs an allegorical interpretation of the text in order to distinguish between genuine and flesh descendants of Abraham. In God's promise to Abraham, the preacher traces two different allegorical lines. He states, "God said to Abraham, 'Your offspring will be not only like stars in heaven, but also like the dusts of the earth . . . " He interprets "the stars" as the genuine descendants of Abraham, and "the dusts" as the flesh descendants.

He states, "Abraham's sons in faith are stars in heaven. The heavenly stars are the sons of Abraham who inherited the nature of Abraham. Do you know why the Scripture compares them with stars? It is because stars are bright. Abraham's spiritual sons have bright minds. Daniel 12:3 says, 'Those who are wise will shine like the brightness of the stars in heaven.' . . . The One who came from Abraham, the Son of Abraham Jesus Christ, the Seed of David, the bright Morning Star gives us victory. Those who are from Abraham by nature are with Christ."

He continues, "The second seeds of Abraham are those who have blood relation with him but do not do what he did. They do not worship the God of Abraham in faith. . . . The Bible compares them with the dust of the earth. . . . Do you know why?"

He answers this rhetorical question by allegorically characterizing the nature of those who are not genuine sons of Abraham: "First, dust is dry. Jews are the sons of Abraham by their blood. But they are sinners, stiff-necked, disobeying people. They do not positively respond to the word of God. . . . They criticize others. . . . They want to trap ministers. . . . Those who have dry hearts always want to criticize. They are always negative thinkers, because spiritually they are dry. Jews are dry. Second, dust is hard. Jews have hardened hearts. . . . St. David said, 'How long do you harden your heart . . . ' Third, dust is cold. Jews have a very cold heart. They are cold to the righteous work and ministry. They like songs, liturgies, but they do not have right life style."

Another of the preacher's main concerns is for present believers in hardship. He states:

> Children of God, "Does the fire of the Holy Spirit touch you?" . . . David, the man of God, danced before the Ark of the Covenant. But Michal daughter of Saul watched it and mocked David. There are Christians who respect themselves but do not want to humble themselves before the Lord at the time of worship . . . Our Lord Jesus died on behalf of us. We should humble ourselves before the Lord. The fire of the Holy Spirit should touch us. But Jews are cold . . . The disciples of Jesus Christ were fired. They were consumed by the Spirit of the Lord. They praised the Lord while they were in prison, and they shook the prison. Isaiah said, "I could not keep silent about Zion. If the fire touches us, we cannot keep silent. We do not fear the sword, the den of lions, and persecution." Here, the preacher metaphorically addresses the suffering of believers.

Identification of Circumcision with Baptism

The place of baptism is theologically defined by the preacher in contrast to circumcision. He states, "God gave the sign of Abraham's covenant in Genesis 17:9. That is why every male of Abraham's offspring was circumcised. It was baptism in the Old Testament . . . After Jesus' first advent, circumcision was changed to baptism. In the New Testament, circumcision and uncircumcision do not work (Gal 5:6). Baptism replaced circumcision . . . Everyone who believes in Jesus Christ and is baptized in his name is saved." This shows the importance of baptism in the EOTC.

The baptism of the EOTC shares much commonality with other Christian churches. However, it has unique procedural aspects. The child is to be baptized forty days after birth if a boy, and eighty days after birth if a girl. This seems to follow the Jewish tradition of purification. The EOTC believes that baptism is the replacement of circumcision.

Concern for Genuine Christian Life

The preacher emphasizes bearing the fruit of righteousness in the life of believers. He states, "It is good to be born from Abraham's seed. But if this does not lead us to the New Testament, and if we do not have our King Jesus in our heart, what is the use of our being Jewish. . . . We may stay in church for long years. We may have knowledge. But these cannot make us the children of Abraham. We must bear the fruits of righteousness (Gal 5:22)."

He expresses his concern for the righteous lifestyle of believers by stating, "God wants us to bear good fruits in order for us not to be cut off from the vine. God wants our spiritual growth. But we are on the opposite side, becoming adulterers, sinners, and evildoers. . . . We think that we will not die, but no one knows what will happen in the future. Please, let us humble ourselves before God."

The preacher goes on to apply the lessons from the text to the life of the Orthodox Christians. He states:

> Jesus preached to the Jews, but they did not accept him (John 8). He taught them that truth gave liberation from spiritual bondage. But they thought as if they did not experience bondage. They said that they were children of God. Many of us enjoy singing at the church, and then go out and enjoy worldly things. After worshipping we enjoy dancing in the world. We fast, but we break it whenever we want. We wear clothes as spiritual persons, but when we go out of the church, we lose our spirituality. If we do not do as our father Abraham did, what advantage, then is there in being an Orthodox member? If we are not separated from idolatry, sexual immorality, division, drunkenness, etc., what advantage, then, is there in being an Orthodox member? God wants our purity rather than our number.

The preacher in this sermon seeks to define Christians as genuine descendants of Abraham, and to exhort godly Christian life. In order to achieve this goal, he employs an allegorical interpretation of the text in order to contrast genuine and physical descendants of Abraham.

Sermon 9—Text: Not Specified; Title: Salvation of the World in Christ

Abstract

When God created the world, it was without any defect. But humans destroyed the beautiful world by disobeying God. Adam and Eve were driven out of the Garden of Eden. The punishment of human sin was death. Since then, all human beings are under the bondage of sin. But the gracious God gave humans hope for salvation. Jesus Christ, the Son of God, came to the world. He became flesh and was crucified. He gave his flesh and blood on the cross for the atonement of the people, as prophesized in the Scripture. The salvation of the world was accomplished once for all in Jesus Christ.

Therefore, the only way humans can be saved is by accepting Jesus Christ as the Savior. There is no other way of salvation in the world apart from our Lord Jesus Christ. Jesus Christ is divine and human. His deity and humanity are united into one (*tewahido*). His humanity and divinity are joined in a mystical union. Jesus Christ has one person and one nature. Even now, he rules human beings in his united deity and humanity. *Tewahido* started in Mary's womb. She was chosen by God to be an instrument.

Major Interpretive Characteristics

This preaching does not focus on one specific text, but draws from different texts in the Bible in order to present the main topic which is "the salvation of the world." Therefore, it is primarily doctrinally oriented, especially focusing on the nature and salvific work of Jesus Christ. In this, it clearly demonstrates the Christology of the EOTC.

This sermon reveals six major characteristics of biblical interpretation in the EOTC. First, it includes traditional formulas. Second, it addresses the human situation. Third, it articulates the doctrine of salvation. Fourth, it employs a prophecy and fulfillment schema. Fifth, it discusses the nature and office of Jesus Christ. Sixth, it presents the doctrine of St. Mary.

Doctrinal Formulas

The preacher begins the sermon with a greeting, which follows a doctrinal formula of the EOTC. He states, "In the name of the Father, the Son, the Holy Spirit, One God. Amen! Father priests, brother deacons, fathers and mothers and to all participants in this assembly, how are you? Praise be to one God!"

The Human Situation

As the background of the salvific work of Jesus Christ, the preacher articulates the status of human beings in creation and their destiny after the Fall. He states, "The world was created by God for humans to live in . . . The earth was created for humans to walk, glorify, and dwell in. . . . When God created the world, it was without any defect. He saw that everything was good and was happy about what he created."

Then, he speaks on the sin of human beings: "If God created such a perfect earth, what happened to it? Constructing a building is hard, but destroying it is easy. Humans destroyed the beautiful earth which had been given to them. That is why we say the world is dead now. The man who was allowed to live in the Garden of Eden was driven out of it. Man was eating different kinds of fruits and living peacefully with animals, but now the fruits became sour and animals also became threats to him."

The preacher defines death in spiritual terms. He states, "The punishment given to this sin is death. When we say death, it does not mean the separation of soul from flesh. This death was made holy by Jesus when he died on the cross. The separation of soul from the flesh is not called death in the Ethiopian Orthodox Church. It is rather called rest for true believers. As a consequence of sin, humans lost the right of being sons and daughters of God, the grace of God was taken away from them, and they were dead spiritually." He states that this is the common destiny of all human beings after Adam: "Everything was under bondage of sin. This sin entered the world through one man, Adam. All human beings, starting from Adam to Moses and from Moses to Christ, are under the bondage. That is why humans are given to death."

He then explains the destiny of the people who died before Christ. He asserts, "The Apostles describe this situation of the world in different ways. Peter calls it prison or the lock-up place where dead people live. People who live in this prison are not heathens only, but also those who walked with God, someone like Abraham or Moses. They were caught by their father's [Adam's] sin. Those people who lived before Christ's death lived in this lock-up. They were like sheep going astray, eaten by beasts, stolen by a thief and even left scattered without a shepherd (1 Pet 2:25). When Jesus died on the cross and his soul separated from his body, he went down there and preached to the spirits in the prison (1 Pet 3:19)." This presents the distinctive EOTC doctrine regarding those who died before the coming of Christ.

The Doctrine of Salvation

The main topic of the sermon is the salvation of the world. After articulating the human situation, the preacher asks, "How can a man come back to his previous state? How can he go back to the Garden of Eden?" These questions reveal that the preacher's view of human salvation is going back to the previous state of human beings in the Garden of Eden.

The preacher states that God gives humans the hope for salvation: "What are we hoping for? It is salvation. How can we get our salvation? God himself prepared the way of bringing salvation to humans . . . " This hope for salvation was given to Adam and Eve: "But God did not drive them out empty-handed. God was gracious towards humans and gave them hope, hope that the offspring of the woman will save them, and hope that the offspring of the woman will eventually crush the serpent. He said to the serpent that 'I will put enmity between you and the woman, and between your offspring and hers. He will crush your head and you will strike his heel' (Gen 3:15)."

He continues, "The Son who was born from the woman St. Mary is our Lord and Savior Jesus Christ. He crushed the head of the Serpent (Satan) on the cross. There is still enmity between the woman's offspring and the serpent until now. One wants to destroy the other."

The preacher underscores that Jesus Christ is the only way of salvation. This theme is repeatedly highlighted in his preaching. He states, "Salvation of the world is accomplished once for all in Christ. And talking about the salvation over and over again is never tiring. This world does not have any other owner apart from our Lord Jesus Christ who raised the fallen world by paying himself as ransom to save us. . . . But people are forgetting God who saved them, and giving glory to different church leaders who did nothing to save them. This shows us how the world is going back to the lost world."

Prophecy and Fulfillment in Christ Schema

The preacher states that the coming of Jesus Christ was prophesied in the Old Testament: "He prepared prophets who would tell the story . . . It is prophesied that the Word of God will come to the world, and the Word itself will become flesh. The Word of God will be crucified and his flesh and blood will atone for people from death. The hope was given to Abraham. God said to Abraham, 'through your offspring all nations on earth will be blessed' (Gen 22:18). Jacob blessed Judah, saying, 'The scepter will not depart from Judah, nor the ruler's staff from between his feet' (Gen 49:10).

He continues, "When Moses was about to die, he said, 'God will raise a prophet like me among you, so listen to what he tells you' (Deut 18:15) . . . It pointed to Jesus Christ. One thousand years before Christ was born, David said, 'I saw a child rolled with cloth in Ephrathah' to implicate Jesus' birth and that he is human. . . . Isaiah also prophesized 700 years before Christ's birth, saying, 'the people walking in the darkness have seen a great light' (Isa 9:2). 'For to us a child is born, to us a son is given' (Isa 9:6)." Thus, the preacher's interpretation is Christo-centric. He asserts that the prophecies in the Old Testament were fulfilled in Jesus Christ.

Office and Nature of Jesus Christ

The preacher states, "Jesus was called Prophet, King and High Priest. He was called a Prophet because he was going around and teaching. . . . He was called King, and his throne is on the cross. He was called High Priest, and he presented himself as sacrificial lamb. He interceded for our sin and asked God for forgiveness of sin while he was on the cross." This reflects the understanding of the office of Jesus Christ in the EOTC, which is shared by the catholic Christian tradition.

> His preaching also clearly articulates the doctrine of *tewahido*. He asserts: God revealed himself in human form to save humans. But humans did not receive him. They tried to give him different names. Sometimes they see him as if he is less than

> human. Sometimes they say that he is human only, and deny his deity. Sometimes they see him as deity only and deny his humanity . . . Jesus became human. And he is the Son of God. In John's Gospel, 'In the beginning was the Word, and the Word was with God, and the Word was God' (John 1:1). 'The Word became flesh and made his dwelling among us' (John 1:14). This Word was united with Virgin Mary (mystical union). He became flesh (human). There is nothing we can add or subtract from this. It does not say, 'He looks like a human.' But 'He is human.' His deity and His humanity are united.

Here the preacher emphasizes the united (*tewahido*) nature of Christ.

He continues, "Mark says, 'The beginning of the Gospel about Jesus Christ, the Son of God.' In his humanity he is just human like us. There is no difference between him and us. In his deity he is like God the Father and the Holy Spirit. He is God and man." He then states, "Paul counts the genealogy of Jesus Christ starting from Abraham to show that Jesus came from this line. From human, but he was the Christ." He continues, "In 1Timothy 3:16, it is the deity the Word who was from the beginning who appeared in body (in flesh) when the angel told Mary that she is going to give birth to a baby. He said, 'He will be great and will be called the Son of the Most High.' It is in this way that salvation came to us."

The preacher also asserts, "If he was only divine, he could not be crucified. And if he was not crucified, he will not save the world. If he was only human, he could not save the world. But Jesus the Son of God became flesh. He became flesh in order to save humans. God himself said, 'This is my beloved Son. Hear him.' It shows his deity. What did Jesus say about himself? 'No one knows the Son except the Father. No one knows the Father except the Son reveals him to someone.' At the last time, the Son of Man will come to judge this world."

Then, the preacher articulates the doctrine of *tewahido*: "Jesus was born by taking flesh and soul from his mother Mary. She gave breastfeeding to him. He was hungry and angry. He was sleeping. He felt sorry for people. He was tired. He was human. That was why he was called Jesus Christ. Jesus is human and Christ, the Messiah. He is man and he is God. *Tewahido* means both man and divine together. . . . One will not destroy the other. *Tewahido* will take place on equal grounds. The humanity and deity are equal. His humanity will hold his deity, and his deity will hold his humanity. They are united in mystical union. We say one person and one nature. *Tewahido* started in St. Mary's womb. Humanity and deity were united. Even now he rules us in his united deity and humanity. While he was in the world, he was in his united deity and humanity." This demonstrates the EOTC's official doctrine of the nature of Christ. As discussed previously, the EOTC rejects the Chalcedonian doctrine of the two natures of Christ, but claims the one nature of Christ.

Doctrine of St. Mary

The preacher speaks on the place of St. Mary in salvation. He states, "When it comes to Mary, what did she conceive? It is the deity. Deity came in the form of human. She gave birth to deity which became flesh, and flesh which became deity. We are saved by the One who was born by St. Mary. He is the Savior, and there is no other Savior."

He asks the rhetorical question, "Why did God become human?" He answers, "He wanted to save humans he created. He became flesh and saved us. Mary became the cause for this salvation. Our church honors her. St. Mary the Virgin was chosen by God to be his instrument. Jesus used the flesh, which he got from Mary, on the cross to save us. In order to save us, she raised and fed him, and went to exile to save him from death. This is the work of salvation." He continues, "When he was crucified, she was with him, but others deserted him. He loved his mother while he was on the cross. He entrusted his mother to the disciple he loved (John) . . . "

He then advocates for the place of St. Mary in the church: "Because of her motherhood the Second International Synod met and gave her honor and called her Holy Mother of God. The Ethiopian Orthodox *Tewahido* Church also accepts the decision. She participated in the salvation. She participated in the message of the gospel. She is a ladder on which we go up and down." This reflects the EOTC's view that St. Mary is a mediator. Thus, her intercession is continually asked in prayer.

THE CHARACTERISTICS OF THE BIBLICAL INTERPRETATION IN THE PREACHING OF THE EOTC

Through the preceding analysis of nine sermons of the EOTC, several prominent characteristics of the EOTC's biblical interpretation, along with underlying factors that markedly influence the reading of the biblical text, are revealed. These include the substantial influence of EOTC tradition, the significance of the EOTC's context, and the various interpretive strategies employed by the EOTC.

Substantial Influence of the Tradition of the EOTC

The analysis of the sermons demonstrates the significance of the EOTC's tradition in its biblical interpretation. The preachers closely follow the tradition of the EOTC in their exegetical work and, therefore, tradition is the most decisive element in their interpretation of the biblical texts. The tradition of the EOTC permeates the sermons as a motivating, driving, and guiding force. In many cases, affirming the tradition of the church becomes the goal of biblical interpretation and preaching.

The influence of tradition is evident in the sermons in that tradition guides the theological assumptions regarding the Bible. There are two primary and connected streams of tradition in the EOTC: doctrine and practice. Both of these streams are evident throughout the sermons. Finally, the influence of the *andemta* commentary tradition is also evident in the analyzed sermons.

Theological Assumptions on the Bible

As discussed in previous chapters, the theological assumptions of the EOTC are one of the most significant elements that influence its interpretation of the biblical text. These theological assumptions have a significant effect on the preachers' interpretive attitudes toward the biblical text. The preachers of the EOTC firmly believe that the Bible is the word of God. They believe that each and every book is written by the human author who was inspired by the Holy Spirit. On this basis, the preachers consistently find the authenticity of their preaching in the authority of the Bible as the sacred word of God.

The presupposition that the Bible is the word of God leads the preachers to assume that everything in the Bible is historical. In the sermons analyzed above, the preachers do not question the historicity of the figures, events, or stories in the Bible. They believe that what is written in the text of the Bible is what genuinely happened in history. This comes from the conviction that the Bible is the word of God and, therefore, everything in it is historically authentic and reliable.

Doctrinal Tradition

Another of the most influential elements in the biblical interpretation of the EOTC, evident in the analyzed sermons, is the doctrinal tradition of the church. It substantially influences the preachers' interpretation of the biblical texts. This influence is found in all the stages of the preachers' interpretive work. EOTC doctrine provides the motivation for their interpretation, directs their choice of interpretive approaches, and guides their way of connecting biblical texts to contemporary circumstances. In many cases, the preachers simply employ the exegetical results found in the tradition of the EOTC. It is, therefore, accurate to state that the outcomes of traditional EOTC biblical exegesis have become part of the EOTC's theology.

As exemplified in the analyzed sermons, the most important doctrinal confessions of the EOTC are articulated in the greeting that opens the sermon. In many cases, the doctrinal formula functions as the introduction of the preaching. It also serves to outline the main topics in the body of the sermon. The greeting articulates EOTC doctrine regarding the Trinity, the Persons of the Trinity, St. Mary, the church, and the Ark of the Covenant.

Trinity

The EOTC doctrine of the Trinity is the most prominent doctrine revealed in the preaching of the EOTC. The preachers consistently begin their preaching by stating the doctrinal formula on Trinity: "In the name of God the Father, God the Son, and God the Holy Spirit, One God. Amen!" This articulates the EOTC understanding that God is one in three and three in one. This foundational doctrinal confession is presumed in all aspects of biblical interpretation in the EOTC. After this initial greeting, the preacher briefly mentions the nature and work of each Person of the Trinity. This is evident in the analyzed sermons.

The Father

God the Father is "Father of the Lord and our Savior Jesus Christ." God is Creator and Sustainer. The preachers clearly state, "God is the Creator of the universe." In one of the analyzed sermons, entitled "What Advantage, Then, Is There in Being A Jew?," the preacher states, "Unchangeable God, who sits on the white throne and rules over all, the God of all saints and fathers, thank you for the peace that you have given us" (Rom 3:1). In another sermon, the preacher states, "You are eternal and unchangeable God, merciful and lovely ruler who sits on the great white throne."

Jesus Christ

In the analyzed sermon entitled, "What Advantage, Then, Is There in Being A Jew?," the preacher states, "I greet you in the name of our God who loved us through his Son Jesus Christ who died on behalf of us." The EOTC sermons contain important doctrinal statements regarding Jesus Christ. Jesus Christ is the Son of God. He is the Word who was with God in the beginning and is God. He incarnated. Jesus Christ is divine and human. His deity and humanity are united into one (*tewahido*). This is a mystical union. Jesus Christ has one person and one nature.

The incarnation of Jesus Christ is for the salvation of the world. Jesus Christ is the Savior. He was crucified. He gave his flesh and blood on the cross for the atonement of the people in the world, as prophesized in the Old Testament. The salvation of the world was accomplished once for all in Jesus Christ. Therefore, the only way for humans to be saved is to accept Jesus Christ as the Savior. Jesus Christ rules creation in his united deity and humanity.

The Holy Spirit

In the analyzed sermon entitled, "Eternal Counselor," the preacher states, "The Holy Spirit has been blessing us till this day. He has blessed us to pass the times in peace. . . . Let it be his will to bless today and teach us."

The sermons of the EOTC articulate the doctrinal understanding of the Holy Spirit. The Holy Spirit is the divine reality dwelling in creatures. He relates them to God. He perfects their salvation. He is always present with us.

The Holy Spirit is Counselor, who comforts and guides us. He continues to do what Jesus Christ did. He is the Spirit of truth, who guides us into the truth, and helps us reach wholeness. He empowers our ministry to bear fruit.

St. Mary

In the sermon entitled, "*Gedaliah*," the preacher begins with this statement of St. Mary: " . . . our mother Virgin Mary . . . you are children of St. Mary . . . her name be blessed forever."

The EOTC doctrine of St. Mary is significant discussion in much of the preaching of the EOTC. This seems to arise due to the challenges from other Christian traditions in Ethiopia that have different doctrinal understandings regarding St. Mary. Thus, EOTC preachers articulate the place and nature of St. Mary for the church and for the faith and life of believers.

St. Mary is confessed as the mother of Jesus Christ. In this sense, she is believed to have a place in salvation. As she is the mother of Jesus Christ, she is also mother of believers in Jesus Christ. Thus, she plays an important role for believers. She is a mediator between God and them. Because of her significance, EOTC preachers emphasize her love, and her purity.

In order to advocate for St. Mary, preachers employ diverse interpretive approaches, particularly symbolic interpretation. EOTC preachers frequently use symbolism in connection with St. Mary. For example, the Ark of the Covenant, which symbolizes God's presence, is also used to signify St. Mary. As the Ark contains the tablets, St. Mary conceived Jesus Christ in her womb. The story of Gideon and his soldiers is another example. They fought against the Midianites with jars and torches in their hands. Here, the jar symbolizes St. Mary and the torch symbolizes Jesus Christ.

The Church

The EOTC understanding of their church is another significant doctrine articulated in the analyzed sermons. EOTC preachers are very interested in promoting the special place of the EOTC. For example, they assert that the church replaces Jerusalem and, therefore, the presence of God is in the church. Thus, the church is the location where believers encounter God's presence. This ecclesiology justifies their respect for the physical church building and its compound.

Another example is the story of the Ethiopian eunuch and its implications. In their view, Ethiopia was the first country to receive baptism in Jesus Christ. Ethiopia became the first Bible reading country. Ethiopia took the first initiative to seek God. Later, the Ethiopian Orthodox Church became the *Tewahido* and, therefore, the true church. They believe that in these ways, the EOTC laid the foundation of Christianity.

The Ark of the Covenant

Tabot also holds a central place in the theology and religious practices of the EOTC. *Tabot* is a replica of the Ark of the Covenant. The EOTC asserts that the original Ark resides in Aksum, and every EOTC church has its sacramental replicas (*tabot*). Theologically, the EOTC affirms that *tabot* is the succession of the Ark. It signifies Zion, which stands for God's presence. It is asserted, therefore, that God's presence is with the EOTC.

Furthermore, *tabot* signifies the sacramental place of the salvation of Jesus Christ. Jesus Christ died on the cross and crushed the devil. He resurrected on the third day. He gave us his flesh to eat and his blood to drink. Those who eat of his flesh and drink of his blood have eternal life. His flesh we eat and his blood we drink require a throne of residence, which is symbolized by the Ark of the Covenant. Thus, the Ark represents the seat of glorification of Jesus Christ, as articulated in the New Testament.

Tradition of Religious Practices

The religious practices of the EOTC, both in daily Christian life and in specific feasts and rituals, are important topics in the preaching of the EOTC. They have a significant impact on the biblical interpretation of the preachers. This is evident in the endeavor of the preachers to deliver the theological meanings of the practices and justify those practices in their sermons.

Emphasis on Daily Christian Life

The EOTC has a strong moral tradition. It highly emphasizes the daily Christian life of believers. The preaching of the EOTC demonstrates such an emphasis, which is in accordance with the tradition of the EOTC. Prayer, fasting, and giving alms are highly recommended as elements of daily Christian life. In one of the sermons, entitled "On Fasting," the preacher states, "With fasting, giving, and righteous work, prayer is good."

Many preachers focus on these as important topics in their sermons, and occasionally devote entire sermons to advocating for or recommending these practices.

In a sermon entitled, "The Necessity of Fasting and Prayer," the preacher states, "Our faces will be shining if we pray and fast . . . Prayer and fasting are our Lord's commandment. When we fast and pray, our hearts are filled with joy." In one of the analyzed sermons, entitled "*Gedaliah*," the preacher states, "The world oppresses the poor and, by so doing, disregards the God who is generous and merciful to the poor." He continues, "If you want to know God, please go visit the poor people who are living on their mats on the street. . . . There you will find him hungry, thirsty, and naked. You must be considerate to the poor."

Furthermore, their preaching shows strong ethical and moral concerns within and outside of the church. Spiritual discipline and a godly life style are commanded, whereas immoralities are criticized and prohibited. Biblical figures are discussed as both positive and negative moral examples. Preachers aim primarily at finding moral lessons from the biblical texts. For example, in the sermon entitled "*Nehushtan*," the preacher uses Hezekiah as a model of faith and life for believers. He states, "We have seen from the king Hezekiah three important things to learn." In contrast, in another sermon entitled "Convenient Time," the preacher uses several biblical figures, such as Judas, Cain, and Amnon, as negative models.

Religious Feasts and Rituals

Throughout many of their sermons, the preachers interpret the biblical texts for the purpose of justifying the traditional religious customs and practices of the EOTC. The first example is *tabot*. As well as its significance in theology, it holds a central place in the practices of the EOTC. *Tabot* stands at the center of EOTC liturgy and plays a significant role in the rituals and ceremonies of EOTC holidays. As discussed previously, *tabot* is located in the church, and it is always kept in the sanctuary. The liturgy of the EOTC is celebrated always with the presence of *tabot* in the church. The sanctity of a church is determined by the presence of *tabot*. Without *tabot*, liturgy cannot be held. The *tabot* is carried around the church courtyard on the patronal feast day.

Additional religious practices are also advocated by EOTC preachers. Some of these practices are founded in EOTC beliefs regarding angles and saints. Angels are the servants of God. They are also mediators between God and people. The angles who appear in the Bible are the ones who continue to work in the daily life of believers. Saints also have a role for believers as models and intercessors between God and believers. This belief justifies both the veneration of angels and saints and the practice of praying to them.

EOTC preachers are also keenly aware of the existence and presence among people of Satan and evil spirits. They believe that the biblical evil spirits work among contemporary people and, therefore, evil spirits are at work behind every evil deed and thing. In the sermon entitled "*Nehushtan*," the preacher states, "You may fight what you see, but God fights enemies that you do not see . . . Satan reveals our secrets. He never covers our sin, but God covers our sin with his mercy." In another sermon, entitled "*Gedaliah*," the preacher states, "Put the small cross on your neck, and the devil will run away."

Another example is sprinkling *tsebal*. In one of the analyzed sermons, the preacher states, "The first hospital for the patient is sprinkling *tsebal* in the church." *Tsebal* is holy water blessed by the priest. It symbolizes purification. The priest sprinkles the water on the people "for the purpose of seeking from God a blessing on those who use it and protection from the powers of darkness."[4] It is also used in order to purify items in the church. Along with baptismal water, *tsebal* is used in many rituals and ceremonies of the EOTC.[5]

In many cases, rituals are combined in the celebration of festivals. The EOTC celebrates *Timkat* (the Feast of the Epiphany) with sprinkling *tsebal* and processions of *tabot*. In this festival, a priest leads the procession as *tabot* is carried to a body of water. The people are sprinkled with *tsebal*. Then, the *tabot* is carried back to the church. Additional rituals have symbolic religious meanings in the EOTC. These include making the sign of the cross, using the cross and crucifix, using ointment, and lighting candles. The preachers of the EOTC use biblical texts to explain these practices, as well.

The significance of doctrinal and religious tradition in the EOTC leads its preaching to be strongly apologetic in its biblical interpretation.

4. Aymro and Joachim, *Ethiopian Orthodox Church*, 72.

5. Ibid.

Typically, the preaching of the EOTC endeavors to theologically and biblically justify and promote its doctrines and practices. Thus, the preaching conveys interpretations of the biblical texts that are already established and passed down as the theological tradition of the church.

The Influence of the Andemta Commentary Tradition

As discussed in the previous chapter, the *andemta* commentary represents the interpretive tradition of the EOTC. The influence of the *andemta* commentary is found in the analyzed sermons of the EOTC. First, many of the sermons directly adopt and deliver the interpretation of the biblical texts found in the *andemta* commentary without any alteration or evaluation.

Preachers occasionally mention the name, *andemta* commentary, explicitly in their preaching. They frequently deliver the explanations of the background stories of the biblical texts from the *andemta* commentary. They often begin their sermons with these stories. Sometimes, these stories comprise crucial parts of the entire sermon.

The influence of the *andemta* commentary is especially evident in the symbolic interpretation of certain biblical figures or objects that are significant to the EOTC. There are several interpretive examples that show the impact of the *andemta* commentary on the sermons. These include the interpretation of *tabot*, the ark of Noah, the story of Isaac and the lamb, and the story of Gideon.

Second, and more significantly, the preachers regard the *andemta* commentary as the interpretive tradition of the EOTC. As such, they assume that the commentary's interpretation is the authentic and authoritative interpretation of the biblical texts. Therefore, there are no significant discrepancies in biblical interpretation between the *andemta* commentary and the sermons of the preachers.

Significance of Context

The preaching of the EOTC demonstrates the contextual nature of the EOTC's biblical interpretation. In other words, the biblical texts are interpreted in the historical and cultural location of the church in Ethiopia. The preaching comes out of Ethiopian culture and shows deep concern for Ethiopian people and issues. It addresses certain significant challenges the EOTC faces in its contemporary context. It demonstrates an appreciation for the history of Ethiopia and advocates for indigenous

Ethiopian Christianity. It seeks to connect the biblical narrative with present Ethiopian circumstances. This contextualization is evident in the analyzed sermons.

Challenges in Ethiopia

The contextual nature of EOTC preaching is expressed in the response to various challenges with which the EOTC is confronted. For example, biblical texts are used in order to fight against religious challenges, such as Islam, Protestant Christianity, and some indigenous idol worship.

The preachers also endeavor to provide answers to a number of significant Ethiopian challenges, such as famine, work ethics, ethnic division, and governmental bribes. In this process, the stories in the biblical texts are occasionally applied directly to the present Ethiopian situation, and occasionally interpreted in such a way as to be relevant to the present Ethiopian situation. In one of the analyzed sermons entitled "Do Not Be Afraid. You Will Not Die," the preacher identifies the contemporary situation of Ethiopia with that of Israel. He states, "When we face many troubles, we are weak and helpless, so our spirits are down . . . However . . . God gives us his power to win our victory. Remember the word of God in times of trouble, 'Don't be afraid; you will not die.'"

Place of Ethiopian History

In EOTC preaching, significant doctrines of the EOTC are contextualized in connection with the history of Ethiopia. The historical event of the role of the Ark of St. George in the battle of *Adwas* against Italy is one example. In one of the analyzed sermons, entitled "*Gedaliah*," the preacher states, "Our forefathers fought against their enemies to bring great respect to this country Ethiopia. They were martyred for the sake of God and proclaimed God's greatness. The Bible says Ethiopia seeks the face of the Lord for her development and prosperity (Ps 68:31). Our forefathers kept Ethiopian boundaries and protected them from foreign colony by carrying the Ark."

Seeking for Ethiopian Connection

EOTC preachers frequently connect Ethiopia with the biblical narratives. For example, the story of King Solomon and Queen Sheba, and their son Menelik is recognized as historically authentic. The Magi in the Gospel of Matthew are identified as Ethiopians. As exemplified in one of the analyzed sermons, entitled "Who Can Speak Of His Descendants?," the narrative of the Ethiopian eunuch is developed into the story of describing the introduction the gospel into Ethiopia. All of these stories seek to rest the present identity of the EOTC in the biblical narrative.

Interpretive Strategies

The preachers of the EOTC employ several interpretive strategies in their sermons in order to achieve their interpretive goals. They locate the meaning of biblical texts in the contemporary context. They employ narrative. They use significant words and phrases as interpretive keys. They utilize various interpretive approaches. These strategies are evident in the analyzed sermons.

Located in Present Application

Typically, EOTC preachers do not give serious attention to the original historical setting of the biblical texts, but rather preach out of concern for the issues in their present context. This approach is guided by their belief in the immediacy of the Bible. However, this does not mean that they disregard the context of the biblical texts, which they occasionally address for various purposes. Nonetheless, they do not view the meaning of the text as residing only in its original context.

When preachers explore the historical and cultural background of the biblical text, they frequently do so as a means of applying the text to the people in their present life situation. This is found in many of the analyzed sermons. Thus, the historical and cultural context of the biblical text is not disregarded, but used according to the purposes of the preacher.

Narrative Orientation

The analysis of the sermons exhibits the importance of narrative in the preaching of the EOTC. Most of the sermons include narratives, mostly biblical and also legendary, which are believed to be historically authentic in the EOTC. In this sense, these stories have become part of the tradition of the church.

Narrative is an important part of the Ethiopian culture. In Ethiopia, messages and lessons are delivered by telling stories. Thus, preachers tend to articulate biblical narratives and connect them to historical and contemporary stories in the Ethiopian context. Stories are told consecutively, and together contribute to conveying the primary message. Not only biblical stories, but also historical and legendary stories, anecdotes, and folk stories, are employed for this purpose. Most of these stories are handed down as the tradition of the EOTC.

In addition, some background story-lines are added to fill "gaps" in the biblical narratives. Two examples of this are in the story of the Samaritan woman and in the story of the woman pouring perfume on Jesus. These stories have also become part of the tradition of the church and are, therefore, accepted as authentic. Thus, understanding and employing narrative is one of the most significant aspects in the EOTC's interpretation of the biblical texts.

This narrative orientation of the EOTC's preaching is demonstrated in the sermon entitled "Convenient Time." The message of this sermon is the command to use convenient time to come to God and, not to sin. In order to deliver this message, the preacher uses stories of different kinds from within and outside of the Bible. All of these stories are consecutively connected and become part of the main narrative.

Interpretive Keys

EOTC preachers frequently employ the interpretive technique in which a word, a phrase, or an idea becomes an interpretive key for biblical texts. The sermon entitled "*Nehushtan*" provides one example. In its contextual context (2 Kgs 18:1–4), the word *Nehushtan* refers to the bronze snake itself. However, the preacher defines it as the breaking down of unclean things, including the bronze snake. This definition functions in the sermon as the interpretive key for every biblical text discussed in the sermon. However, the preacher did not create this interpretation. It is an established interpretive tradition in the EOTC.

The sermon entitled "Convenient Time" provides another example. Here, the idea of "convenient time" is the interpretive key. All of the stories, biblical and extra-biblical in the sermon are interpreted in the light of "convenient time." They are used as positive and negative examples in order to deliver the preacher's message to use the time for glorifying God rather than for committing sin.

Various Interpretive Approaches

As exemplified in the analyzed sermons, the preachers of the EOTC employ different interpretive approaches in accordance with their exegetical goals. Typically, the biblical texts are interpreted as they are written in the Bible. This derives from the conviction that each and every biblical text is the word of God. Even when other interpretive methods are adopted for certain purposes, the literal sense of the text comprises the basis for these methods. However, this does not mean that other interpretive approaches are denied for the sake of literal interpretation.

For example, various kinds of allegorical approaches to the biblical texts are employed in EOTC sermons. The preachers use allegorical interpretation in order to draw spiritual meanings from the text. For example, in the sermon entitled, "The Ark of Noah," which is not analyzed in this research, every figure and event in the narrative is allegorically interpreted. In the sermon entitled, "Do Not Be Afraid. You Will Not Die," the behaviors of Gideon and his soldiers are interpreted allegorically.

In addition, the allegorical approach is used in order to offer practical moral lessons to believers. In the sermon on Gideon and his soldiers, in order to find moral lessons the preacher allegorically interprets various objects and events in the biblical text, such as the hole, getting out of the hole, the ways of drinking water, entering the middle, and empty jars. In this sense, the EOTC does not use allegory in order to establish a philosophical system, in contrast to Alexandrian allegorical interpretation.

The preachers of the EOTC also frequently adopt typological interpretations of the biblical text. For example, preachers use the prophecy and fulfillment schema in Old and New Testament texts. Stories and persons in the Old Testament prefigure those in the New Testament. This approach is especially focused on the person and work of Jesus Christ, and also on St. Mary. For example, in the sermon entitled "Who Can Speak of His Descendants?" the preacher states that in Isaiah 53, the prophet Isaiah prophesized about Jesus, including his nature, emptiness, suffering, and death. In the same sermon, the preacher asserts that the virgin in Isaiah 7:14 prefigures Mary in Matthew 1:21.

In addition, EOTC preachers frequently employ symbolic interpretation of the Bible. This symbolic interpretation is especially prevalent in the interpretation of certain biblical texts. In particular, specific objects, figures, and events in the Bible are employed to represent spiritual truths that have significant implications for the EOTC. These include Adam and Eve, Paradise, the trees in the Garden of Eden, Abel and Seth, the Ark of Noah, the Ark of the Covenant, Zion, Jesus Christ, the Cross, and St. Mary. For example, in the sermon entitled, "The Ark of Noah," Noah symbolizes Jesus Christ, and the ark symbolizes St. Mary. In the sermon entitled, "Do Not Be Afraid. You Will Not Die," the jar and the torch carried by Gideon and his soldiers signify, respectively, St. Mary and Jesus Christ.

Another example is found in the ecclesiology of the EOTC. In the sermon entitled, "*Nehushtan*," Jerusalem in the Old Testament signifies the church, and it is identified with the EOTC. Zion in the Old Testament symbolizes the eschatological reign of God among his people, and the EOTC identifies it with *tabot*.

As shown in the discussion above, adopting any one specific interpretive approach is not the main concern of the preacher. Rather, the main concern is how to effectively deliver the primary message through using different interpretive approaches. The focus is not on interpretive creativity or novelty, but how the established interpretive tradition of the EOTC is employed to convey the preacher's message. The preachers adopt the outcomes of interpretation passed down as the tradition of the church. This again demonstrates the significance of the EOTC's tradition in the biblical interpretation of the church.

SUMMARY

In this chapter, I proposed that the biblical interpretation of the EOTC is most practically revealed in the preaching of the EOTC. It addresses particular theological and practical issues in the context of the EOTC and demonstrates the significant influence of EOTC tradition in the church. In order to substantiate my proposal, I analyzed nine sermons that exemplify preaching in the EOTC. Through this investigation, several distinctive characteristics of and significant influences on the biblical interpretation of the EOTC have been identified.

First, the sermons demonstrate the significance of EOTC tradition in the interpretation of biblical texts. The preachers of the EOTC firmly believe that the Bible is the word of God, and this theological assumption is the basis for their interpretive attitude toward the biblical texts. In addition, the doctrinal tradition of the church substantially informs all stages of the preachers' interpretive work. The religious traditions of the EOTC are also significant in its preaching, which is evident in the endeavor of the preachers to theologically define and justify them. The sermons also show the significant influence of the *andemta* commentary.

The tradition of the EOTC holds a central place in the biblical interpretation of the EOTC. It functions as the interpretive key in the EOTC's reading of the Bible. It sets the goal of the biblical interpretation, guides interpretive principles, and determines the use of exegetical approaches.

Thus, specific exegetical approaches for certain texts are already fixed and established by the traditional interpretation of the EOTC. In other words, what matters is not the exegetical method *per se*, but the theology that motivates the interpreter to adopt that method. In many cases, the meaning of the text has been determined and passed down as tradition, and thereby become part of the theology of the EOTC. In their sermons, the preachers faithfully convey this traditional interpretation.

Second, the sermons of the preachers demonstrate the contextual nature of the EOTC's biblical interpretation. The preaching comes out of Ethiopian culture and shows deep concern for Ethiopian people and issues. It addresses certain significant challenges the EOTC faces in its contemporary context. It demonstrates an appreciation for the history of Ethiopia and advocates for indigenous Ethiopian Christianity. It seeks to connect the biblical narrative with present Ethiopian circumstances.

The historical and cultural context of Ethiopia is the very stage on which the tradition of the EOTC has been shaped and developed. In that context, the EOTC has established its own tradition of biblical interpretation. Therefore, the tradition of the EOTC itself has contextual nature.

The contemporary situation of believers in Ethiopia is the very context in which the preachers choose biblical texts. In this context the preachers interpret and produce their sermons. They address the faith and life issues of believers and those of the Ethiopian people as a whole. They seek to give answers to those questions, and exhort their audiences to practice their messages. Therefore, the historical and cultural context of Ethiopia is the very place in which the preachers interpret biblical texts and also carry out their preaching.

Third, the preachers of the EOTC employ several interpretive strategies in their sermons in order to achieve their interpretive goals. They locate the meaning of biblical texts in the contemporary context. They employ narrative. They use significant words and phrases as interpretive keys. They utilize various interpretive approaches.

This chapter is significant for the overall argument of this monograph. The preaching of the EOTC demonstrates effectively the biblical interpretation of the EOTC. It reveals, in the most practical sense, the distinctive characteristics of the EOTC's biblical interpretation. It reveals that the biblical interpretation of the EOTC has been shaped and developed by the EOTC's tradition in the historical and cultural context of Ethiopia.

The biblical interpretation of the EOTC notably demonstrates the contextual nature of biblical interpretation. It reveals the significant influence of tradition and context in biblical interpretation. Thus, the EOTC provides a compelling historical example of contextual reading of the Bible, which has been shaped and developed under the substantial influence of the EOTC's tradition in the historical and cultural context of Ethiopia.

Conclusion

In this conclusion, I will present a summary, implications for theological interpretation, and contributions of the research. Then, I will offer suggestions for further study. I will close this monograph by making some concluding remarks.

SUMMARY OF FINDINGS

I have argued in this monograph that tradition and context decisively shaped the way the Ethiopian Orthodox *Tewahido* Church has interpreted the Bible across the centuries. The biblical interpretation of the EOTC has been shaped and developed under the substantial influence of the EOTC's tradition in the historical and cultural context of Ethiopia. Thus, it is a compelling example of contextual reading of the Bible. Here, I present the findings that demonstrate the thesis of this monograph.

First, all theology is contextual theology. Theology is always embedded in culture and, therefore, context-laden. Authentic theology is formed and developed by the people of a faith community in a particular historical and cultural location. There is no universal or perennial theology that can be applied to any particular context.

There are dangers in approaching contextual theology by using models of contextualization. Such models, frequently amounting to ideal types, often do not fit a people's real-life situation. In addition, using models of contextualization frequently imposes the theology of cultural outsiders, who have foreign theological concepts and categories, on cultural insiders. It prevents the people in a culture from being the agents, doing theology in their context. The discussion of contextual theology must be descriptive rather than normative: it must seek to discover and describe what happens when the people encounter the gospel in their context.

In addition, tradition plays a critical role in theology. As a set of guiding and regulating principles, it significantly influences the way in which theology is done. There are multiple church traditions in the world, which share commonalities as part of the Christian church and, at the same time, have particular contours. Thus, in the discussion of theology, it is vital to explore the theology of each tradition. Constructing contextual theology is not merely a matter of creating a new theology, but of exploring the existing theologies already contextualized in particular locations.

Second, biblical interpretation is also contextual. People read the biblical texts in a particular historical and cultural context. The first basis for contextual biblical interpretation is the "situatedness" of human understanding. The social location of the reader critically influences the interpretation of the biblical texts. Narrativity is another basis for the contextual reading of the Bible. Human beings are characterized by narrativity and the Bible has a narrative structure. The interpreter's encounter with the biblical narratives in the context of their narratives of life makes possible particular understandings of the text. It brings about new narratives of formation and transformation in life.

Tradition functions as the primary interpretive principle for the interpretation of the Bible. It engages every stage of interpretive work. People read the Bible within their tradition. Theological tradition, particularly the Rule of Faith, is regarded not as an obstacle to understanding the biblical texts, but as the basis on which the texts can be explored. Biblical interpretation practiced by local churches in their particular locations contributes to a more wholesome understanding of the Bible for the global church.

Third, the EOTC is a hermeneutical community which has its own way of interpreting the biblical texts. The EOTC has developed a living tradition during its survival over nearly two millennia, because of its ability to continually negotiate its way forward by accepting or rejecting internal and external influences in its historical and cultural context. These internal and external influences include Ethiopian primal, Hebraic-Jewish, Apostolic, Syriac, and Egyptian Coptic traditions. These traditions have been through the process of contextualization in Ethiopia, and have shaped the unique tradition of the EOTC. Ethiopian nationalism has functioned as the guiding principle underlying Ethiopian contextualization.

The EOTC continues to exemplify how a church with a long history and tradition addresses new challenges and maintains its distinctive tradition in the dynamic interaction of its local and global contexts. Thus, the EOTC offers a wonderful example of contextualization in which a church effectively forms and develops its unique tradition from various traditional stands. Notably, the living tradition of the EOTC, along with the context of the church, plays a critical role in the biblical interpretation of the EOTC.

Fourth, the EOTC has developed its own way of reading the biblical texts under the substantial influence of its tradition in the historical and cultural context of Ethiopia. Primarily, the biblical interpretation of the EOTC is contained in the *andemta* commentary. The *andemta* commentary is a traditional and theological commentary. It is also a systematic and practical commentary. It was formed and developed under the influence of various theological and exegetical traditions, such as Alexandrian, Antiochene, and Syriac.

In particular, Syriac symbolic interpretation has significantly influenced Ethiopian biblical interpretation. This effect is noticeable in Ethiopian literature, including the *andemta* commentary. The EOTC employs symbolism in the interpretation of significant biblical and theological concepts. For example, the Ark of the Covenant holds a central place in Syriac symbolic interpretation and, consequently, in Ethiopian biblical interpretation.

However, these traditions were assimilated into the *andemta* commentary by scholars in the Ethiopian historical and cultural context. Thus, these Ethiopian scholars created the unique exegetical tradition that passed from generation to generation. This tradition continues to influence the interpretive work of the EOTC.

Finally, the biblical interpretation of the EOTC is most practically revealed in the preaching of the EOTC. It addresses the particular theological and practical issues in the context of the EOTC under the significant influence of the tradition of the church. Through the investigation of the preaching of the EOTC, certain significant and distinctive characteristics of the EOTC's biblical interpretation along with important influential interpretive factors have been identified.

The sermons analyzed in this monograph demonstrate the significance of the tradition of the EOTC in its reading of biblical texts. The traditional theological assumption that the Bible is the inspired word of God is the element that underlies their basic interpretive attitude toward the biblical texts. Thus, the tradition of the EOTC substantially influences the preachers' interpretation of the biblical texts. This tradition is both doctrinal and practical. In addition, the influence of the *andemta* commentary is evident in the sermons of the EOTC. The preachers regard the *andemta* commentary as the EOTC's interpretive tradition and, therefore, they assume that the commentary's interpretation is the authentic interpretation of the EOTC.

The tradition of the EOTC holds a central place in the EOTC's biblical interpretation in several crucial areas. It functions as the interpretive key in the EOTC's reading of the Bible. It sets the goals of biblical interpretation, and establishes guiding interpretive principles. It also determines the use of exegetical approaches. In many cases, the preachers simply employ the exegetical results found in the tradition of the EOTC.

In addition, the sermons demonstrate the contextual nature of the EOTC's biblical interpretation. The biblical texts are interpreted in the historical and cultural context of the church in Ethiopia. The preaching of the EOTC essentially depends on this contextual interpretation of the biblical texts. It comes out of the Ethiopian cultural context, appreciates the traditional culture, and advocates for indigenous Ethiopian Christianity. The sermons show a deep concern for the Ethiopian people, and address issues that are significant for the EOTC in its contemporary context.

In sum, the findings of this research demonstrate the significance of tradition and context in biblical interpretation. The biblical interpretation of the EOTC has been shaped and developed under the substantial influence of the EOTC's tradition in the historical and cultural context of Ethiopia. The tradition of the EOTC and the contemporary context of Ethiopia continue to significantly influence the interpretive work of the church. Thus, the EOTC provides a compelling historical example of contextual biblical interpretation.

IMPLICATIONS FOR THEOLOGICAL INTERPRETATION OF THE BIBLE

In this section, I will locate the findings of this monograph in a broader hermeneutical discussion, and demonstrate that the discussion of the EOTC's biblical interpretation has significant implications for the theological interpretation of the Bible. First, I will consider recent discussion of theological interpretation. Second, I will discuss the biblical interpretation of the EOTC in terms of recent discussion of theological interpretation. Finally, I will offer some suggestions for the development of the EOTC's theological interpretation.

Theological Interpretation

Recently, there has been a growing interest in the theological interpretation of the Bible among theologians and ministers. The dominance of the historical-critical approach to biblical texts in the post-Enlightenment era greatly diminished theological interpretations and has, therefore, had a significant negative impact on the Christian church. Theological interpretation of the Bible has reemerged in response to the serious deficiencies of historical criticism. As Green notes, "Here at the turn of the 21st century, theological interpretation is moving into the limelight after hundreds of years of shadowy exile from academic biblical and theological studies."[1]

Although theological interpreters have presented different definitions and understandings of theological interpretation, some common aspects are found in recent scholarly discussions. Typically, theological interpreters are not interested in developing a certain kind of interpretive method. Vanhoozer asserts that theological interpretation "is not a form of merely historical, literary, or sociological criticism preoccupied with (respectively) the world 'behind,' 'of,' or 'in front of' the biblical text."[2] In other words, theological interpretation is not a matter of methods, but of assumptions, aims, and sensibilities in addressing the biblical texts. In short, theological interpretation is defined as interpreting the biblical texts "theologically."

This broad definition of theological interpretation has some important implications. First, the interpretive work in theological interpretation is based on certain theological assumptions. The foundational assumption of theological interpretation is that the Bible is the word of God. While recognizing the dual authorship (divine and human) of the Bible, this interpretive approach holds that God is the Bible's primary author.

Subsequently, the audience of the Bible is the people of God, the church. Reading the Bible in the Christian context is listening for what God says to the church. Thus, theological interpreters read the Bible as

1. Green, "What Is Theological Interpretation?," 1.

2. Vanhoozer, "Introduction," 19.

the canon of the Christian church. Green states, "Theological interpretation is identified especially by its self-consciously ecclesial location."[3] Regarding the concern and aim of theological interpretation, Wood states, "Theological hermeneutics asks more specifically how the text may be Christianly understood and what the aims of a deliberate Christian use of it might be."[4] This is, as Green articulates, to read the Bible as Scripture.[5] In other words, theological interpretation of biblical texts is the Christian reading of the Bible with theological assumptions regarding its author, text, and readers.

Second, theological interpretation places priority on theological concerns over other concerns, such as historical, philosophical, literary, socio-cultural, or linguistic. Fowl asserts that "The key to interpreting theologically lies in keeping theological concerns primary to all others."[6] Green presents theological concerns as "the role of Scripture in the faith and formation of persons and ecclesial communities."[7] In other words, theological interpretation is concerned with the formation or transformation of the faith community. Furthermore, it aims at proclaiming the gospel to the world for the furtherance of the kingdom of God.

Third, theological interpretation is guided by theology in its interpretive work. Gracia states, "Theology governs . . . the interpretation of revealed texts."[8] He explains, "Theology is not only a hermeneutical tool for interpretation, but more importantly, it is the ultimate determining factor of scriptural meaning."[9] Theological interpretation recognizes the essential role of theology in the interpretation of biblical texts. Thus, theological tradition is regarded not as an obstacle to understanding the biblical texts, but as the basis on which the texts can be explored.

Finally, theological interpretation of the Bible means engaging and inhabiting the Bible, not just cognitively understanding the meaning of the texts. Theological interpretation is a way of life guided by the Bible. Fowl, borrowing from St. Augustine, states: "Theological interpretation of Scripture will involve those habits, dispositions, and practices that

3. Green, *Practicing Theological Interpretation*, 2.

4. Wood, Foundation of Christian Understanding, 9.

5. Green discusses in detail the meaning and way of reading the Bible as Scripture in his book, *Seized by Truth: Reading the Bible as Scripture* (2007).

6. Fowl, "Further Thoughts on Theological Interpretation," 126.

7. Green, *Practicing Theological Interpretation*, 4.

8. Gracia, *How Can We Know What God Means?*, 144.

9. Gracia, "Meaning," 499.

Christians bring to their varied engagements with Scripture so they can interpret, debate, and embody Scripture in ways that will enhance their journey toward their proper end in God."[10]

Theological interpretation was the standard way of interpreting biblical texts in the pre-modern era. Therefore, recent discussion and development of theological interpretation states that it is reforming biblical interpretation to time-honored interpretive practices in Christian history. More significantly, I would argue, theological interpretation is not a type of biblical interpretation, but the nature of biblical interpretation itself. Persons read the Bible theologically. However else they may read the Bible, all persons bring certain theological assumptions. Therefore, the recent development of theological interpretation can be regarded as the conscious correcting of biblical interpretation.

However, recent scholarly discussions of theological interpretation have yet to develop in practically applicable ways. It appears that these discussions remain primarily at the theoretical level. Theological interpreters focus on discussing the philosophical and theological bases of theological interpretation. In order to develop theological interpretation, the discussion must address the particulars of theological interpretation in specific theological contexts.[11]

In addition, recent scholarly discussions of theological interpretation tend toward theological universalism, which is often evident in Western theology. It appears that scholars do not attend to the reality that there are many different theological traditions, and many different theological contexts. In order to develop theological interpretation, the following questions must be asked: "what theology?" and "in what context?" Green asserts, "The question remains, though, of which context. In reality, biblical texts are always read 'in context'—that is, in *some* context."[12] He also notes, "In this way, theological interpretation of Scripture participates in the well-known mantra "context, context, context."[13] Different theological traditions read the Bible with different theological perspectives in different contexts. Therefore, the theological tradition

10. Fowl, *Theological Interpretation of Scripture*, 14.

11. Joel B. Green's book, *Practicing Theological Interpretation: Engaging Biblical Texts for Faith and Formation* (2011) moves in this direction by discussing in detail his own Wesleyan biblical hermeneutics.

12. Green, *Practicing Theological Interpretation*, 13.

13. Ibid., 42.

and context of a particular faith community must be considered in the discussion of theological interpretation.

In other words, theological interpretation presents a general orientation and mode of biblical interpretation: reading the Bible theologically. However, the outcome of reading the Bible theologically might be quite different, because the Bible is read from the perspective of different theologies and in different contexts. Accordingly, in order to develop theological interpretation, it is necessary to have examples of theological interpretation from among particular Christian churches in the world.

The EOTC's Theological Interpretation of the Bible

In this regard, the biblical interpretation of the EOTC, addressed in this monograph, provides a fruitful historical and contemporary example of theological interpretation. The EOTC has employed theological interpretation throughout its history. For example, it has its own traditional and theological commentary: the *andemta* commentary. As the preaching of the EOTC demonstrates, theological interpretation is also the basic mode of the EOTC's contemporary biblical interpretation.

In addition, the biblical interpretation of the EOTC demonstrates the substantial influence of the theological tradition in biblical interpretation. The theological tradition of the EOTC provides interpretive goals, determines the use of exegetical methods, and functions as the guiding principle of biblical interpretation. In sum, the EOTC's biblical interpretation is a historical manifestation of theological interpretation of the Bible in the particular context of Ethiopia. Thus, the EOTC's theological interpretation provides valuable insights and practical guidance for the development of theological interpretation.

The theological interpretation of the EOTC has several distinctive interpretive characteristics that demonstrate its contextuality. First, the EOTC's theological interpretation has a strong doctrinal and communal orientation. Doctrinal tradition is the determining element in the EOTC's biblical interpretation. In many cases, the exegesis of certain biblical texts is already established and is passed on as the theological tradition of the church. Thus, exegetical novelty is not welcomed. In addition, the biblical interpretation of the EOTC is the task of the church as a hermeneutical community. Thus, individual interpretations of biblical texts are not encouraged, because they risk deviation from the authentic teaching of the church. This orientation toward doctrinal and communal unity in the interpretation of the Bible characterizes the EOTC's theological interpretation.

The second distinctive characteristic of the EOTC's theological interpretation is found in its symbolic hermeneutical approach. The sermons of EOTC preachers demonstrate that the biblical interpretation of the EOTC moves from symbol to history. It starts with actual physical symbols (e.g., the Ark of the Covenant, the temple, Jerusalem, Mary, baptism, etc.) and then moves to the historical meaning. This is the exact opposite of the approach in typical Protestant preaching, which moves from history to meaning and/or symbol. The symbolic approach to the biblical text enables EOTC preachers to present multivalent symbolic meanings of the biblical text. The meaning is not located in history, or in the text itself. The meaning is located in multiple symbolic interpretations. This is the approach from which the *andemta* commentary presents multiple meanings of a biblical text.

These symbols are frequently used to define a sacred space where God is present. This is exemplified in the EOTC's interpretation of "the church." The physical building and compound of an EOTC church symbolize the sacred place where God's presence is encountered. In order to validate this theology, the EOTC employs symbolic interpretation of Jerusalem. The biblical Jerusalem symbolizes the EOTC church. The perception of St. Mary is another important example of symbolic interpretation. In order to advocate for the nature and place of St. Mary in EOTC theology, the EOTC symbolically interprets biblical figures and objects, in relation to St. Mary. For example, the Ark of the Covenant, which signifies the presence of God, is identified with St. Mary, the mother of Jesus Christ.

Another important example of symbolic interpretation in the EOTC is found in the *tabot*. *Tabot* symbolizes and guarantees the presence of God in the EOTC. Accordingly, the presence of *tabot* in a church is evidence of authenticity of that church. This symbolic interpretation justifies the existence of *tabot* in the church and the role of *tabot* in liturgy and festivals of the EOTC. Thus, the EOTC's biblical interpretation begins with the theological significance of symbols and proceeds to their historical meanings.

The third significant characteristic of the EOTC's theological interpretation is its Christocentric focus. The central template of the EOTC's biblical interpretation is the prophecy-fulfillment schema, in relation to Christ. In order to highlight the person and salvific work of Jesus Christ, the EOTC employs various interpretive methods, including symbolic, allegorical, and typological. For example, the narrative of Noah's Ark is symbolically interpreted in order to emphasize the person and work of Jesus Christ. The *andemta* commentary on Genesis 6–8 presents several examples: the ark as the cross, Noah as Christ; the ark as baptism, Noah as the baptized; the ark as the church, Noah as the believers; the ark as the resurrection, Noah as the dead who are raised.

Another example of the EOTC's Christocentric focus is the use of allegory in the interpretation of "the jar and the fire" in Gideon's narrative: the "fire" is Jesus Christ; he is the glory and the beauty of the world. A third example is found in the interpretation of Isaiah 53 with the schema of prophecy and fulfillment: the prophet Isaiah prophesized about Jesus, including his nature and his redemptive work. These examples demonstrate that the biblical interpretation of the EOTC employs diverse exegetical methods in order to achieve its Christocentric interpretive goals.

The fourth significant characteristic of the EOTC's theological interpretation is found in application. The interpretive strategies of the EOTC are employed to facilitate the application of biblical texts to the contemporary situation. As noted previously, the contemporary application is organic to the preaching of the EOTC. In this, it differs from typical Protestant preaching, in which application is tacked on at the end. Western interpreters start with history and then face the challenge of how to make that history meaningful. The organic application in EOTC preaching is a result of its movement from symbol to meaning. In their interpretation of biblical texts, EOTC preachers begin with theological significance, rather than with history.

Thus, in the EOTC's hermeneutical approach, there is no artificial dichotomy of meaning and significance, or meaning and application, which is frequently found in the exegetical and homiletic approaches of Protestant churches. There are significant problems with the attempt to establish the meaning of a biblical text first, and then apply it to the present context. The attempt to establish the meaning of a biblical text generally results in ever-growing complexity and conflicts regarding the supposed fixed meaning. Frequently, in the process of moving from meaning to application, external factors (e.g., psychology, counseling, education, or economics) come into play, which inform the fixed textual meanings.

In contrast, the biblical interpretation of the EOTC assumes that the figures and objects in the Bible have direct spiritual meanings for the contemporary readers of the Bible. They are directly applied to the present situation of believers with the use of various interpretive strategies, including allegorical, symbolical, and typological interpretation. This interpretive practice is made possible by the EOTC's belief in the immediacy of the Bible. That is, God speaks now and here to his people through the Bible.

In sum, the biblical interpretation of the EOTC is a fruitful example of theological interpretation. It illuminates contextual ways of interpreting biblical texts, and demonstrates that theological interpretation can take many different shapes. Protestant churches may gain many valuable lessons from the biblical interpretation of the EOTC.

Suggestions for the Development of the EOTC's Theological Interpretation

Simultaneously, however, there are some limitations to overcome in the EOTC's biblical interpretation. First, the EOTC's symbolic interpretation is limited only to certain significant doctrines of the church. The EOTC does not expand its dynamic interpretive approaches to other important areas in the faith and life of believers. Particularly, given the current changing local and global context, the EOTC is required, through its interpretation of the Bible, to address issues that are critical for the people of Ethiopia. If the EOTC can apply its interpretive approaches to diverse issues in its context, it will help enrich the understanding of biblical texts for the people of Ethiopia. Doing so will also contribute to the biblical interpretation of the global church.

Second, it appears that the attitude of the EOTC in its biblical interpretation is overly defensive. Most preachers endeavor to justify the EOTC's theological tradition, including its doctrines and religious practices. Given the church's historical situation of isolation and hardship, this is understandable. However, the current global context is one in which the EOTC can proactively participate in the hermeneutical dialogue among Christians traditions throughout the world. The EOTC can teach and learn from other church traditions in interpreting biblical texts. In addition, the EOTC needs to pay attention to the charge that it is "overly contextualized." While the theological universalism found in the West, particularly in historical criticism, must be overcome, the theological isolationism found in the EOTC must be overcome, as well.

There are currently signs of positive change in the EOTC. In particular, scholars of EOTC theological schools are increasingly receptive to the theologies of other church traditions. Many academic writings in these schools refer to Protestant theological scholars. The leaders of these schools often invite scholars of Protestant theology to come and teach their students. This type of cooperation will open doors for different church traditions in Ethiopia to teach and learn from each other.

CONTRIBUTIONS

This monograph is a historical case study of contextual biblical interpretation through the exploration of the EOTC's reading of the Bible. I have demonstrated the significance of tradition and context in biblical interpretation. This monograph will contribute to several important areas of study.

First, this research will contribute to the study of contextualization, especially the EOTC's tradition and its contextualization. The EOTC successfully contextualized biblical interpretation in the historical and cultural context of Ethiopia. Consequently, it offers a fascinating example of contextualization. However, the EOTC's heritage has not been well recognized by Christian traditions outside of Ethiopia. Thus, valuable insights and practical lessons can be gained through the study of the EOTC.

This particular research presents an appropriate methodology in the study of contextualization. I argued that the appropriate approach to constructing contextual theology is descriptive rather than normative. Therefore, I employed a descriptive approach in the investigation of the EOTC's biblical interpretation. As a result, I was able to discover the characteristics of the EOTC's biblical interpretation. Accordingly, this research provides an example of effective investigation of contextual biblical interpretation.

Second, this research will contribute to recent discussion regarding theological interpretation of the Bible. The EOTC has exercised theological interpretation throughout its history. Therefore, this study of the EOTC's biblical interpretation has elucidated the nature and practice of theological interpretation. In particular, it has highlighted the significance of tradition, along with the significance of context in biblical interpretation. In contemporary religious studies the significance of tradition has frequently been overlooked. This research has demonstrated the substantial influence of tradition in the EOTC's biblical interpretation and, thereby, demonstrated the significance of tradition in overall biblical interpretation.

Third, this research has presented a practical way of exploring the biblical interpretation of a church: an analysis of preaching in the church. The preaching of the EOTC reveals the characteristics of the biblical interpretation of the church. This is a rare attempt in the study of biblical interpretation. This approach can also be employed in the investigation of the biblical interpretations of other Christian churches.

Last, in the religious context of Ethiopia, this study will help foster the theological dialogue between the EOTC and the Protestant churches. Believers in the EOTC will more clearly understand their own biblical interpretation. Believers in the Protestant churches will gain significant hermeneutical insights into the EOTC's biblical interpretation, which is in line with the Ethiopian tradition and cultural context, rather than uncritically importing Western modes of biblical interpretation. This will promote mutual understanding and acceptance among the EOTC and the Protestant churches as parts of the Christian church.

SUGGESTIONS FOR FUTURE STUDY

I have explored the biblical interpretation of the EOTC through the examination of the *andemta* commentary and the EOTC's preaching. Yet, there are different ways in which to investigate the biblical interpretation of the EOTC. As discussed in this monograph, the tradition of the church, especially the theological tradition, has a substantial influence on the EOTC's reading the Bible. The EOTC's theological tradition is both explicitly and implicitly contained in two important areas: liturgy and icons. Thus, both of these areas would merit further study.

Study of Liturgy in the EOTC

Liturgy holds a central place in the faith and practice of the EOTC. As a living tradition, the EOTC's liturgy reveals the preservation of the faith of the EOTC. Practically, liturgy is the very heart of the EOTC's worship. As noted previously, the liturgy of the EOTC consists of two main parts. The first part is the Synaxis which includes the reading of the Epistles and Gospels. The second part is the Anaphora, which includes the reading of the Canon of the church. The EOTC has fourteen Anaphoras, some of which are sung while others are read aloud by priests.

All of the rituals and activities in the liturgy have theological meaning. In particular, anaphoras most explicitly articulate the theology of the EOTC. Therefore, it is vital to investigate the liturgy of the EOTC in order to grasp its theology. The liturgy discloses how the EOTC interprets certain biblical texts. More significantly, the study of liturgy will be valuable in its exploration of how the theology contained in the liturgy influences the biblical interpretation of the EOTC. This will more clearly demonstrate the characteristics of the EOTC's biblical interpretation.

Study of Icons in the EOTC

Icons are artistic expressions of the faith, order, and teaching of the EOTC. Icons hold a significant position in the life and faith of Ethiopian people. Believers in the EOTC have great respect for icons. Icons are an essential element in the liturgy, as well as the building design, of the church. Icons are used in ceremonies and festivals in the church, and believers occasionally march on the street with icons. Believers also use icons for devotional purposes.

Icons have an educational function, as well. They are used to teach people who are unable to read the stories of the Bible. Believers learn through icons about the lives, devotions, and struggles of biblical and historical figures, including martyrs. This educational function is not limited to those who are illiterate, but applied to all believers. Icons are very powerful instruments used to teach and build-up believers in the EOTC.

Thus, Ethiopian icons contain the theology of the EOTC. In other words, icons are windows through which the theology of the EOTC may be found. In terms of biblical interpretation, icons express many biblical figures and stories in artistic ways. They reveal how the EOTC interpreted biblical texts in the historical and cultural context of Ethiopia. Accordingly, the study of Ethiopian icons will contribute to the exploration of the biblical interpretation of the EOTC.

FINAL REMARKS

Believers gather together in church for worship. They sing, pray, cite creeds, eat bread and drink wine, read the Bible. They experience the word of God, interpreted according to the church's tradition and addressed to issues in the context of the faith community, in preaching. They find the meaning of their faith and life. They are consoled in their suffering, encouraged to go forward through their hardship, challenged to leave evil things and behaviors, and exhorted to live a godly life. They are motivated to follow the way of God, given in the Bible.

A local reading of the Bible reveals certain aspects of God's truth. The biblical interpretations of local faith communities throughout the world contribute together to enrich our understanding of God's truth in the Bible. Hermeneutical communities in various contexts can teach and learn from each other through their interpretations of the Bible. Therefore, constructing contextual biblical interpretation must be a mutual dialogue, rather than an arbitrary monologue. Biblical interpretation is a journey taken together, as we listen to others' stories of God and tell our own. By so doing, we enhance our knowledge of God and build-up the body of Christ.

The EOTC is a companion in our journey toward God, and a conversation partner in our talk about God. It shows how a local church with a unique tradition reads the Bible in the context of a particular faith community. It also reveals how the word of God has powerfully worked among the believers in their life situations. It is impressive, as well, that the biblical interpretation of the EOTC demonstrates many commonalities, as well as differences, with other Christian churches in the world, despite its long isolation and lack of global recognition. I believe this is the work of the Holy Spirit, the Author of the Bible and the Sustainer of the one, holy, catholic, and apostolic Church.

Bibliography

Alaka, Imbakom Kalewold. *Traditional Ethiopian Church Education*. Translated by Menghestu Lemma. New York: Teachers College Press, 1970.

Aymro, Wondmagegnehu and Joachim Motovu, eds. *The Ethiopian Orthodox Church*. Addis Ababa: The Ethiopian Orthodox Mission, 1970.

Barram, Michael. "The Bible, Mission, and Social Location: Toward a Missional Hermeneutic." *Interpretation: A Journal of Biblical Theology* 43 (2007) 42–58.

Bartholomew, Craig G. "Uncharted Waters: Philosophy, Theology and the Crisis in Biblical Interpretation." In *Renewing Biblical Interpretation*, edited by Craig Bartholomew et al., 1–39. Grand Rapids: Zondervan, 2000.

Barton, John. *The Nature of Biblical Criticism*. Louisville, KY: Westminster John Knox, 2007.

Belai, Giday. *Ethiopian Civilization*. Addis Ababa: B. Giday, 1992.

Bevans, Stephen B. *Models of Contextual Theology*. Maryknoll, NY: Orbis, 2003.

Breck, John. *Scripture in Tradition: The Bible and Its Interpretation in the Orthodox Church*. Crestwood, NY: St Vladimir's Seminary Press, 2001.

Brock, Sebastian. *St. Ephrem the Syrian: Hymns on Paradise*. Crestwood, NY: St. Vladimir's Seminary Press, 1990.

———. "St. Ephrem the Syrian on Reading Scripture." *The Downside Review* 125.438 (2007) 37–50.

Budge, E. A. Wallis. *The Kebra Nagast: The Glory of Kings*. Lexington, KY: Chakra Healing Sounds, 2011.

———. *The Queen of Sheba and Her Only Son Menyelek*. London: Medici Society, 1922.

Burnett, Richard E. "Historical Criticism." In *Dictionary for Theological Interpretation of the Bible*, edited by Kevin J. Vanhoozer. Grand Rapids: Baker Academic, 2005.

Clark, Elizabeth A. *History, Theory, Text: Historians and the Linguistic Turn*. Cambridge, MA: Harvard University Press, 2004.

Coe, Shoki. "In Search of Renewal in Theological Education." *Theological Education* 9.4 (1973) 233–43.

Collins, John J. *The Bible after Babel: Historical Criticism in a Postmodern Age*. Grand Rapids: Eerdmans, 2005.

———. *Encounters with Biblical Theology*. Minneapolis, MN: Fortress, 2005.

Conn, Harvie M. "Contextual Theologies: the Problem of Agendas." *Westminster Theological Journal* 52 (1990) 51–63.

———. "Contextualization: Where Do We Begin?" In *Evangelicals and Liberation*, edited by Carl E. Armerding, 90–119. Grand Rapids: Baker, 1997.

Cook, Albert. *History Writing: The Theory and Practice of History in Antiquity and in Modern Times*. Cambridge: Cambridge University Press, 1988.

Cowley, Roger. "The 'Blood of Zechariah' (Mt 23:35) in Ethiopian Exegetical Tradition." In *Ethiopian Exegetical Tradition. Studia Patristica* 18.1 (1985) 293–302.

———. *Ethiopian Biblical Interpretation: A Study of Exegetical Tradition and Hermeneutics*. Cambridge: Cambridge University Press, 1988.

———. "Mämher Esdros and His Interpretations." In *Sixth International Conference of Ethiopian Studies*, edited by Gideon Goldenberg, 41–69. Tel-Aviv: A. A. Alkema, 1980.

———. "New Testament Introduction in the Andemta Commentary Tradition." *Ostkirchliche Studien* 26 (1977) 144–92.

———. "Old Testament Introduction in the Andemta Commentary Tradition." *Journal of Ethiopian Studies* 12 (1974) 133–75.

———. "Preliminary Notes on the baläandem Commentaries." *Ostkirchliche Studien* 26 (1971) 9–20.

———. *Traditional Interpretation of the Apocalypse of St. John in the Ethiopian Church*. Cambridge: Cambridge University Press, 1983.

den Biesen, Kees. *Simple and Bold: Ephrem's Art of Symbolic Thought*. Piscataway, NJ: Gorgias, 2006.

Dietrich, Walter and Ulrich Luz, eds. *The Bible in a World Context: An Experiment in Contextual Hermeneutics*. Grand Rapids: Eerdmans, 2002.

Diodore of Tarsus. "Commentary on the Psalms, Prologue." In *Biblical Interpretation in the Early Church*. Translated and edited by Karlfried Froehlich, 82–86. Philadelphia: Fortress, 1984.

———. "Preface to the Commentary on Psalm 118." In *Biblical Interpretation in the Early Church*. Translated and edited by Karlfried Froehlich, 87–94. Philadelphia: Fortress, 1984.

Dobbs-Allsopp, F. W. "Rethinking Historical Criticism." *Biblical Interpretation* 7 (1999) 235–71.

Donahue, John R. "Modern and Postmodern Critical Methods of Biblical Study." In *Scripture: An Ecumenical Introduction to the Bible and Its Interpretation*, edited by Michael J. Gorman, 147–62. Peabody, MA: Hendrickson, 2005.

Douglas, J. A. "Introduction." In *The Teaching of the Abyssinian Church*, edited by A. F. Matthew and J. A. Douglas, vii–xl. London: Faith Press, 1936.

Dyrness, William A. *The Earth Is God's: A Theology of American Culture*. Eugene, OR: Wipf & Stock, 1997.

———. *Invitation to Cross-Cultural Theology: Case Studies In Vernacular Theologies* Grand Rapids: Zondervan, 1992.

———. *Learning about Theology from the Third World*. Grand Rapids: Academia, 1990.

———. *Poetic Theology: God and the Poetics of Everyday Life*. Grand Rapids: Eerdmans, 2011.

———. *Senses of Devotion: Interface Aesthetics in Buddhist and Muslim Communities*. Eugene, OR: Cascade, 2013.

Enns, Peter. *Inspiration and Incarnation: Evangelicals and the Problem of the Old Testament*. Grand Rapids: Baker Academic, 2005.

Fabella, Virginia. "Contextualization." In *Dictionary of Third World Theologies*, edited by Virginia Fabella and R. S. Sugirtharajah, 58–9. Maryknoll, NY: Orbis, 2000.

Fairbairn, Donald. "Historical and Theological Studies, Patristic Exegesis and Theology: The Cart and the Horse." *Westminster Theological Journal* 69 (2007) 1–19.

Fiorenza, Elisabeth Schüssler. "Biblical Interpretation and Critical Commitment." *Studia Theologica* 43 (1989) 5–18.

Fisher, Walter R. "Narrative as a Human Communication Paradigm: the Case of Public Moral Argument." *Communication Monographs* 51 (1984) 1–22.

———. "The Narrative Paradigm: An Elaboration." *Communication Monographs* 52 (1985) 347–67.

Foutz, Scott. "Theology of Slavery: Western Theology's Role in the Development and Propagation of Slavery." *Quodlibet* 2.1 (2000). Online: http://www.quodlibet.net/articles/foutz-slavery.shtml.

Fowl, Stephen E. "Further Thoughts on Theological Interpretation." In *Reading Scripture with the Church: toward a Hermeneutic for Theological Interpretation*, edited by A. K. M. Adam et al., 125–30. Grand Rapids: Baker Academic, 2006.

———. *Theological Interpretation of Scripture*. Eugene, OR: Cascade, 2009.

Frei, Hans W. *The Eclipse of Biblical Narrative: A Study in Eighteenth and Nineteenth Century Hermeneutics*. New Haven, CT: Yale University Press, 1974.

Froehlich, Karlfried. *Biblical Interpretation in the Early Church*. Philadelphia: Fortress, 1984.

Fyfe, Christopher and Andrew F. Walls, eds. *Christianity in Africa in the 1990s*. Edinburgh: University of Edinburgh, 1996.

Gadamer, Hans-Georg. *Truth and Method*. Translated by Joel Weinsheimer and Donald G. Marshall. New York: Continuum, 2004.

Garcia, Miguel Angel. *Ethiopian Biblical Commentaries on the Prophet Micah*. Äethiopistische Forschungen 52. Wiesbaden: Harrassowitz Verlag, 1999.

———. "Ethiopian Traditional Biblical Interpretation." *African Christian Studies* 12.2 (1996) 1–8.

Geertz, Clifford. *The Interpretation of Cultures*. New York: Basic Books, 1973.

Girma, M. A. "Whose Meaning?: A Critical Look at Wax and Gold Tradition as a Philosophical Foundation for a Unique Ethiopian Hermeneutics." *Sophia* 50.1 (2011) 175–87.

Goldsmith, Martin, "Contextualization of Theology." *Themelios* 9.1 (1983) 18–23

Gracia, Jorge J. E. *How Can We Know What God Means?: The Interpretation of Revelation*. New York: Palgrave, 2001.

———. "Meaning." In *Dictionary for Theological Interpretation of the Bible*, edited by Kevin J. Vanhoozer, 492–99. Grand Rapids: Baker Academic, 2005.

Green, Joel B. "Context." In *Dictionary for Theological Interpretation of the Bible*, edited by Kevin J. Vanhoozer, 130–33. Grand Rapids: Baker Academic, 2005.

———. "The (Re-)Turn to Narrative." In *Narrative Reading, Narrative Preaching: Reuniting New Testament Interpretation and Proclamation*," edited by Joel B. Green and Michael Pasquarello, 11–36. Grand Rapids: Baker Academic, 2003.

———. *Practicing Theological Interpretation: Engaging Biblical Texts for Faith and Formation*. Grand Rapids: Baker Academic, 2011.

———. *Seized by Truth: Reading the Bible as Scriptures*. Nashville: Abingdon, 2007.

———. "What Is Theological Interpretation? (Theological Interpretation)." Accessed February 5. http:/www.sites.google.com/site/theologicalinterpretation, 2010.

Greene-McCreight, Kathryn. "Rule of Faith." In *Dictionary for Theological Interpretation of the Bible*, edited by Kevin J. Vanhoozer, 703–4. Grand Rapids: Baker Academic, 2005.

Greer, Rowan. *The Captain of Our Salvation: A Study in the Patristic Exegesis of Hebrews*. Tubingen: J. C. B. Mohr, 1973.

———. "The Christian Bible and Its Interpretation." In *Early Biblical Interpretation*, edited by James L. Kugel and Rowan A. Greer, 107–208. Library of Early Christianity 3. Philadelphia: Westminster John Knox Press, 1986.

Griffith, Sidney H. *'Faith Adoring the Mystery': Reading the Bible with St. Ephrem the Syrian*. Milwaukee, WI: Marquette University Press, 1997.

Haleblian, Krikor. "The Problem of Contextualization." *Missiology* 11.1 (1983) 95–111.

Harvey, Van A. *The Historian & the Believer: The Morality of Historical Knowledge and Christian Belief*. Urbana, IL: University of Illinois Press, 1966.

Haskell, Rob. "Introduction: Aims and Themes of the Project." In *Local Theology for the Global Church: Principles for an Evangelical Approach to Contextualization*, edited by Matthew Cook et al., ix–xxiv. Pasadena, CA: William Carey Library, 2010.

Haskell, Thomas L. *Objectivity Is Not Neutrality: Explanatory Schemes in History*. Baltimore, MD: The Johns Hopkins University Press, 1998.

Hastings, Adrian. *The Church in Africa* 1450–1950. Oxford: Clarendon, 1994.

Hiebert, Paul G. *Anthropological Insights for Missionaries*. Grand Rapids: Baker, 1985.

Hirsch, E. D. Jr. *The Aims of Interpretation*. Chicago, IL: The University of Chicago Press, 1976.

———. *Validity in Interpretation*. New Haven, CT: Yale University Press, 1967.

———. "Meaning and Significance Reinterpreted." *Critical Inquiry* 11 (1984) 202–25.

Holmes, Stephen R. *Listening to the Past: The Place of Tradition in Theology*. Grand Rapids: Baker Academic, 2002.

Holy Trinity Theological College. *Introduction to the History of the Ethiopian Orthodox Tewahedo Church*. Unpublished manuscript. Addis Ababa: Holy Trinity Theological College, 2007.

Hubbard, David Allen. "The Literary Sources of the Kebra Nagast." PhD diss., University of St. Andrews, 1956.

Hwang, C. H. "A Rethinking of Theological Training for the Ministry in the Younger Churches Today." *The S. E. Asia Journal of Theology* 4.2 (1962) 7–34.

Hyatt, Harry Middleton. *The Church of Abyssinia*. London: Luzac, 1928.

Jenkins, Philip. *The Next Christendom: The Coming of Global Christianity*. Oxford: Oxford University Press, 2002.

Jennings, Willie James. *The Christian Imagination: Theology and the Origins of Race*. New Haven, CT: Yale University Press, 2010.

Jenson, Robert W. "Scripture's Authority in the Church." In *The Art of Reading Scripture*, edited by Ellen F. Davis and Richard B. Hays. Grand Rapids: Eerdmans, 2003.

Johnson, Luke Timothy. "Imagining the World Scripture Imagines." *Modern Theology* 14.2 (1998) 165–80.

Kaplan, Steven. "Finding the True Cross: The Social-Political Dimensions of the Ethiopian Meskel Festival." *Journal of Religion in Africa* 38 (2008) 447–65.

Keshishian, Aram I. "The Oriental Orthodox Churches." *The Ecumenical Review* 46.1 (1994) 104–8.

Kessis, Kefyalew Merahi. *The Contribution of the Orthodox Tewahedo Church to the Ethiopian Civilization*. Addis Ababa: K. K. Merahi, 1999.

Kraft, Charles H. *Anthropology for Christian Witness* .Maryknoll, NY: Orbis, 2003.

Krentz, Edgar. *The Historical-Critical Method.* Eugene, OR: Wipf & Stock, 1975.

Kuhn, Thomas S. *The Structure of Scientific Revolutions*, 3rd ed. Chicago: University of Chicago Press, 1996.

Lane, Anthony N. S. "Tradition." In *Dictionary for Theological Interpretation of the Bible*, edited by Kevin J. Vanhoozer, 809–12. Grand Rapids: Baker Academic, 2005.

Lee, Ralph. "Symbolic Interpretations in Ethiopic Ephremic Literature." PhD diss., University of London, 2011.

Levine, Donald N. "Ethiopia: Identity, Authority, and Realism." In *Political Culture and Political Development*, edited by Lucian W. Pye and Sidney Verba, 245–81. Princeton, NJ: Princeton University Press, 1965.

———. *Greater Ethiopia: The Evolution of a Mutiethnic Society.* Chicago: University of Chicago Press, 1974.

———. *Wax and Gold: Tradition and Innovation in Ethiopian Culture.* Chicago: Chicago University Press, 1965.

Luzbetak, Louis J. *The Church and Culture: New Perspectives in Missiological Anthropology.* Maryknoll, NY: Orbis, 1988.

MacIntyre, Alasdair. *After Virtue*, 2nd ed. Notre Dame, IN: University of Notre Dame Press, 1984.

Maggay, M. P. and W. A. Dyrness. "Culture and Society." In *Global Dictionary of Theology*, edited by William A. Dyrness and Veli-Matti Kärkkäinen, 217–23. Downers Grove, IL: IVP Academic, 2008.

Meyendorff, John. *Catholicity and the Church.* Crestwood, NY: St. Vladimir's Seminary Press, 1983.

Muto, Shinichi. "Early Syriac Hermeneutics." *The Harp: A Review of Syriac and Oriental Studies* 11/12 (1998–99) 45–65.

Niebuhr, H. Richard. *Christ and Culture.* New York: Harper & Row. 1951.

Noll, Mark A. *The New Shape of World Christianity: How American Experience Reflects Global Faith.* Downers Grove, IL: IVP Academic, 2009.

Novick, Peter. *That Noble Dream: The "Objectivity Question" and the American Historical Profession.* Cambridge: Cambridge University Press, 1998.

O'Keefe, John J. and R. R. Reno. *Sanctified Vision: An Introduction to Early Christian Interpretation of the Bible.* Baltimore, MD: Johns Hopkins University Press, 2005.

Ortner, Sherry B. *Anthropology and Social Theory: Culture, Power, and the Acting Subject.* Durham: Duke University Press, 2006.

Paddison, Angus. *Theological Hermeneutics and 1 Thessalonians.* Cambridge: Cambridge University Press, 2005.

Padilla, C. René. "The Interpreted Word: Reflections on Contextual Hermeneutics." *Themelios* 7.1 (1981) 18–23.

Patte, Daniel. *Ethics of Biblical Interpretation: A Reevaluation.* Louisville, KY: Westminster John Knox, 1995.

Pawlikowski, John T. "The Judaic Spirit of the Ethiopian Orthodox Church: A Case Study in Religious Acculturation." *Journal of Religion in Africa* 4 (1972) 178–99.

Pedersen, Kirsten Stoffregen. "The Amharic *Andemta* Commentary on the Abraham Stories: Genesis 11:24—25:14." In *The Book of Genesis in Jewish and Oriental Christian Interpretation*, edited by Judith Frishman and Lucas Van Rompay, 253–61. Lovanii: Peeters, 1997.

———. *Traditional Ethiopian Exegesis of the Book of Psalms.* Äethiopische Forschungen 36. Wiesbaden: Harrassowitz Verlag, 1995.

Pelikan, Jaroslav. *The Christian Tradition: A History of the Development of Doctrine, Vol. 1. The Emergence of the Catholic Tradition (100–600).* Chicago: University of Chicago Press, 1971.

———. *The Vindication of Tradition.* New Haven, CT: Yale University Press, 1984.

Provan, Iain W. "Knowing and Believing: Faith in the Past." In *"Behind" the Text: Historical and Biblical Interpretation*, edited by Craig Bartholomew et al., 229–66. Scripture and Hermeneutics Series. Grand Rapids: Zondervan, 2003.

Provan, Iain W., et al. *A Biblical History of Israel.* Louisville, KY: Westminster John Knox, 2003.

Rae, Murray A. "Creation and Promise: Toward a Theology of History." In *"Behind" the Text: Historical and Biblical Interpretation*, edited by Craig Bartholomew et al., 267–99. Scripture and Hermeneutics Series. Grand Rapids: Zondervan, 2003.

———. "Texts in Context: Scripture and the Divine Economy." *Journal of Theological Interpretation* 1.1 (2007) 23–45.

Rah, Soong-Chan. *The Next Evangelicalism: Freeing the Church from Western Cultural Captivity.* Downers Grove, IL: InterVarsity, 2009.

Rufinus of Aquileia. *The Church History of Rufinus of Aquileia.* Books 10 and 11. Translated by Philip R. Amidon. New York: Oxford University Press, 1997.

Schreiter, Robert J. *Constructing Local Theology.* Maryknoll, NY: Orbis, 1985.

———. "Foreword to the Revised and Expanded Edition." In *Models of Contextualization*, by Stephen B. Bevans, ix–xi. Maryknoll, NY: Orbis, 2003.

Sedmak, Clemens. *Doing Local Theology: A Guide for Artisans of a New Humanity.* Maryknoll, NY: Orbis, 2006.

Segovia, Fernando F. and Mary Ann Tolbert, eds. *Reading from This Place (Vol. 1): Social Location and Biblical Interpretation in the United States.* Minneapolis, MN: Fortress, 1995.

Segovia, Fernando F. "Culture Studies and Contemporary Biblical Criticism: Ideological Criticism as Mode of Discourse." In *Reading from This Place (Vol. 2): Social Location and Biblical Interpretation in Global Perspective*, edited by Fernando F. Segovia and Mary Ann Tolbert, 1–17. Minneapolis, MN: Fortress, 1995.

Segura-Guzman, Osias. "The Practice of Theology." In *Local Theology for the Global Church: Principles for an Evangelical Approach to Contextualization*, edited by Matthew Cook et al., 125–42. Pasadena, CA: William Carey Library, 2010.

Shaw, R. Daniel. *Transculturation: The Cultural Factor in Translation and Other Communication Tasks.* Pasadena, CA: William Carey Library, 1988.

Shenk, Calvin E. "The Ethiopian Orthodox Church: A Study in Indigenization." *Missiology* 14.3 (1988) 259–78.

———. "Reverse Contextualization: Jesuit Encounter with the Ethiopian Orthodox Church." *Direction* 28.1 (1999) 88–100.

Shenk, Wilbert. "Theological Education in Historical and Global Perspective." In *Theology in Missionary Perspective: Lesslie Newbigin's Legacy*, edited by Mark T. B. Laing and Paul Weston, 221–43. Eugene, OR: Pickwick, 2012.

Simonetti, Manlio. *Biblical Interpretation in the Early Church: An Historical Introduction to Patristic Exegesis.* Edinburgh: T. & T. Clark, 1994.

Siu, Paul. "Theologizing Locally." In *Local Theology for the Global Church: Principles for an Evangelical Approach to Contextualization*, edited by Matthew Cook et al., 143–64. Pasadena, CA: William Carey Library, 2010.

Smith, Barbara Ann. "The Role of the Ethiopian Orthodox Church in Affirming the National Identity of Her People: Historical Observations." *Journal of the International Theological Center* 26.2 (1999) 169–89.

Song, C. S. *In the Beginning Were Stories, Not Texts: Story Theology*. Eugene, OR: Cascade, 2011.

———. *Tell Us Our Names: Story Theology from an Asian Perspective*. Maryknoll, NY: Orbis, 1984.

Steinmetz, David G. "The Superiority of Pre-Critical Exegesis." In *The Theological Interpretation of Scripture: Classic and Contemporary Readings*, edited by Stephen E. Fowl, 26–38. Cambridge: Blackwell, 1997.

Sternberg, Meir. *The Poetics of Biblical Narrative: Ideological Literature and the Drama of Reading*. Bloomington, IN: Indiana University Press, 1985.

Stott, John R. W. "The Bible in World Evangelism." In *Perspective on the World Christian Movement*. Revised ed., edited by Ralph D. Winter and Steven C. Hawthorne, 3–9. Pasadena, CA: William Carey Library, 1992.

Stott, John R. W. and Robert T. Coote, eds. *Gospel and Culture: The Papers of a Consultation on the Gospel and Culture Convened by the Lausanne Committee's Theological and Education Group*. Pasadena, CA: William Carey Library, 1979.

Straus, Steve. "The Role of Context in Shaping Theology." In *Contextualization and Syncretism: Navigating Cultural Currents*, edited by Gailyn Van Rheenen, 99–128. Pasadena, CA: William Carey Library, 2006.

Swain, Scott. "A Ruled Reading Reformed: The Role of the Church's Confession in Biblical Interpretation." *International Journal of Systematic Theology* 14.2 (2012) 177–93.

Tanner, Kathryn. *Theories of Culture: A New Agenda for Theology*. Minneapolis, MN: Fortress, 1997.

The Ethiopian Orthodox Church. *The Church of Ethiopia: A Panorama of History and Spirituality*. Addis Ababa: The Ethiopian Orthodox Church, 1970.

———. A *Short History, Faith and Order of the Ethiopian Orthodox Tewahedo Church*. Addis Ababa: The Ethiopian Orthodox Church, 1983.

Theological Education Fund (TEF) Staff. *Ministry in Context: The Third Mandate Programme of the Theological Education Fund (1970-77)*. Bromey, Kent: T.E.F. Fund, 1972.

Tillich, Paul. *Theology of Culture*. New York: Oxford University Press, 1964.

Troeltsch, Ernst, "Historiography." In *Encyclopedia of Religion and Ethics*, vol. 6, edited by James Hastings , 716–23. Edinburgh: T. & T. Clark, 1913.

———. *Religion in History. Fortress Texts in Modern Theology*. Translated by James Luther Adams and Walter F. Bense. Minneapolis, MN: Fortress, 2007.

———. *Writings on Theology and Religion*. Translated and edited by Robert Morgan and Michael Pye. Atlanta, GA: John Knox, 1977.

Ukpong, Justin S. "Inculturation Hermeneutics: An African Approach to Biblical Interpretation." In *The Bible in a World Context*, edited by Walter Dietrich and Ulrich Luz, 17–32. Grand Rapids: Eerdmans, 2002.

———. "What is Contextualization?" *Neue Zeitschrift für Missionswissenschaft* 43 (1987) 161–68.

Ullendorff, Edward. *Ethiopia and the Bible*. Oxford: Oxford University Press, 1968.

———. "Hebraic-Jewish Elements in Abyssinian (Monophysite) Christianity." *Journal of Semitic Studies* 1 (1956) 216–56.

Vähäkangas, Mika. "Modeling Contextualization in Theology." *Swedish Missiological Themes* 98.3 (2010) 279–306.

Vanhoozer, Kevin J. "Introduction: What Is Theological Interpretation of the Bible?" In *Dictionary for Theological Interpretation of the Bible*, edited by Kevin J. Vanhoozer, 19–25. Grand Rapids: Baker Academic, 2005.

———. *Is There a Meaning in This Text?: The Bible, the Reader, and the Morality of Literary Knowledge*. Grand Rapids: Zondervan, 1998.

Van Rompay, Lucas. "The Christian Syriac Tradition of Interpretation." In *Hebrew Bible/Old Testament: The History of Its Interpretation. Vol. 1. From the Beginnings to the Middle Ages (Until 1300)*, edited by Magne Sæbø, 612–41. Gottingen: Vandenhoeck & Ruprecht, 1996.

Wall, Robert W. "Reading the Bible from within Our Traditions: The 'Rule of Faith.' In Theological Hermeneutics." In *Between Two Horizons: Spanning New Testament Studies & Systematic Theology*, edited by Joel B. Green and Max Turner, 88–107. Grand Rapids: Eerdmans, 2000.

Wallace-Hadrill, D. S. *Christian Antioch: A Study of Early Christian Thought in the East*. Cambridge: Cambridge University Press, 1982.

Ward, Graham. *Cultural Transformation and Religious Practice*. Cambridge: Cambridge University Press, 2005.

White, Hayden. *The Content of the Form: Narrative Discourse and Historical Representation*. Baltimore, MD: Johns Hopkins University Press, 1987.

Williams, D. H. *Evangelicals and Tradition: The Formative Influence of the Early Church*. Grand Rapids: Baker Academic, 2005.

Wood, Charles M. *The Formation of Christian Understanding: An Essay in Theological Hermeneutics*. Philadelphia: Westminster, 1981.

Yesehaq. *The Ethiopian Tewahedo Church: An Integrally African Church*. New York: Vantage, 1989.

Young, Frances. *The Art of Performance: Towards a Theology of Holy Scripture*. London: Darton, Longman and Todd, 1990.

———. "The Fourth Century Reaction against Allegory." In *Studia Patristica*, vol. 30, by Elizabeth A. Livingstone, 120–25. Leuven: Peeters, 1997.